Positive Psychology
Theory, Research and Applications

D1214919

Praise for this book

"This accessible, yet comprehensive, book provides an excellent new resource in the area of positive psychology. Students, researchers and practitioners alike will benefit from the skilful and lively integration of theory, research and application. The authors are prominent members of the international positive psychology movement and as such are able to deliver a confident, practical and overarching assessment of the area, integrated into psychology more widely."

Angela Clow, University of Westminster, UK

"In Positive Psychology, Hefferon and Boniwell offer a comprehensive and up-to-date overview of this new science. The topics in this book stretch from personal well-being to resilience to workplace application. The authors have wisely included features such as personal reflections, assessments, and activities that offer positive psychology students and enthusiasts a more engaged way to connect with the material. Positive Psychology is a fine read and a storehouse of information."

Dr. Robert Biswas-Diener, Managing Director, Positive Acorn and Part-time instructor, Portland State University, USA

"This is an exceptional book that synthesizes more than a decade of positive psychology research into chapters that are engaging, accessible, and educational. Hefferon and Boniwell demonstrate a mastery of the literature through the ways in which they have marshalled the evidence from research and practice into this invaluable resource. This book will become an essential reference guide for researchers, educators and practitioners of positive psychology around the world."

Professor Alex Linley, Founding Director, Capp

"This book is a valuable resource for students looking for an introduction to Positive Psychology, but also wanting to get a comprehensive and updated overview of this innovative approach to the study of human behaviour and experience. It provides a broad coverage of the most relevant theories and constructs developed within Positive Psychology, and of their relevance for intervention and application in the most diverse life domains. Hefferon and Boniwell use a rigorous though accessible and friendly style of presentation. By means of effective learning supports, they stimulate readers' active engagement in critical reflections on each topic. The authors address the several issues and open questions which still characterize Positive Psychology as a relatively recent domain through a balanced and objective approach."

Antonella Delle Fave, University of Milano, Italy

"Kate Hefferon and Ilona Boniwell have produced the first textbook which has set out purposefully to support students and teachers in higher education in the exciting new area of positive psychology. The authors have experience of teaching the lectures described in each chapter and the book is written in a way that students will find engaging and fun. Each chapter has clear learning objectives, mock essay questions, measurement tools, summaries and a guide to further resources. The content has been well researched and the early chapters cover the main concepts of positive psychology such as emotions, happiness, wellbeing, optimism, and resilience. The later chapters are more novel and cover interventions and applications all with a critical eye. Of particular note is the chapter on the body in positive psychology – a topic which is frequently omitted from the 'thoughts and feelings' approach of other texts in this area. I would strongly recommend this book to all students and teachers of psychology."

Nanette Mutrie, Professor of Exercise and Sport Psychology, Strathclyde University, UK

Positive Psychology

Theory, Research and Applications

Kate Hefferon, PhD and Ilona Boniwell, PhD

 Open University Press

Open University Press
McGraw-Hill Education
McGraw-Hill House
Shoppenhangers Road
Maidenhead
Berkshire
England
SL6 2QL

email: enquiries@openup.co.uk
world wide web: www.openup.co.uk

and Two Penn Plaza, New York, NY 10121-2289, USA

First published 2011

Copyright © Kate Hefferon & Ilona Boniwell 2011

All rights reserved. Except for the quotation of short passages for the purposes of criticism and review, no part of this publication may be reproduced, stored in a retrieval system, or transmitted, in any form or by any means, electronic, mechanical, photocopying, recording or otherwise, without the prior written permission of the publisher or a licence from the Copyright Licensing Agency Limited. Details of such licences (for reprographic reproduction) may be obtained from the Copyright Licensing Agency Ltd of Saffron House, 6-10 Kirby Street, London, EC1N 8TS.

A catalogue record of this book is available from the British Library

ISBN-13: 978-0-335-24195-8 (pb) 978-0-335-24194-1 (hb)
ISBN-10: 0-335-24195-6 (pb) 0-335-24194-8 (hb)
eISBN: 978-0-335-24196-5

Library of Congress Cataloging-in-Publication Data
CIP data applied for

Typeset by Aptara Inc., India
Printed in the UK by Bell and Bain Ltd, Glasgow.

Fictitious names of companies, products, people, characters and/or data that may be used herein (in case studies or in examples) are not intended to represent any real individual, company, product or event.

The *McGraw-Hill* Companies

Contents

Preface

Purpose of the book

As lecturers on the only English-speaking European MSc course in positive psychology we were shocked at how little there was in the way of a proper, encompassing textbook for undergraduate students. Thus, this book represents a resource for all students, whether in psychology or other fields, to refer to. In addition, the textbook provides lecturers who are new to the area with a comprehensive and clear structure for teaching a module in positive psychology.

Tone of the book

Our background is very different from those of you who are just starting positive psychology. Indeed, both of us were studying and researching within the topic areas before they came under the umbrella term of positive psychology. This ultimately means that we have a more critical, multidisciplinary approach to the topics within the discipline. Major differences between our book and other textbooks within positive psychology include:

- A message of balance. Kate Hefferon's work in trauma, cancer and growth has firmly solidified the perspective that positive psychology must focus on negative events in life as well as the positive. We both hold this viewpoint and it will be present throughout the text.

- Broadening of research methods. As primarily qualitative researchers we have huge issues with American researchers' preoccupation with the 'scientific method'. Indeed, it seems ironic to have a science based on human wellbeing that reduces people to simple numbers and averages. Qualitative research allows us to see a richer, deeper side to the story and should be used in conjunction with quantitative methodologies.

- Critical perspective. Europeans have traditionally been trailblazers in the psychological sciences, with their critical and unfettered perspectives. By including several exercises as well as a critical perspective throughout, we endeavour to maintain this important reputation.

- The book has a fun and engaging voice while still adhering to academic evidence. We want this to be fun, informative and educational for you, the reader, and we have taken a great deal of time to ensure that this is possible.

Structure of the book

The textbook is divided into 11 chapters, representing 11 lectures across a 12-week semester (inclusive of a reading break). Institutions that run longer semesters can separate the chapters or concentrate on one of the topics in more detail. Not only are the chapters full of information on the theories of positive psychology, they are also packed with exercises to help meld together research and the application of the discipline. The chapters finish with exercises for you to use and implement in daily life. Furthermore, each chapter provides lists of suggested reading and web resources to enable you to continue learning about its specific topic.

Beginning of chapters

We have arranged the book so that you begin learning from the outset. We start each chapter with clear learning objectives that help orientate you to the material in the chapter. Next, we offer you three mock essay questions that we believe are appropriate for the chapter content. We would ask you to keep an eye out for the content that would be useful when answering these questions.

Throughout the chapter

Throughout each chapter we have included several learning/interest boxes that will help you on your journey. The first box to look out for is:

> ### Think about it…
>
> These boxes are peppered throughout the book to get you thinking about the concepts and theories we have just relayed to you. This is a great way to collate what you've learned and critically reflect on the subject matter.

The second type of box to look out for is:

> ### EXPERIMENTS
>
> We have also included sections within the textbook detailing the appropriate groundbreaking research studies that link to the theories discussed. We have chosen sharp, quirky one-liner titles to describe the studies, which you will hopefully find funny and easy to remember.

Finally, when we need to recap or refresh our knowledge of general psychology issues, look out for:

time out

These boxes take you on a time out to relearn topics such as epistemology, validity, reliability and the brain. You should know this general psychology information already but you may need a refresher.

End of chapter

From teaching an applied positive psychology course, we know that you need more than just being talked at, or given a book to read. The end of each chapter includes several ways for you to become active in your learning process. You will find the following sections there:

- *Chapter summary.* Just as we provide learning objectives at the start of each chapter, we also summarize all that you should now know after reading it. This way, you will have a concise overview of the information.

- *Suggested resources.* We have provided links and explain the usefulness of each one for your benefit. Have a look at them and see which will be most helpful to you in your learning.

- *Measurement tools section.* No psychological science is complete without an assortment of psychometric tools, so we have included, with the permission of the original authors, several widely used positive psychology tools at the end of each chapter for you to try out and reflect on. Make sure you take the time to complete these, as experience is very important in the learning process.

Kate Hefferon
Ilona Boniwell

Acknowledgements

I would like to thank my family for their support and friendship. They truly mean the world to me. I would also like to thank Ilona for her friendship, time and playful nature, which make for a wonderful collaboration (Kate).

I would like to thank Kate for her dedication to the project, for diving deep into all available studies, and for her enthusiasm and passion to create a really good piece of work (Ilona).

Every effort has been made to trace and acknowledge ownership of copyright and to clear permission for material reproduced in this book. The publishers will be pleased to make suitable arrangements to clear permission with any copyright holders whom it has not been possible to contact.

List of Figures, Tables and Questionnaires

Figures

Tables

Questionnaires

Flow Experience Questionnaire
Life Orientation-Revised (LOT-R)
Generalized Self-Efficacy Scale (GSE)
Changes in Outlook Questionnaire (CiOQ)
Self-Determination Scale (SDS)
Person–Activity Fit Diagnostic
International Physical Activity Questionnaire (IPAQ)

Guided Tour

[box excerpt]

time and banked to create a 'protective reservoir' upon which a person can draw from during unpleasant or distressing times (more about this in Chapter 2).

The engaged life focuses on flow, engagement, absorption and wellbeing, while the meaningful life encompasses service to something higher than the self. Thus, individuals can find happiness with the pursuit of all three 'lives'. At present, the concept of authentic happiness is more a theory than a causal recipe for happiness (Rashid, 2009a). As positive psychology continues to grow and develop more longitudinal databacks, we will know more about how these three 'lives' work in harmony to enhance wellbeing.

Think about it...

Sheldon (2009) defines authenticity as 'emotional genuineness, self-refinement and psychological depth'. Humanists originally believed that you couldn't study such abstract concepts, whereas other theorists, such as Freud believed that one could never be authentic.

1 Do you agree or disagree with these arguments?

2 Can you think of a time when you have been truly authentic or inauthentic to your self?

3 How do you know when you are being truly authentic?

The origins of modern-day positive psychology

The person regarded as being responsible for the creation of the positive psychology movement is Martin E. P. Seligman, a professor at the University of Pennsylvania. After decades of experimental research and success with his learned helplessness theory, Seligman was appointed President of the American Psychological Association (APA) in 1998. It was during his inauguration at the

Think about it...

These boxes are peppered throughout the book to get you thinking about the concepts and theories discussed. This is your chance to step back and critically reflect on the subject matter.

Experiments

It's not all theory. If you want to learn about the most influential positive psychology experiments to date, watch out for these succinct boxes, which expand your knowledge through real-life examples related to the main body of the chapter.

[box excerpt]

- creating new avenues for control; or
- accepting current circumstances (Thompson, 2002).

PLANTS

Langer and Rodin, both Yale Professors, argued that nursing homes are de-escalation live environments for those who live there. They conducted a study that gave patients some control over small decisions in their lives. The researchers split the members of the nursing home into two groups: the responsibility-induced group (RII) and the control group. At a floor meeting, the RII residents were told they had choices on the arrangement of furniture, visiting hours, entertainment and they were given a small plant to care for. The other group (control group) had a floor meeting where they were told that the nurses would take care of their every need, what entertainment to expect, what visiting hours were set, how many hours are arranged and that nurses would care for their plants. They tested the floors on several pre-post measures and the RII group reported better moods, enhanced alertness and much more active. However, the disturbing results came 18 months after the intervention was finished. Pre-intervention, the nursing home reported a 25 per cent mortality rate in six 18 month period. This time, they found that the participants who were in the RII group had a 50 per cent lower mortality rate than the control group (15 per cent versus 30 per cent). The difference in mortality between groups as well as to previous baseline measures was believed to be the result of giving control and chance to the participants.

See Langer and Rodin (1976) for the original article.

Locus of control (LOC) was developed as a concept in 1966 by Rotter and since then has been examined by many researchers against hundreds of diverse dependent variables. People with a strong internal locus of control believe that the responsibility

[box excerpt]

Time out section below to consider their emotions. At present, the literature shows a strong correlation between dispositional global positive affect and extraversion (Costa and McCrae, 1980; Shiota et al., 2006).

The two most robust relationships with happiness and personality are extraversion and neuroticism, will be shown predicting wellbeing up to ten years later. People who are extraverted are more likely to experience positive emotion and more intense positive emotion. In addition, our attachment style or relationships may have an impact on our ability to feel positive emotions. Not surprisingly, secure attachment has been associated with higher levels of positive affect to a greater relationships (more anxious attachment. Neuroticism on the other hand, is consistently linked to depression and low levels of wellbeing.

Five personality traits

According to Costa and McCrae (1992) there are five main personality traits that individuals possess to some degree or another. These include:

1 **Extraversion:** individuals who score high on extraversion tend to be sociable. Introverts are just as what there is something collective going on. It is often said to be classically considered to more reserved, quiet, shy and prefer to be alone.

2 **Agreeableness:** individuals who score high on agreeableness tend to be pleasant, compassionate and sympathetic to others' needs. Low-scorers tend to be antagonistic, suspicious, critical and slightly hard-nosed.

3 **Conscientiousness:** individuals who score high on conscientiousness tend to have high levels of grit, meaning they are industrious, diligent, efficient and reliable. Low scorers tend to be inattentive, also more moody, and sometimes unreliable.

4 **Neuroticism:** individuals who score high on neuroticism tend to experience high levels of anxiety, insecurity and can be emotionally volatile. Low scorers tend to be more tranquil, steady and composed.

5 **Openness to experience:** individuals who score high on openness to experience tend to be original and artistic. Low-scorers tend to be more conventional and unoriginal.

Shiota et al. (2006) reviewed the correlation between one's positive emotions and one's ability to engage across 12 areas: joy, contentment, pride, love, compassion,

Time Out

Stop at these boxes and take the opportunity to re-cap or refresh your knowledge on general psychology issues. These are all based on key topics, such as epistemology, validity, reliability, the brain, etc.

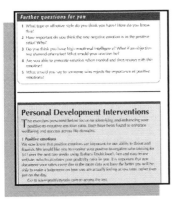

Further Questions for You

At the end of each chapter, further questions invite discussion of key topics. Interacting with these questions will help you meld together research and application, as your pin down your response.

Personal Development Interventions

These exercises explore how the principles of each chapter apply to or impact you. As you reflect on the different tasks over a number of days, you will learn how the perspectives expressed in the chapter work in the real world.

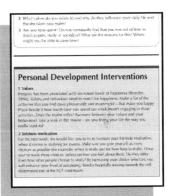

Measurement Tools

Handily, we have included an assortment of psychometric tools, including well-used measuring tools that are essential for collecting data for your positive psychology studies. As you measure your responses with the scales provided, you can put into action the analysis skills you are learning. Each section also teaches you the main benefits and limitations of measuring data with its specific tool.

CHAPTER 1

Introduction to Positive Psychology

❖ LEARNING OBJECTIVES

Positive psychology is the study of topics as diverse as happiness, optimism, subjective wellbeing, and personal growth. The opening chapter has two goals: (1) to describe and critically examine the emergence and development of this new field in recent years and (2) to orientate students to some of the topics studied by positive psychologists. At the end of the chapter you will have the opportunity to complete questionnaires on some of the main topics in positive psychology.

List of topics

- The scope and aim of positive psychology.
- The history of positive psychology.
- How we measure happiness.
- The good life and authenticity.
- Humanistic psychology.
- Where positive psychology stands today.

MOCK ESSAY QUESTIONS

1 Critically discuss the differences between 'positive' psychology and 'psychology as usual'.
2 Is positive psychology as different from humanistic psychology as it claims to be?
3 Why might we need positive psychology?

What is positive psychology?

In today's world, society is facing extremely tough challenges in the form of global warming, natural disasters, economic recession, unprecedented homelessness, terrorism and the draining continuation of war. With all this sadness and horror, where in the world does a science based on testing happiness, wellbeing, personal growth and 'the good life' fit into the modern-day agenda?

This textbook will take you through the new science of positive psychology, which aims to 'understand, test, discover and promote the factors that allow individuals and communities to thrive' (Sheldon et al., 2000). Positive psychology focuses on wellbeing, happiness, flow, personal strengths, wisdom, creativity, imagination and characteristics of positive groups and institutions. Furthermore, the focus is not just on how to make individuals happy, thereby perpetuating a self-centred, narcissistic approach, but on happiness and flourishing at a group level as well. We will look at how individuals and groups thrive and how increasing the wellbeing of one will have a positive effect on the other, leading to a win-win situation.

What we hope to demonstrate, throughout this textbook, is that positive psychology is not simply the focus on positive thinking and positive emotions. It's much more than that. Indeed, the area of positive psychology is focused on what makes individuals and communities flourish, rather than languish. Flourishing is defined as 'a state of positive mental health; to thrive, to prosper and to fare well in endeavours free of mental illness, filled with emotional vitality and function positively in private and social realms' (Michalec et al., 2009: 391). Indeed, existing figures show that only 18 per cent of adults meet the criteria of flourishing, 65 per cent are moderately mentally healthy and 17 per cent are languishing. Unsurprisingly, flourishing has several positive correlates such as academic achievement, mastery goal setting, higher levels of self-control and continued perseverance (Howell, 2009). Thus, a science that focuses on the development and facilitation of flourishing environments and individuals is an important addition to the psychological sciences.

> ### Think about it...
>
> Why have you decided to take this module? What was it about the syllabus that attracted you? Past experiences? A certain topic? Take a moment to reflect on this.

Positive psychology concentrates on positive experiences at three time points: (1) the past, centring on wellbeing, contentment and satisfaction; (2) the present, which focuses on concepts such as happiness and flow experiences; (3) the future, with concepts including optimism and hope. Not only does positive psychology distinguish between wellbeing across time points but it also separates the subject area into three nodes:

- the subjective node, which encompasses things like positive experiences and states across past, present and future (for example, happiness, optimism, wellbeing);
- the individual node, which focuses on characteristics of the 'good person' (for example, talent, wisdom, love, courage, creativity); and
- the group node, which studies positive institutions, citizenship and communities (for example, altruism, tolerance, work ethic) (Positive Psychology Center, 1998).

Contrary to criticism, positive psychology is not a selfish psychology. At its best, positive psychology has been able to give the scientific community, society and individuals a new perspective on existing ideas as well as providing empirical evidence to support the phenomenon of human flourishing. Above all, though, positive psychology has challenged and rebalanced the deficit approach to living while connecting its findings to many different disciplines. Throughout this textbook you will see how inducing positive emotions, committing acts of kindness and enhancing social connections enable individual and societal flourishing, demonstrating the usefulness of the discipline for individual, group and community wellbeing.

Authentic happiness and the good life

What is the good life? Socrates, Aristotle and Plato believed that when people pursued a virtuous life, they would become authentically happy. Epicurus and later utilitarians preached that happiness was indeed the abundance of positive feelings and pleasures. Positive psychology has traditionally conceptualized authentic happiness as a mix of *hedonic* and *eudaimonic* wellbeing (Seligman and Csikszentmihalyi, 2000). Hedonic happiness encompasses high levels of positive affect and low levels of negative affect, in addition to high subjective life satisfaction (Diener, 1999). Eudaimonic wellbeing focuses more on the creation of meaning and purpose in life, although the distinction between these two concepts is subject to debate (Kashdan et al., 2008; Keyes and Annas, 2009; Tiberius and Mason, 2009).

The notion of 'authentic happiness' has been further broken down by Seligman to indicate a life that is a combination of a *pleasurable life,* an *engaged life* and a *meaningful life.* The pleasurable life encompasses feelings of positive emotions (for example, joy, gratitude, serenity, interest, hope, pride, amusement, inspiration, awe and love – Fredrickson, 2009), which are integral components to our success and wellbeing. Positive emotions widen our thought processes, which can be built up over time and banked to create a 'protective reservoir' upon which a person can draw from during unpleasant or distressing times (more about this in Chapter 2).

The engaged life focuses on flow, engagement, absorption and wellbeing, while the meaningful life encompasses service to something higher than the self. Thus, individuals can find happiness with the pursuit of all three 'lives'. At present, the concept of authentic happiness is more a theory than a causal recipe for happiness (Rashid, 2009a). As positive psychology continues to grow and develop more longitudinal databanks, we will know more about how these three 'lives' work in harmony to enhance wellbeing.

Think about it...

Sheldon (2009) defines authenticity as 'emotional genuineness, self-attunement and psychological depth'. Humanists originally believed that you couldn't study such abstract concepts, whereas other theorists, such as Freud believed that one could never be authentic.

1   Do you agree or disagree with these arguments?

2   Can you think of a time when you have been truly authentic or inauthentic to your self?

3   How do you know when you are being truly authentic?

The origins of modern-day positive psychology

The person regarded as being responsible for the creation of the positive psychology movement is Martin E. P. Seligman, a professor at the University of Pennsylvania. After decades of experimental research and success with his learned helplessness theory, Seligman was appointed President of the American Psychological Association (APA) in 1998. It was during his inauguration at the 107th Annual Convention of the APA in Boston, Massachusetts, 21 August 1999, that Seligman decided to introduce his agenda to correct the trajectory of modern day 'pathologically focused' psychology. Since Seligman's presidential position, he has become a figurehead for the positive psychology movement and continues to gain support from research funds and governments across the world to include positive psychology theories and practices into daily life.

ROSES

Although not an experiment, the story of Seligman and his rose garden has become a folk legend in the discipline of positive psychology. By his account, positive psychology started from an epiphany he experienced while attending to his rose garden. His daughter, who was five at the time, had been trying to get her father's attention. Seligman turned to her and snapped. Unhappy with this response, his daughter asked him whether or not he remembered how she used to whine when she was three and four? She told him that when she turned five she decided to stop – and if she was able to stop whining, then he was able to stop being a grouch! This revelation of developing what was right, rather than fixating on what was wrong, sparked what Seligman would go on to promote during his career as APA president: that we should be teaching our children and ourselves to look at our strengths rather than weaknesses.

See Seligman and Csikszentmihalyi (2000) for the original account.

Psychology as usual (pre-1998)

Unbeknown to the general psychology population, there were *three tasks* of psychology prior to World War Two. These were to: (1) cure mental illness; (2) enhance the lives of the normal population; and (3) study geniuses. Due to the aftermath of two world wars and the return of many psychologically impaired soldiers, research funding focused on its first agenda, with the other two nearly forgotten[1] (Linley, 2009).

We must acknowledge that this funding for mental disorders has been immensely successful, as at least 14 disorders can now be cured or considerably relieved (Seligman and Csikszentmihalyi, 2000). Unfortunately, these fixations on pathology led to psychology becoming a 'victimology'. Instead of viewing humans as proactive, creative, self-determined beings, psychologists viewed humans as passive individuals subjected to external forces (Seligman and Csikszentmihalyi, 2000).[2] Hence, the main difference between post-World War Two psychology and today's positive psychology is in the question asked: 'Why do these individuals fail?' versus 'What makes some individuals succeed?'

66 The message of the Positive Psychology movement is to remind our field that it has been deformed. Psychology is not just the study of disease, weakness, and damage; it also is the study of strength and virtue. Treatment is not just fixing what is wrong; it also is building what is right. Psychology is not just about illness or health; it is about work, education, insight, love, growth, and play. And in this quest for what is best, Positive Psychology does not rely on wishful thinking, self-deception or hand-waving; instead it tries to adapt what is best in the scientific method to the unique problems that human behaviour presents in all its complexity.

– (Seligman, 2002b). **99**

Think about it…

From 1972 to 2006, the ratio of depression research publications to wellbeing publications was 5:1. We challenge you to undertake your own calculations on PsychInfo, to see where the ratio is currently at today.

time out

Depression and mental illness

Depression and mental illness are still important issues within our society and positive psychology researchers do not negate this. Indeed, statistics indicating the occurrence of depression were and are still worrying. Depression was ten times higher in 2009 than it was in 1960, with the mean age for depression today being 14.5 (compared to 29.5 in 1960). Furthermore, at any one time, about 2 per cent of the population is suffering from depression and 14 per cent of us will experience depression by the age of 35 (compared to 2 per cent in the 1950s) (Keyes and Michelac, 2009).

The results of the Global Burden of Disease Study (1996) found depression to be among the top five illnesses contributing to disability in life adjusted years (the total number of years a person lives with disabilities). Indeed, mental disorder came only second to cardiovascular disease.

Mental illness costs the USA over $40 billion per annum and this figure continues to rise (Keyes and Michelac, 2009). Staggering new statistics suggest that up to 50 per cent of us will experience some mental disorder in our lifetime. Furthermore, once we have experienced a mental disorder we are far more likely to experience another again in the future. The rise in documented occurrences may also be due to the reduced stigma involved in seeking help for depression in addition to public awareness of mental disorders.

Disease model debate

Originally, the idea of positive psychology was to move away from the disease (medical) model (Figure 1.1), which fixated on moving people from a −8 to −3 or severely depressed to mildly depressed. Positive psychology, on the other hand, situated its focus on people who fell at +3 (languishing) and helped to raise them to a +8 (flourishing). We find this model an easy, simple visual when teaching our students to differentiate between the 'main aims' of positive psychology.

Psychosis, neuroticism Depression, disorder	Wellbeing, contentment, bliss Excitement, cheerfulness
− ——————————————————— **0**	——————————————————— +
Focus on flaws Overcoming deficiencies Avoiding pain Running from unhappiness Neutral state (0) as ceiling	Focus on strengths Building abilities Seeking pleasure Engaging happiness No ceiling (you can keep going)

FIGURE 1.1 Disease/health model

Of course, the analogy is simple and did the trick at a time when clarification between the psychologies was needed. However, this theoretical model assumes that people can be at zero; but what is zero? And what does it really mean to be +3? The model assumes that positive psychology cannot help those on the negative end of the scale. However, we now have evidence that positive psychology interventions can benefit people who are diagnosed as clinically depressed in addition to the normal population (Sin and Lyubomirsky, 2009).

Furthermore, the diagram calls into question the meaning of health. What exactly is 'health' and when do we exhibit mental health versus mental illness?[3] Since 1948, the World Health Organization has defined health as 'a state of complete physical, mental and social wellbeing and not merely the absence of disease or infirmity' (World Health Organization, 1948: 200). In 1958, Austrian psychologist Marie Jahoda wrote her major contribution to psychology, titled *Ideal Mental Health*, which listed six criteria or six characteristics found within the normal population: (1) efficient self-perception; (2) realistic self-esteem and acceptance; (3) voluntary control of behaviour; (4) true perception of the world; (5) sustaining relationships and giving affection; and (6) self-direction and productivity. She argued that these six criteria were needed to establish 'positive mental health'. Her studies were amongst the first to attempt to operationalize positive functioning and her findings are not far divorced from what we know about mental health and wellbeing today.

Corey Keyes, a shining example of a positive sociologist, has spent years looking at the relationship between mental health and mental illness. His work brought him to conclude that the two are not on the same continuum, and that they are two separate continuums. Thus, the absence of mental illness does not equate to the presence of mental health. As research has continually found that the absence of mental health is as damaging as the presence of mental illness, Keyes proposed two strategies for tackling mental disorder: (1) the promotion and maintenance of mental health;[4] and (2) the prevention and treatment of mental illness (Keyes and Michalec, 2009).

History of positive psychology

One of the criticisms of positive psychology is that the ideas are not new. Even the term 'positive psychology' was used by Abraham Maslow, many decades before Seligman (Maslow, 1954: 201). However Seligman has done a phenomenal job of bringing the thoughts and ideas of past researchers, philosophers and scientists back to our consciousness. We have identified four groups of individuals who were looking at 'the good life' before the discipline of positive psychology even existed. Let's begin with the Ancient Greeks . . .

Greeks

Aristotle's (384–322 BCE) greatest contribution to philosophy is arguably his work on morality, virtue and what it means to live a good life. As he questioned these topics, he concluded that the highest good for all humanity was indeed eudaimonia (or happiness). Ultimately, his work argued that although pleasure may arise from engaging with activities that are virtuous, it is not the sole aim of humanity (Mason and Tiberius, 2009).

Utilitarianism

Utilitarianism, created by Jeremy Bentham and carried on by John Stuart Mill, is a philosophy that argued that the right act or policy from government is that which will cause 'the greatest good for the greatest number of people', also known as the 'greatest happiness principle', or the principle of utility. Utilitarianism was the first sector that attempted to measure happiness, creating a tool composed of seven categories, assessing the quantity of experienced happiness (Pawelski and Gupta, 2009). Whereas philosophers before had assumed that happiness was not measurable, utilitarianism argued and attempted to demonstrate that it was indeed possible. Pawelski and Gupta (2009) proposed that utilitarianism influences some areas of positive psychology today, such as subjective wellbeing and the pleasurable life. Ultimately, positive psychology accepts that while pleasure is a component of overall wellbeing, it is not enough, and the inclusion of eudaimonic pursuits is necessary as a complement to utilitarian philosophy.

William James

A brilliant scholar, William James is best known for his contribution to psychology through his widely read text, *The Principles of Psychology* (James, 1890). James originally trained as a medical doctor at Harvard University, Boston, USA, before becoming interested in religion, mysticism and epistemology (Pawelski, 2009). His chapter, 'The Emotions', is most relevant for positive psychology to acknowledge. He suggests there that emotions come after we have physically acted out. For example 'common-sense says, we lose our fortune, are sorry and weep; we meet a bear, are frightened and run; we are insulted by a rival, are angry and strike. The hypothesis here to be defended says that this order of sequence is incorrect . . . that we feel sorry because we cry, angry because we strike, afraid because we tremble . . .' (James 1890: 1065–6). This was one of the first examples, if not the very first example, of writing to connect emotions and expressions together. His years of intertwining physiology, psychology and philosophy still have an impact in philosophical issues surrounding the mind, the body and the brain today.

Humanistic psychology

Humanistic psychology emerged in the late 1950s and early 1960s as a backlash to the predominant psychological theories of psychoanalysis, behaviourism and conditioning. The humanistic movement introduced and solidified qualitative inquiry as an imperative paradigm to research human thought, behaviour and experience, adding a holistic dimension to psychology. In a nutshell, humanistic psychology is the psychological perspective that emphasizes the study of the whole person. Humanistic psychologists believe that: (1) individuals' behaviour is primarily determined by their perception of the world around them and their personal meanings; (2) individuals are not solely the product of their environment or their genes; and (3) individuals are internally directed and motivated to fulfil their human potential.

The main drive of humanistic psychology was to focus on mental health, specifically positive attributes such as happiness, contentment, ecstasy, kindness, caring, sharing and generosity. Humanists felt that, unlike their behaviourist cousins, humans had choice and responsibility for their own destiny. This perspective ultimately views life as a process, with all humans beholding an innate drive for growth and fulfilment of potentials. The humanists even went as far as to include spiritual proprieties of the self, the world and wellbeing; an area that is controversial even in today's scientific societies.

So, even back then, psychologists were aware of the deficit in research on the positive side of life. Some positive psychologists have argued that the reason why the humanistic discipline never really took off stems from the fact that it never developed a respectable empirical basis. This lack of theoretical basis led to encouraging a narcissistic preoccupation with the self and self-improvement at the expense of societal welfare (Seligman and Csikszentmihalyi, 2000).

time out

Abraham Maslow

Abraham Maslow was one of several eminent psychologists who embodied the humanistic movement and what it stood for. Maslow was a very famous psychologist across many disciplines and actually coined the term 'positive psychology' (Maslow, 1954: 201). Mostly known for his model of a 'hierarchy of needs', Maslow emphasized the need for psychology to focus on human potentialities rather than just human deficiencies (Bridges and Wertz, 2009). Thus, he desired a more positive approach toward psychology. His major contributions to psychology as a whole were his theories on motivation, needs, self-actualization and peak experience.

The science of psychology has been far more successful on the negative than on the positive side; it has revealed to us much about man's shortcomings, his illnesses, his sins, but little about his potentialities, his virtues, his achievable aspirations, or his psychological height.

(Maslow, 1954: 201)

Unfortunately, positive psychology didn't start off on the right foot with its humanistic cousins. In the beginning, there was a clear drive to separate positive psychology from the humanistic discipline, claiming a major difference in methodological inquiry. Positive psychology is the scientific study of wellbeing, and therefore uses the scientific method to test hypotheses. We believe that there is much that positive psychology can learn from and continue to learn about the humanistic movement and this need to separate from the humanistic appears divisive and unnecessary.

Humanistic psychology criticizes positive psychology for its short-sighted drive to separate itself from the humanistic discipline, as by adopting this approach, it has left out vital areas of research and methods of inquiry (qualitative) that limit the generalization of its main findings. Furthermore, humanistic psychologists feel that to prove that positive psychology is indeed 'scientific' it has overcompensated and stuck to quantitative inquiry. This is a very important historical fact that students must be aware of when undertaking their studies in positive psychology. We truly believe that in order to understand where we are in positive psychology we have to know where we have come from.

Can we measure happiness?

This is one of the most fundamental questions for positive psychology. Indeed, much of the reason why the topics and concepts within positive psychology were not previously studied was because they were believed to be ephemeral and too difficult, if not impossible, to study and measure. By creating and testing scientific measurement tools as well as experimental methods, scientists/psychologists have taken philosophical concepts of virtue and happiness and put them to rigorous, scientific testing.

You will read repeatedly how positive psychology is a science, not a self-help technique that uses the scientific method to understand human thoughts, feelings and behaviours. When psychology was first making its way into history, its practitioners wanted to adopt the same scientific rigour as the natural sciences, such as biology and chemistry. These sciences are based on objective testing and the positivist epistemological paradigm. This epistemology uses experimentation, logical deduction and rational thought to examine the world whereby knowledge is obtained by direct, objective observation. Facts and knowledge lead to laws and predictions for human nature and can determine causal relationships (cause and effect).

time out

Epistemology
Epistemology is a branch of philosophy concerned with the acquisition of knowledge. A multitude of philosophical viewpoints surround methodological paradigms. Researchers must therefore choose which epistemological position they believe best suits their research question. The four main paradigms include: post-positivism, constructivism (social constructionism), advocacy/participatory and pragmatism.

There are, however, several critiques of the scientific method, to which we will allude throughout the textbook. First of all, it does not acknowledge historical, cultural and societal factors. In reducing people to numbers and averages, this method 'oversimplifies' human behaviour and neglects the individual (Langdridge, 2004a, 2004b). Furthermore, positive psychology, in its attempt to be considered a 'proper science' has separated itself from the use of qualitative methods, which are imperative adjunct methods of data collection, used to explain and explore topics and results within the discipline.

> ## Think about it…
>
> What do you consider to be 'good evidence'? What is truth? Can research be totally objective? Write down your answers and think of examples to argue your points. (Adapted from Forrester, 2010: 19.)

Where is positive psychology today?

As mentioned, the positive psychology movement has gained massive momentum over the past years. After Seligman's speech, researchers gathered in Akumal, Mexico, from 1999 to 2002, to discuss development of the new area of positive psychology. At the same time, researchers were holding national and international summits from Lincoln, Nebraska to Washington DC, which continued to thrive (Linley, 2009).

There are currently hundreds of undergraduate classes in positive psychology across the world as well as two Masters programmes in applied positive psychology, the first founded in 2005 by Seligman at the University of Pennsylvania, and the second founded in 2007 at the University of East London, UK.[5] Italy, Portugal and Mexico are currently creating Masters courses in positive psychology in their own languages.

At present, there are several conferences offered by the European Positive Psychology Network (Boniwell, 2009). The First World Congress of Positive Psychology was held on 18–21 June 2009 in Philadelphia, Pennsylvania, USA. Finally, a sign of the strength of the movement lies in the fact that positive psychology boasts its own academic, peer-reviewed journal, *Journal of Positive Psychology,* founded in 2006.

In the UK, several positive psychology resources contribute to the positive psychology research base. We work within the London Partnership for Positive Psychology in Practice (LP4), which provides access to leaders in the field of positive psychology as well as opportunities for collaboration of research and consultancy. Furthermore, the Centre for Applied Positive Psychology at Warwick, UK, runs online short courses on positive psychology as well as consultancy projects.

Positive psychology's place

The discipline of psychology can be divided into a vast number of different areas. The American Psychological Association has 56 branches, while the British Psychological Society recognizes nine chartered areas of psychology: clinical, counselling, educational, forensic, health, neuro-psychology, occupational, sport and exercise, and teachers/researchers in psychology. However, where exactly does positive psychology fit within the accepted psychology disciplines?

There is disagreement regarding whether positive psychology is a separate discipline in itself or if it encompasses the entire field of psychology. For example, Figure 1.2 shows how positive psychology can be situated within mainstream psychological disciplines. Other links can be drawn to humanistic psychology, psychiatry, sociology, biology and other subject areas. However, whether or not positive psychology will become a separate discipline remains to be seen.

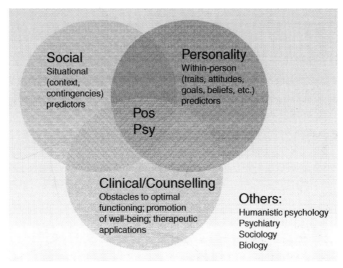

FIGURE 1.2 Positive psychology in relation to 'psychology as usual'

Positive psychology has rapidly grown in the past few years and spans a multitude of areas and disciplines. You only have to look at the mind map in Figure 1.3 to gain a sense of how this area is spreading.

Think about it…

What might be missing from this mind map? As you go through this textbook, create your own visual mind map, which will help you understand the many links within positive psychology.

Positive psychologists would argue that psychology should also expand its focus to improve child education by making greater use of intrinsic motivation, positive affect and creativity; improve psychotherapy by developing approaches

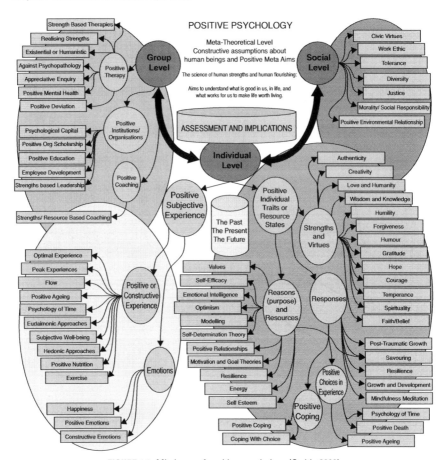

FIGURE 1.3 Mind map of positive psychology (Smith, 2008)

that emphasize hope, meaning and self-healing; improve family life by better understanding the dynamics of love, parenthood and commitment. They would argue that it should improve work satisfaction across the lifespan by helping people to find authentic involvement, experience states of flow and make genuine contributions in their work; that it should improve organizations and societies by discovering conditions that enhance trust, communication, and altruism; and that it should improve the moral character of society by better understanding and promoting the spiritual impulse.

One thing to note is that many researchers in these areas of expertise were working on them before positive psychology was even born. What suddenly makes some of these areas now 'positive psychology' rather than say clinical or sport psychology? For example, since the early 1980s, research has been conducted on how coaches and athletes can achieve peak performance. From the vast amount of data collected, theories about motivation, planned behaviour, mastery and success have been cross-fertilized with other areas of psychology. In particular, sport psychology and performance psychology appear to seek the same outcome. Sport tends to look at the best performers and adapt their strategies to those who can improve further, as does positive psychology, which looks at those who are flourishing and shares this information with the normal population. The authors believe that collaboration with these two areas is essential for positive psychology.

Topics we will cover in this textbook

Areas with significant amounts of research include subjective wellbeing, positive affect, hope, optimism, resilience, post-traumatic growth, goals, meaning and strengths (Snyder and Lopez, 2007). Each chapter is created to cover similar or connected areas of positive psychology.

More specifically, Chapter 2 focuses on the concepts of *positive emotions* and *emotional intelligence*. Chapter 3 discusses *hedonic happiness* and the concept of *subjective wellbeing* (SWB). Following from this, Chapter 4 questions the concept of SWB with *eudaimonic* theories, including *psychological wellbeing* and *self-determination theory*. No course on positive psychology would be complete without studying the theory of *optimism, positive illusion* and *hope* (Chapter 5). Chapter 6 focuses on *resilience, post-traumatic growth, wisdom* and positive *ageing*. Chapter 7 fixes on *meaning* and *goal theories* and their association with wellbeing. The last few chapters focus more on the applied nature of positive psychology, looking at *strengths* and *interventions* and how we can apply them within corporate organizations, schools, health centres and therapeutic surroundings. The last chapter looks at the discipline from a more critical viewpoint, with scholarly predictions of where this new and exciting discipline will end up.

So, from our review of positive psychology yesterday, today and tomorrow, we hope we've shown you that the topics have history and decades of research behind them. They were in fruition before the umbrella term and will, hopefully, continue to be so in the future, whether or not the movement solidifies its place in psychology. Positive psychology has definitely identified groups of fragmented researchers focusing on the positive side of human behaviour, thought and feelings and given them a common thread. Indeed, some scientists may be positive psychologists and not know it (Diener, 2003).

Summary

Reflecting on the learning objectives, you should now understand the main aims of positive psychology and its components. More specifically:

- Positive psychology is the science of wellbeing and optimal functioning.
- There are three levels to positive psychology: the subjective node, the individual node and the group node.
- Positive psychology has a rich history within ancient Greek philosophy, humanism and several areas of mental health.
- Humanistic psychology is a close cousin of positive psychology, the main difference being positive psychology's focus on the use of the scientific method.
- We will cover a wide variety of topics, ranging from positive emotions to trauma and growth.
- Positive psychology is not simply a 'happiology'; it is intended as a supplement to 'psychology as usual'.

Suggested Resources

www.positivepsychology.org.uk
This is our positive psychology UK website, which focuses on leading positive psychology researchers and their findings.

www.authentichappiness.org
The original 'go to' website, authentic happiness is a place where you can access all of the leading positive psychology tools, participate in research and learn about current research from Seligman himself.

www.ippanetwork.org
This is a website dedicated to researchers in positive psychology, with access to full membership reserved for psychologists and MSc graduates in positive psychology. Details of conferences are available to the public.

www.enpp.eu
This is the European Network for Positive Psychology, with highlighted representatives for countries within Europe, as well as their conference details and abstract submission deadlines.

www.cappeu.com
A work-based applied centre in Warwick – this is ideal for those looking to see the applied nature of positive psychology in business.

www.neweconomics.org
A leading research/policy think tank based in London.

Further questions for you

1 What do you feel is novel about positive psychology?
2 If this is positive psychology, does that mean all other psychology is negative? Discuss.
3 Why do you think positive psychology is needed in today's society?
4 Which topics do you relate to and why?
5 What do you think the potential dangers of positive psychology are?

Personal Development Interventions

Before we start the course, we would like you to think about your current state of happiness. How happy are you? Try out the following exercises to help raise awareness around your current happiness levels and how you can potentially improve them.

1 This is an interesting exercise about a rapidly growing therapeutic intervention, quality of life therapy (Frisch, 2006). It is known as 'the happiness pie'. To do this, you should get a sheet of blank paper and draw a large circle, or happiness pie, to represent your life and to what you allocate your energy to, such as family, health, exercise, goals, spiritual practices, work and play. As you reflect on these, make 'slices' into the pie to reflect how much energy you devote to each. Does the size of each slice represent the importance of that slice? For example, if family is very important to you and yet it represents only a small fraction of the pie, then maybe it's time to start thinking of how to scale back other areas and increase this particular one. Finally, list five ways in which you can make time for these slices and thereby increase your wellbeing.

2 The second exercise we would like you to do is something that you may already do instinctively. This is simply putting a name and some structure to your daily routine. If you do not already do this, then you're in for a big surprise (Seligman et al., 2005).

   This exercise is called 'three good things' and was developed to enhance one's sense of gratitude. For the next week, before you go to bed, write down three good things that happened to you that day. The 'things' do not have to be monumental, such as winning the lottery or graduating, and it is surprising how hard it can be at the start. Eventually, you will start to see and appreciate the smaller things in life that add up over time.

We would suggest that after you have done the 'three good things' exercise for one week, you continue for the remainder of the course. Use the gratitude scale below to document your 'before' and 'after' gratitude scores.

Measurement Tools

Before we start asking you to fill out questionnaires, we would like you to review the 'time out' section below to refresh your memory about what constitutes a 'good' questionnaire. Remember, the data collected are only as good as the questionnaire used to collect them. Enjoy!

time out

Assessing quality within questionnaires

The following section will review the main components involved in creating a good quality questionnaire (Howitt and Cramer, 2008). These components are found throughout psychology – keep them in mind as you go through the Measurement Tools sections.

Reliability: this is what we use to assess if something is consistent. For example, the ability of a questionnaire to produce the same results under the same conditions. It asks whether or not the test is measuring something relatively unchanging: are the scores stable over time? Reliability is a necessary but not sufficient condition of a questionnaire.

- *Inter-/intra-rater reliability* assesses whether the scores are consistent across/within raters.
- *Test/retest reliability* assesses whether or not the scores are consistent across time. What about practice effects/mood states? Some test results can be expected to change.
- *Internal consistency:* this considers whether the items are intercorrelated. The Cronbach's alpha method splits the test into all possible halves,

correlates all scores and averages the correlations for all splits. In psychology we generally accept a cutoff of 0.7 with anything above 0.8 deemed as reliable.

Validity: this refers to whether or not the questionnaire measures what it is intended to measure. Validity is a necessary but not sufficient condition of a questionnaire. You can think of validity as accuracy – does the questionnaire hit the 'bull's eye'? There are several types of validity. These include:

- *Content/face validity:* How representative are your items? How well do they relate to the construct being measured at face value?
- *Criterion validity:* Is the questionnaire measuring what it intends to measure?
- *Predictive validity:* If we use the questionnaire in a variety of settings, would it predict an appropriate outcome? For example, tests in mathematical ability should predict success in maths examinations.
- *Concurrent validity:* Does it correlate well with other, already validated measures of the same construct? Comparison with real world observations?
- *Construct validity:* A higher level concept is applied to a test that fulfils predictions that would be made given the nature of the construct it purports to operationalize.
- *Convergent validity:* Measures of constructs that theoretically *should* be related to each other are, in fact, observed to be related to each other.
- *Discriminant validity:* Measures of constructs that theoretically *should* not be related to each other are, in fact, *observed* not to be related to each other.
- *Factorial validity:* Is your factor structure valid? Does it make intuitive sense? If items cluster into meaningful groups, factorial validity can be inferred.

Tips on making your own questionnaire:

- Each item should contain only *one* complete thought or idea.
- Items should be succinct, rather than long.
- No complex sentences. The language of the items should be simple, accessible, clear and direct.
- No double negatives.
- No items that are likely to be endorsed by almost everyone or by almost no one.
- No items that are ambiguous and may be interpreted in more than one way.
- No items which clearly contain a socially desirable response.
- Item content and language should be suitable for people of different ages, meaningful across the socioeconomic gradient, for men and women, and not culture-specific.

Think about it…

What is the value of assessment? What about social desirability? What is your previous experience with assessments?

The Gratitude Questionnaire-Six Item Form (GQ-6)

(McCullough, Emmons and Tsang, 2002)

Directions

Using the scale below as a guide, write a number on the line preceding each statement to indicate how much you agree with it.

1 = strongly disagree
2 = disagree
3 = slightly disagree
4 = neutral
5 = slightly agree
6 = agree
7 = strongly agree

____ 1. I have so much in life to be thankful for.
____ 2. If I had to list everything that I felt grateful for, it would be a very long list.
____ 3. When I look at the world, I don't see much to be grateful for.
____ 4. I am grateful to a wide variety of people.
____ 5. As I get older I find myself more able to appreciate the people, events, and situations that have been part of my life history.
____ 6. Long periods of time can go by before I feel grateful to something or someone.

Scoring

Add together your scores for items 1, 2, 4, and 5. Reverse your scores for items 3 and 6. Add the reversed scores for items 3 and 6 to those for items 1, 2, 4, and 5. This is your total GQ-6 score. This number should be between 6 and 42.

Interpretation

If you scored 35 you scored higher than 25 per cent of the 1224 individuals who took the GQ-6 on the Spirituality and Health website. If you scored 38 out of 42, you scored higher than 50 per cent of them. If you scored 41 out of 42, you scored higher than 75 per cent. If you scored 42 or higher, you scored among the top 13 per cent.

For more cultural and contextual norms, please refer to www.psy.miami.edu/faculty/mmccullough/gratitude/GQ-6-scoring-interp.pdf.

Review

This questionnaire documents your level of gratitude. It contains six items on a seven-point Likert scale. Overall, the scale yields a high internal consistency (0.82) and is positively correlated with positive emotions, life satisfaction, vitality, optimism, empathy, sharing and forgiving. It is negatively related to depression and stress.

The scale has low-to-moderate correlations with self-deceptive and impression-management scales (McCullough et al., 2002).

Notes

1 The Veterans Administration (1946) and the National Institute of Mental Health (1947) were established at this time.
2 Contrary to criticisms, positive psychology does not refer to all other disciplines as 'negative psychology'. Positive psychologists use the term 'psychology as usual' instead.
3 Mental disorder/mental illness is defined as 'a persistent deviation from normal functioning that is sufficient to cause emotional suffering and role impairment, diminishing an individual's capacities to execute their responsibilities as a parent, spouse or employee' (Keyes and Michalec, 2009: 612).
4 In 2004, WHO included Mental Health Promotion (MHP) as a key agenda for the development of healthy individuals.
5 Ilona Boniwell founded this programme, on which both authors of this textbook currently teach.

CHAPTER 2

Understanding Emotions

❖ LEARNING OBJECTIVES

This chapter will examine the origin and functions of positive affect and positive emotions. Some theorists hold that positive affect is simply a function of people's progress towards goals. Others have argued that positive emotions have constructive functions: they facilitate learning, creativity and play. These and other theories will be reviewed and critiqued. The chapter also focuses on the construct of emotional intelligence, which has received much popular and research attention since 1996. You can turn to the end of the chapter to complete questionnaires relevant to the identification of positive emotions.

List of topics

- The definitions of emotions and mood.
- The science behind positive affectivity and neuroscience.
- The power of the 'positivity ratio'.
- The broaden-and-build theory of positive emotions.
- The influence of genetics and personality on emotions.
- Two main theories within emotional intelligence.

MOCK ESSAY QUESTIONS

1 Critically discuss the extent to which positive emotions can be said to have beneficial (and harmful) effects.

2 Critically discuss the contribution of positive psychology to our understanding of emotional intelligence.

3 Compare and contrast the 'ability' and the 'mixed' models of emotional intelligence.

Defining emotions

We would like you to stop for a minute and reflect upon the last time you felt 'really happy'. Have you done this? What did you think of? How do you now feel? Keep that feeling with you as we go through the chapter. Hopefully, you are now in a perfect place to learn about the interesting area of positive emotions.

Emotions are part of being human. In fact, when we are unable to feel emotions, either good or bad, doctors put in place drastic measures to understand why and to intervene. An emotion can be defined as a 'psychological state defined by subjective feelings but also characteristic patterns of physiological arousal thought and behaviours' (Peterson, 2006: 73). Emotions tend to focus on a specific event or circumstance during the past, present or future. However, emotions are likely to be short lived and we are aware of them at the time of occurrence.

Moods, on the other hand, are different from emotions as they are 'free floating or objectless, more long-lasting and occupy the background consciousness' (Fredrickson and Losada, 2005: 121). Thus moods, unlike emotions, tend to be unfocused and enduring.

When psychologists began studying emotions, they focused on the term 'hedonic capacity', which refers to our ability to feel good (Meehl, 1975). Today, researchers focus on 'affectivity', which is defined as 'the extent to which an individual experiences positive/negative moods' (Peterson, 2006: 62). Positive affect is the extent to which someone experiences joy, contentment, and so on, whereas negative affect is the extent to which someone experiences feelings such as sadness or fear.

Furthermore, the same events that you or I may experience will bring about different emotional responses due to individual differences in the brain (Davidson, 2003). These differences are termed our affective style. Affective style is defined as 'a broad range of individual differences in different parameters of emotional reactivity . . . including a) threshold to respond, b) the magnitude of the response, c) the rise time to the peak in the response, d) recovery function of the response and e) the duration of the response' (Davidson, 2003: 657–8). These individual differences in brain activity have been found to remain stable over time (Tomarken et al., 1992). Scientists have also looked at the brains of resilient individuals when faced with potential threats. They have found that more resilient individuals tend to have less activity in areas of the brain that deal with worry (orbitofrontal cortex) (Waugh et al., 2008).

Basic human emotions

Paul Ekman (2003), a leading researcher on the study of human emotions and expression, posits that there are six basic human emotions found throughout the world, across gender, age and culture. These include: anger, disgust, fear, joy, sadness, and surprise. Another theorist, Izzard, argues that we have ten basic emotions including: anger, contempt, disgust, distress, fear, guilt, interest, joy, shame and surprise. Of course other researchers have offered alternative theories, however these are the most robust.[1]

So for those of us who can, and do, feel emotions on a regular basis, what impact do they have on our life, our thinking, behaviours and overall wellbeing and why do we have them in the first place? Well, the evolutionary benefits of negative emotions are clear: they narrow our thought-action repertoires (or, simply speaking, what we think about and the range of actions we are engaged in) to those that best promoted our ancestors' survival in life-threatening situations. They are also associated with specific action tendencies. Thus, fear makes us want to run, and anger makes us want to thrash out at the aggressor.

The human brain's ability to hone in on real or potential danger is a left-over by-product of evolutionary and adaptive tendencies. Humans and animals have a tendency or bias towards attending to negative rather than positive stimuli. Thousands of years ago, people survived if they were able to selectively attend to danger or dangerous situations that could lead to extinction of their genetic line. Although once useful, this selectivity can lead us to narrow in consciously on what is wrong, rather than what is right with ourselves and the world around us. However, recent studies have shown that people who score high on self-reported experiences of positive emotions have an attention bias toward positive information (Strauss and Allen, 2006).

But what use are positive emotions and do they have any action repertoires? This leads us to the 'broaden-and-build' theory of positive emotions. Fredrickson commenced work on her groundbreaking and widely accepted theory of the broaden-and-build functions of positive emotions (Fredrickson, 2001) in the early 1990s. Her research, in several laboratory-controlled experiments, has demonstrated that positive emotions broaden our thought-action repertoires, undo negative emotions and build resilience (Cohn and Fredrickson, 2009).

The broadening effect

Fredrickson's positive emotions lab has repeatedly tested the broadening effects of positive emotions. They propose that when we experience one of the main positive emotions, our minds tend to open up – or broaden – and we are able to think 'outside the box'. This is important because when we broaden our thinking patterns we tend to get a bird's-eye view of our situation, which can help generate alternative solutions to the tasks at hand. We also become more creative, with positive emotions being found to enhance verbal creativity tasks.

The building effect

Positive emotions do not only open our mind to alternative strategies – research has shown that the experience of positive emotions coupled with the broadening effect has the ability to build personal resources, which we are able to dip into when needed. These include intellectual resources (problem solving, being open to learning), physical resources (cardiovascular health, coordination), social resources (we can maintain relationships and create new ones) and psychological resources (resilience, optimism, sense of identity and goal orientation).[2] As these develop, they induce more positive emotions that continue building the resources in an upward spiral (see Figure 2.1).

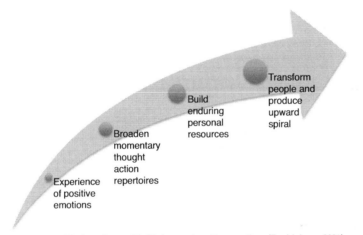

FIGURE 2.1 The broaden-and-build theory of positive emotions (Fredrickson, 2001)

The undoing effect

The next time you are faced with a stressful experience, think about the undoing effect of positive emotions. The undoing effect is simply the theory that 'positivity can quell or undo cardiovascular after-effects of negativity' (Fredrickson, 2009: 105). Thus, when we feel anxiety or stress or any other negative emotions, experiencing positive emotions can help our bodies return to normal physiological functioning significantly faster than any other types of emotion (Fredrickson and Levenson, 1998). Research is now under way to discover whether or not this extends to cognitive tasks, such as pattern recognition (Falkenstern et al., 2009).

(handwritten margin note: 3:1 Ratio development →)

BUTTERFLIES

Unfortunately, we are not talking about the beautiful butterflies that appear in springtime. No, this butterfly was the result of a very intricate mathematical equation that was conducted by Losada and Fredrickson (2005) to come up with the ideal ratio of positive to negative emotions for flourishing business teams. Losada studied 60 high-performing (n = 15), medium (n = 26) and low-performing (n = 19) business teams for the experience of positive interaction to negative interaction, whether they inquired or told (inquiry-advocacy) and whether their speech was about themselves or others. Losada created a nonlinear dynamics model of observed interactions and found that business teams that had a 6:1 positive to negative interaction, with more inquiry than advocacy and that discussed more about others than themselves, were high performing. This study then led to the collaboration with Barbara Fredrickson, who used this technique to identify the optimal positive-to-negative emotion ratio for human flourishing as 3:1.

See Fredrickson and Losada (2005) for the original article.

Which positive emotions are important?

From decades of research across many populations, ten positive emotions are the most widely researched, as well as experienced in daily life. In order of occurrence, Fredrickson's top ten positive emotions include: joy, gratitude, serenity, interest, hope, pride, amusement, inspiration, awe and love (Fredrickson, 2009). Love is unique in that it encompasses all other nine emotions and can be elicited through the presence of the others. Therefore, love is arguably the most experienced human emotion.

Think about it…

Fredrickson makes it clear that emotions are individual and can be elicited at different times for different people. Try and think of one of her top ten emotions. Don't overanalyse – just think about it . . .

When was the last time I felt this feeling?
Where was I?
What was I doing?
What else gives me that feeling?
Can I think of still more triggers?
What can I do to cultivate this feeling?

(Fredrickson, 2009: 40)

Emotions don't all occur in the same way. The circumplex model of emotions (Russell, 1980; Larsen and Diener, 1992) (Figure 2.2) postulates that emotions exist in a circumplex across two dimensions, highlighting frequency and intensity as the two organizing principles. There are issues with this model, mainly based on the fact that it was created using self-reported data and not mixed with objective markers. Furthermore, have we generalized human emotions to the extent that we can say that these are the only dimensions available?

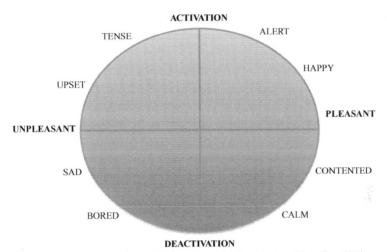

FIGURE 2.2 The circumplex model of emotions (cited in and adapted from Carr, 2004)

Furthermore, researchers have suggested that there may be two different types of positive affect itself (Gilbert et al., 2008). The first may be linked to the dopaminergic system, which controls drive/seeking, whereas the other may be linked to the opiate/oxytocin system, which induces soothing/contentment. Gilbert et al. (2008: 182) found that positive affect was indeed mediated by three underlying factors: activated positive affect, relaxed positive affect and safe/content positive affect, with the latter negatively correlating highest with depression, anxiety, stress, self-criticism and insecure attachment.

Where do positive emotions come from?

If positive emotions are essential for success and wellbeing, it is important to understand where they come from. There are currently two main theories as to how positive emotions come about:

- via our material brains (Davidson, 2003; Davidson et al., 2003) and
- via our perceived rate of progress towards important goals (Carver and Scheier, 1990).

time out

Mind–body dualism

Greek philosophers Aristotle and Plato discussed the human self in terms of three separate entities: the mind, body and the soul. It wasn't until René Descartes came along in the seventeenth century, with his famous quote 'I think therefore I am' that society began a longstanding debate between the existence of the immaterial mind (consciousness, self-awareness) and material body (brain-intelligence) (eventually know as Cartesian dualism).

According to scientists, the separation debate is considered outdated, with research showing that it is a complex interaction between both – the body and the mind affecting each other. Within the brain, researchers have identified that the primary somatosensory cortex is responsible for the transference of sensory information from the body to the brain (Ratey, 2001).

Looking to our brains

Relatively speaking psychology, in its entirety, is a new science. Furthermore, positive psychology is just a baby in comparison to the other well established schools of thought. One of the biggest criticisms of psychology from its 'hard science' cousins is that it relies (a lot) on self-reports as a measure of reality or truth.[3]

Since the 1990s, however, psychology has made leaps and bounds in terms of the creation of machinery to access the brain and its functioning. For example, psychologists can determine which parts of the brain are being used or which cells are firing via functional magnetic resonance imaging (fMRI). This allows scientists to access all parts of the brain with low invasiveness. Alternatively, if cost and access to such high-tech machinery is limited, psychologists can use electroencephalography (EEG), which is like a hat with multiple suction caps that people place on their heads, so that the behaviour of neurons can be monitored. Ultimately, these machines allow cognitive psychologists and neuropsychologists access to the brain in an attempt to match other physiological or emotional markers (Ratey, 2001).

Electroencephalography and fMRI helped scientists to establish that the two key components in the brain in relation to the experience of positive emotions appear to be the prefrontal cortex (PFC) and the amygdala. The prefrontal cortex is home to emotions and emotional regulation whereas increased activity in the amygdala can predict higher levels of negative affect (Davidson, 2001). The PFC enables the generation of goals and pathways to achieve them (Davidson, 2003). It monitors

The brain

Within our magical, wonderful brain there are several systems that are linked to the experience of happiness. The brain can be separated into three categorises including:

Reptilian: the oldest part of the brain structure, which we share with our ancestors. It controls basic functioning such as temperature regulation, sleeping and waking.

Paleomammalian: this section includes the limbic system and also controls movement for survival, as well as some elements of emotions.

Neomammalian: also known as the cortex, this is the latest evolutionary component in the brain, which enables abstract thinking, planning, and control of lower functioning skills (Ratey, 2001).

Specific parts of the brain responsible for the regulation of happiness include:

The reward system: this is responsible for inducing feelings of pleasure.

The pleasure system: this recognizes what the person is doing, seeing or listening to is good.

Dopamine: this is the key neurotransmitter involved in the pleasure centre. Limited levels of dopamine can subdue levels of motivation whereas high levels of dopamine can lead to mania (Ackerman, 2009).

Ventral tegmental area (VTA): in collaboration with the substantia nigra, the VTA is the key area of the dopamine system.

Nucleus accumbens: this component of the brain is a very important player in the reward system of the brain. Part of the limbic system, it is thought to be 'the pleasure centre as it holds the highest concentration of dopamine neurotransmitters'. Addictive drugs (for example, cocaine) target this area.

Prefrontal cortex: this area of the brain is responsible for working memory.

Orbital frontal cortex: this is the area of the brain where decisions are made.

(Ratey, 2001)

daily experiences in relation to long-term goals, sometimes initiating delayed gratification. Individuals who have low activation in the left PFC are therefore not able to initiate goal-directed behaviour or regulate impulses. Furthermore, people who have increased activation in their right PFC report difficulties in regulating emotions.

From early research documenting the effects of brain damage (Gainotti, 1972;

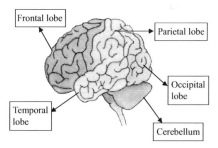

FIGURE 2.3 Basic components of the brain
Source: Original illustration by A. Howitt (2010).

time out

Sackeim et al., 1982), researchers have discovered the link between the anterior left-side PFC and positive affect. Specifically, when we experience positive affect, this section of the brain is activated, and vice versa when we feel anxiety or depression (Wheeler et al., 1993; Davidson et al., 2000). Our brain is therefore divided into two systems – the approach system (positive affect) and the avoidance system (negative affect) (Davidson and Irwin, 1999).

These systems and emotions are directly linked to goal attainment. Thus, when we engage in behaviour that is

FIGURE 2.4 The pleasure centre
Source: Original illustration by A. Howitt (2010).

bringing us towards a desired goal, we will feel increased positive affect. However, when we are faced with a threat, we will attempt to remove ourselves from the situation, and likely feel negative affect in response. The behavioural activation system (BAS) is more sensitive and responsive to incentives, making people more extraverted and impulsive, whereas the behavioural inhibition system (BIS) is more sensitive and responsive to threats – arousing anxiety and neurosis.

So what is it that makes the brain develop a certain affective style? Multiple theories exist, including the impact of social influences, activation patterns, neurogenesis and gene expression (Davidson et al., 2000). There is mounting evidence for the first theory, via research on plasticity. Specifically, scientists have found that rodents that are raised in a nurturing environment have significant changes to the circuitry of their PFC and amygdala (emotion and emotion regulation areas) in relation to control groups. Furthermore, the evidence also suggests that changes in this area do not have to happen from birth. Enriching environments later on in life can also have a significant impact on the circuitry of the emotion and regulation areas of the brain (Davidson et al., 2003).

Emotions, goals and discrepancy theory

So why are goals so important to human beings? Affective neuroscientists believe that whether we engage the BAS or BIS will determine affect. Charles Carver and Michael Scheier have spent the past few decades researching goals and self-regulation and their effects on emotional wellbeing. (More on goals in

trying to get to our goals

Chapter 7.) Their control-theory perspective is based on behaviour and self-regulation. When we set ourselves a goal (large or small, physical or mental) this becomes our 'reference value'. We then engage in what is known as a discrepancy loop, trying to minimize the distance between where we are and where we want to be (Carver and Scheier, 1990).

Carver and Scheier (1990–2009) posit that we are always thinking and behaving in relation to a goal. As we go through a day, our life, an event and so forth, we are constantly assessing our current state in relation to some standard or desired goal. If there is discrepancy between where people are and where they want to be (reference value), they will adjust their behaviour in hopes of getting closer to the reference value.

Sometimes, however, there are outside influences or impediments that stand in the way of us attaining our goals. Individuals need to make adjustments, either to their expectancies or environmental circumstances, to override these impediments. It is imperative to note that it is the rate of progress, rather than the progress per se that determines whether we experience positive or negative emotions: 'negative emotion comes from inadequate progress towards a goal, whereas positive affect comes from progress towards future success' (Carver and Scheier, 1990: 27).

interesting theory

Positive emotions and other people

When we feel positive emotions, we feel connected to others and actually allow ourselves to open up and include others into our sense of self (Waugh and Fredrickson, 2006). Positive emotions make us feel less as two and more as one. This inclusion side effect has tremendous impact on personal relationships with others. Not only do we see others as part of our self-concept but we are also more likely to understand other people's complexities and perspectives, which in turn will enhance the relational bond (Waugh and Fredrickson, 2006).

Cross-cultural research shows that feeling positive emotions is not a selfish endeavour. In fact, by experiencing positive emotions we are able to take a broader perspective, recognizing others' viewpoints and not just our own, thereby developing stronger relationships with others. This connection to others expands beyond people that we already know. In fact, Fredrickson has found evidence that inducing positive emotions can help with combating and almost eliminating own-race bias. Own-race bias is the psychological phenomenon that people are not good at recognizing members of other races, which can feed racism and segregation. Furthermore, there is also evidence that suggests that positive emotions can affect cross-cultural perspective taking, with people who feel higher levels of positive emotions being able to take a larger perspective and exhibit greater feelings of sympathy and compassion for someone from a dissimilar cultural context (Nelson, 2009).

Positive emotions and race bias

Get everyone your pic for Christmas :)

Good Stuff

Think about it...

The next time you are feeling a little blue, seek out your favourite person. Research shows that simply by looking at our favourite person, there are several documented immediate physiological and psychological benefits, such as invigoration, enhanced immune system functioning and mood states. So make a date today with your favourite person and get those positive emotions flowing! (Matsunaga et al., 2008)

Attenuation to positive emotions

It is important to make it clear that people who experience positive emotions and have resilient tendencies are still able to feel sadness and anxiety, just as much as anyone else. It appears, however, that they are able to draw on resources to help them out much faster than those who do not experience these positive emotions (Fredrickson, 2009).

Positive attenuation is also essential in protecting against depressive symptoms. Resilient individuals have a unique ability to maintain and regulate positive emotions. Dysphoric and non-dysphoric individuals react just the same to emotions; however, it appears that there is a difference in the ability to maintain and regulate these emotions rather than in the ability to react in the first place (McMakin et al., 2009).

By pursuing positive emotion-eliciting activities, we accrue resources (psychological, social, and so forth) that enhance our odds for survival and reproduction. Positive emotions not only mark or signal health and wellbeing, but also produce health and wellbeing. As mentioned, the optimal ratio is three positive emotions to one negative emotion.[4] Individuals who score higher on levels of positive affect tend to report better marriages and job satisfaction, more engagement with physical activity and better sleep patterns. However, we must be wary of such cross-sectional work as we are still not able to determine which comes first – is it that people sleep better and therefore experience more positive affect or vice versa? More research is needed to determine causal links to the variables.

Personality and positive emotions

Personality is a hot topic within psychology and is concerned with individual differences in how we think, feel and act. Personality can be defined as 'Distinctive and relatively enduring ways of thinking, feeling and acting that characterize a person's response to life situations' (Passer and Smith, 2006: 420). Most areas of psychology uses the NEO Big Five traits of personality (see the 'time out' section below) to correlate their concepts. At present, the literature shows a strong correlation between dispositional global positive affect and extroversion (Costa and McCrae, 1980; Shiota et al., 2006).

The two most robust relationships with happiness and personality are extraversion and neuroticism, with extraversion predicting wellbeing up to ten years later. People who are extraverted are more likely to experience positive emotions and more intense positive emotions. In addition, our attachment style in relationships may have an impact on our ability to feel positive emotions. Not surprisingly, secure attachment has been associated with higher levels of positive affect in romantic relationships versus insecure attachment. Neuroticism, on the other hand, is consistently linked to depression and low levels of wellbeing.

time out

Five personality traits

According to Costa and Macrae (1992) there are five main personality traits that individuals possess to some degree or another. These include:

1 **Extraversion:** individuals who score high on extraversion tend to be sociable, talkative and join in when there is something collective going on. Low scorers tend to be classically considered as more reserved, quiet, shy and prefer to be alone.

2 **Agreeableness:** individuals who score high on agreeableness tend to be pleasant, compassionate and sympathetic to others' needs. Low scorers tend to be untrusting, suspicious, critical and slightly hard nosed.

3 **Conscientiousness:** individuals who score high on conscientiousness tend to have high levels of grit, meaning they are industrious, diligent, efficient and reliable. Low scorers tend to be inattentive, idle, unsystematic and sometimes unreliable.

4 **Neuroticism:** individuals who score high on neuroticism tend to experience high levels of anxiety, insecurity and can be emotionally volatile. Low scorers tend to be more tranquil, steady, and composed.

5 **Openness to experience:** individuals who score high on openness to experience tend to be original and artistic. Low scorers tend to be more conformist and uncreative.

Shiota et al. (2006) reviewed the correlations between seven positive emotions known to engage survival fitness: joy, contentment, pride, love, compassion, amusement and awe. When correlated with the Big Five, all seven correlate positively with extraversion. Conscientiousness tended to be correlated with agency-focused emotions such as joy, contentment and pride. Agreeableness correlated with love and *in teresting - more research needs to be done with younger people (?) Do we stay w/bd- Personalitics?*

compassion. Awe was strongly linked to openness as well as amusement, joy, love and compassion. Neuroticism was negatively correlated with love, contentment, pride and joy. These correlations remained after comparison with peer reports.

Other links to personality traits and enhanced wellbeing include optimism, assertiveness, emotional stability, loneliness and self-esteem. However, despite the interesting links, positive psychology has yet to show a clear-cut causal relation between personality and positive life outcomes (Holder and Klassen, 2009). Furthermore, the majority of research into personality and positive life experiences/outcomes has been done on adults, thus future research needs to include all ages in order to determine stronger and causal links. Ultimately, Holder and Klassen (2009) argue that the benefit of understanding personality and wellbeing will enhance researchers' ability to match interventions to personality type, thereby tailoring the interventions and hopefully achieving maximum potential.

The face and positive emotions

Does smiling have anything to do with our ability to experience positive emotions? The presence of a Duchene smile has been regarded as an objective measure of genuine happiness/positive emotions. Studies that have looked at the incidence of Duchene smiling have found positive correlations between Duchene smiling and duration of grief after bereavement, less negativity, greater competence, more positive ratings from others and greater wellbeing in later life (Harker and Keltner, 2001). Also, Johnson et al. (2010) found experimental evidence that when people smile genuinely (as detected through facial muscular tracking), their thought patterns are immediately broadened.

YEARBOOKS

Did you smile in your yearbook photo? And was it a genuine (Duchene) or a fake smile (Pan-American)? This small detail may be important in predicting your future wellbeing. Dacher Keltner and LeeAnne Harker, researchers at the University of California at Berkeley, analysed the smiles in the photos of 141 high-school seniors (age 18) from a 1960 yearbook from Mills College. Those that were smiling were contacted at three subsequent time points (age 27, 43 and 52) and questioned on their satisfaction with life and marital satisfaction. Even 30 years later, the females that expressed a genuine Duchene smile at the age of 18, were more likely to have married and stayed married as well as reporting higher levels of wellbeing and life satisfaction.

See Harker and Keltner (2001) for the original article.

Emotional intelligence

Emotional intelligence (EI) is a widely used phrase within pop psychology. Salovey and Mayer (1990: 189) define EI as the 'ability to monitor one's own and others' feelings and emotions, to discriminate among them, and to use this information to guide one's thinking and action.' Ultimately, researchers believe that emotions have use (Davidson, 2003) and are not present for idle purpose. Our emotions are good at sending us messages to let us know how we feel about people and situations. Emotional suppression can be detrimental to our wellbeing, thus attempts to become more aware of emotions are important (Mayer and Salovey, 1993; Mayer et al., 2001, 2004).

After the groundbreaking theory of multiple intelligences (Gardner, 1993), people began to see that intelligence was not simply about IQ, but several kinds of intelligence, including:

- linguistic intelligence;
- logical-mathematical intelligence;
- spatial intelligence;
- bodily-kinaesthetic intelligence;
- musical intelligence;
- interpersonal intelligence;
- intrapersonal intelligence;
- naturalist intelligence.

At present, there are two distinct groups of models of emotional intelligence: the ability EI models and mixed EI models. The following section will focus on these two types of models with a specific focus on the ability model framework, which we perceive to be the most robust in terms of objective classifications.

 ## The Ability Model

Pioneers in emotional intelligence testing include John Mayer and Peter Salovey who, in collaboration with their colleague David Caruso, developed the Mayer–Salovey–Caruso EQ Model,[5] a 141-item, task-based emotional intelligence test (MSCEIT) (Mayer et al., 2003). Although EI became popular via Daniel Goleman (1996), the theory and research behind EI had been the work of these three men. According to their model, EI is a set of competencies or mental skills that include four stages (Bracket et al., 2009). This section will review the branches outlined from Mayer and Salovey's work and suggest some questions we can ask ourselves that will help enhance our emotional intelligence quotient.

Perceiving emotions

The first branch is 'perceiving': the ability to recognize emotions either in yourself or in others. Questions to ask yourself include: How do you feel? How do others feel? By recognizing these subtle emotional cues, individuals are better equipped to deal with social circumstances.

Using

The second branch is entitled 'using emotions', which is the ability to use emotions to facilitate your mood. Thus if you need to edit your papers or perform surgery, you can bring yourself down into a calm, unaroused state in order to narrow your focus. Conversely, if you need to write a creative essay, you can bring yourself up, either by music or self-talk, to enhance positive feeling and thereby facilitate broader thinking patterns (remember broaden and build). Questions to help develop this include: How does your mood influence thinking? How is it affecting your decision-making?

Understanding

The third branch is 'understanding emotions', and people who are high in this aspect are able to understand that emotions are highly complex – they do not just come neatly packaged. You are not just mad or just hurt, happy or sad – you can be a mixture of all these feelings all at once. They also recognize that emotions can change over time. Thus, when you are angry you don't always stay angry. That anger can change into another emotion such as shame or regret. When trying to develop this area, ask yourself: Why are you feeling this? What do these emotions mean? What has caused that for you? Where is that going to go?'

Managing

The final last branch is 'managing emotions' and this is the ability to manage, or self-regulate, your emotions. Thus, you can identify when and where it is inappropriate to express certain emotions and wait until the appropriate time. For example, if someone tries to be cheeky during class and this angers us, it would be highly inappropriate to turn round and scream at the student. Highly emotionally intelligent individuals would recognize that there is a time and place for certain emotions and manage them accordingly. Furthermore, this branch deals with managing emotions in others. People who score high in this are able to manage other people's emotions in addition to their own. However, just because people can manage their own emotions does not necessarily mean they can manage the emotions of others. In order to develop this area, ask yourself: What can you do about it? How can these emotions be regulated?

Ultimately, EI seems to predict several outcomes such as wellbeing, self-esteem, more pro-social behaviours, less smoking and alcohol-use, enhanced positive mood, less violent behaviour, greater academic eagerness and higher leadership performance (Salovey et al., 2002; Brackett et al., 2009).

Mayer and Salovey's ability model seems to have more support than Goleman's model. In addition, ability measures of emotional intelligence seem to be more reliable than self-report measures, which are open to many problems.

Mixed Models of EI

According to Goleman, EI is defined as 'the ability to adaptively perceive, understand, regulate, and harness emotions in the self and others' (Goleman, 1996; Schutte et al.,

2002). Hence, EI mixed models view EI as a combination of perceived emotional skills and personality. According to Goleman, EI matters because of its ability to predict academic, occupational and relationship success better than traditional IQ (Goleman, 1996). However, longitudinal data are needed to confirm any causal relationships between performance and EI (Roberts et al., 2001).

According to Goleman's theory of intelligence there are five main areas within the concept including:

- managing emotions, where one engages in reframing anxiety and attempting to dismiss feelings of distress;
- using emotion for self-motivation, where one becomes proficient in delaying gratification for future success;
- recognizing emotions in others, where one has the ability to exhibit empathy, which is important for social relationships;
- managing emotions in others, where one is able to help others with their distress or encourage motivation;
- emotional self-awareness, where one is able to understand and identify one's own emotions.

In order to measure this type of EI, researchers use the Emotional and Social Competence Inventory, or ESCI (2007). However, a major issue with EI self-reports is that they can be potentially inaccurate, unavailable to conscious interpretation, vulnerable to the influence of social desirability, deception and impression management (Roberts et al., 2001). Furthermore, Goleman's work has been branded as simply pop psychology (Mayer et al., 2008), which has overshadowed his contribution to the area of EI.

The Bar-ON model of emotional-social intelligence (ESI)

As one further example of a mixed model, the Bar-ON model of emotional-social intelligence views emotional intelligence as the skill of being able to understand yourself and those around you as well as an ability to interact and connect with others. The Bar-ON is another self-report measurement tool that aims to test individuals' emotional and social skills. Criticisms of this test include reports of high levels of deception (Grubb and McDaniel, 2007; Day and Carroll, 2008).

One big question is whether or not EI is separate from personality traits. Research on personality traits argues that EI self-report measures are too strongly related to several personality traits such as neuroticism, extraversion and agreeableness (Davies et al., 1998). For example, those who are neurotic rather than emotionally stable will have issues trying to identify emotions in themselves and others. Furthermore, their vocabulary and ability to identify emotions will be stunted. Extraverts, on the other hand, have excellent communication skills and are able to convey their emotions to others well. Likewise, people who score high on agreeableness will be proficient in displaying acts of empathy. Thus a problem with EI is that it may not be unique and may be too highly associated with personality to be seen as a separate construct.

Overall, the development of EI, from an ability model perspective, is highly beneficial for an individual's wellbeing.

Summary

Reflecting on the learning objectives, you should now understand the concept of positive emotions and emotional intelligence. More specifically:

- Emotions are short lived, in our consciousness and focus on a specific event, whereas moods are unfocused and enduring.
- We all have an affective style, which refers to our tendency to experience more positive or negative moods.
- Research has shown that we should be aiming for 3:1 positive to negative emotions if we are to flourish.
- The experience of positive emotions can help broaden our thoughts and build resources in order to gain resilience.
- The influence of genetics and personality on emotions.
- There are two types of models within emotional intelligence research: ability and mixed.

Suggested Resources

http://www.paulekman.com/
To see the application of emotion and facial expression research, check out Paul Ekman's website.

www.positivityratio.org
As mentioned, this is where you can take the positivity ratio test and monitor your ratio for the next month.

http://psyphz.psych.wisc.edu/web/index.html
This is the link to the Laboratory for Affective Neuroscience, run by groundbreaking researcher Dr Richard Davidson.

http://danielgoleman.info/
This is Daniel Goleman's official website with links to his books and assessment tools.

www.ebpsych.com
This is a link to one of the leading businesses in emotional intelligence. If you fancy getting your EQ tested via the MSCEIT, contact the providers via this link.

Further questions for you

1 What type of affective style do you think you have? How do you know this?

2 How important do you think the one negative emotion is in the positive ratio? Why?

3 Do you think you have high emotional intelligence? What if an objective test showed otherwise? What would your reaction be?

4 Are you able to generate emotion when needed and then reason with this emotion?

5 What would you say to someone who rejects the importance of positive emotions?

Personal Development Interventions

The exercises presented below focus on identifying and enhancing your positive-to-negative emotion ratio. Both have been found to enhance wellbeing and success across life domains.

1 Positive emotions

We now know that positive emotions are important for our ability to thrive and flourish. We would like you to monitor your positive-to-negative ratio (aiming for 3:1) over the next two weeks using Barbara Fredrickson's free and easy-to-use website, which calculates your positivity ratio for you. It is important that you document your ratios every day as the more data you have the better you will be able to make a judgement on how you are actually feeling across time, rather than just on the day.

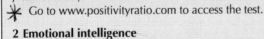 Go to www.positivityratio.com to access the test.

2 Emotional intelligence

How would you like to increase your emotional intelligence? The following exercises are aimed to help you expand your EQ through developing each of the four components of the ability model. Try them out over the upcoming week.

Perceiving: The next time you are talking with a friend, make sure you take the time to see if his or her facial expressions match the conversation. If you are happy all the time, don't assume that others are. Take the time to look and listen.

Using: The next time you go to write an essay, take heed of the scientific findings that positive moods enable creative thinking whereas neutral moods enhance editing and analytical thinking. Use this knowledge in your writing-up process.

Understanding: The next time you are angry, stop and write down why you feel this. Try to follow that emotion back as far as it will go. The anger may be an emotion that started out as hurt or sadness. Trace the chain of emotions to get to the source of the problem.

Managing: The next time you feel like immediately exploding with anger, think about whether or not this is the appropriate emotion to display given the situation you are in. We need to manage our emotions and regulate them so that they are expressed in appropriate social contexts. Reflect on your thoughts and how you actually handled the situation.

Measurement Tools

Positive and Negative Activation Schedule (PANAS)

(Watson et al., 1988)

Directions

This scale consists of a number of words that describe different feelings and emotions. Read each item and then mark the appropriate answer in the space next to that word. Indicate to what extent you felt this way *in the last week*. Use the following scale to record your answers:

1	2	3	4	5
very slightly or not at all	a little	moderately	quite a bit	extremely

5 interested		___ scared
4 distressed		___ hostile
4 excited		___ enthusiastic
2 upset		___ proud
___ strong		___ irritable
___ guilty		___ alert

___ ashamed	___ attentive
___ inspired	___ jittery
___ nervous	___ active
___ determined	___ afraid

Scoring

To score this scale, simply add the positive items (interested, alert, excited, inspired, strong, enthusiastic, proud, active, attentive, and determined) and retain a summative score for these. Do the same for the negative items and compare them.

Interpretation

Your scores for the positive affect items should outweigh the negative scores (hopefully in a 3:1 ratio).

Review

This is a widely used scale developed by Watson and Tellegen in the late 1980s. It is used across psychological and physical activity research. It is based on monitoring 20 emotion adjectives (ten positive and ten negative). The scale can be administered using different temporal instructions, ranging from 'right now' to 'in the last week/month/year'. The creators believe that when researchers use a shorter time frame they are tapping into emotional responses whereas a longer time frame will highlight mood or personality differences. The internal consistency is quite high (0.86–0.90) and the PANAS has acceptable divergent validity, with good correlations between negative affect and measures of distress and psychopathology. Criticisms of the PANAS include that several of the items on this tool are not actually emotions (for example, alert) and several important positive emotions for wellbeing are missing from the scale (love, contentment) (Shiota et al., 2006).

Scale of Positive and Negative Experience (SPANE)

(Diener et al., 2009)

Directions

Please think about what you have been doing and experiencing during the past four weeks. Then report how much you experienced each of the following feelings, using the scale below. For each item, select a number from 1 to 5, and indicate that number on your response sheet.

1 Very rarely or never
2 Rarely
3 Sometimes
4 Often
5 Very often or always

_____ Positive
_____ Negative
_____ Good
_____ Bad
_____ Pleasant
_____ Unpleasant
_____ Happy
_____ Sad
_____ Afraid
_____ Joyful
_____ Angry
_____ Contented

Scoring[6]

To calculate positive feelings (SPANE-P) you need to add the scores for the six items: positive, good, pleasant, happy, joyful, and contented. The score can vary from 6 (lowest possible) to 30 (highest positive feelings score).

To calculate negative feelings (SPANE-N) you need to add the scores for the six items: negative, bad, unpleasant, sad, afraid and angry. The score can vary from 6 (lowest possible) to 30 (highest negative feelings score).

To calculate affect balance (SPANE-B) you must now subtract the negative feelings score from the positive feelings score. The resulting difference score can vary from −24 (unhappiest possible) to 24 (highest affect balance possible).

Interpretation

If you scored 24 or above, this is a very high score, which assumes that you hardly experience the negative feelings mentioned, if you experience them at all, and very often or always have all of the positive feelings.

Review

This is a new scale developed by some of the authors of the Satisfaction with Life Scale (SWLS) (Diener et al., 1985). It contains 12 items, which are argued to focus on a broad rage of both positive and negative emotions equally (Diener et al., 2009).

Notes

1 It is interesting how, within both lists, the majority are negative emotions.
2 Interestingly, new research has looked at the potential for positive emotions to build religious and spiritual resources in addition to the others mentioned (Saroglou et al., 2008).
3 The concepts of truth and objectivity were discussed in Chapter 1.
4 At 12:1 the ratio tips and appears to become detrimental.
5 EI refers to emotional intelligence whereas EQ refers to emotional quotient. They are used here interchangeably.
6 This is adapted from http://s.psych.uiuc.edu/~ediener/SPANE.html. Please go to the website for further information regarding this tool.

CHAPTER 3

Happiness and Subjective Wellbeing across Nations

❖ LEARNING OBJECTIVES

Happiness is not a superficial topic; it has a real benefit for those who experience it in balanced ratios. This chapter will focus on the notion of happiness, specifically on the concept of subjective wellbeing (SWB), how we measure wellbeing and the most recent findings on the correlates and predictors of happiness within cultures from around the world.

List of topics

- Definitions of happiness and subjective wellbeing (SWB).
- How we measure SWB.
- Global happiness polls.
- Highest and lowest SWB-scoring countries.
- Hedonic adaptation and the hedonic adaptation prevention model.
- The burden of choice and its role in influencing our wellbeing.

MOCK ESSAY QUESTIONS

1 Critically evaluate the available research evidence on the correlates and predictors of subjective wellbeing.

2 Critically evaluate the merits and shortcomings of the concept of subjective wellbeing as a way of conceptualizing and measuring happiness.

3 Do we always return to our set point of happiness following positive or negative events?

Introduction

Misguided critics of positive psychology often refer to it as a so-called 'happiology'. As you will hopefully see, by the end of this textbook and throughout, this is not the case. Positive psychology openly accepts the importance of negative emotions and does not attempt to deny their existence. Just as mainstream psychology became too negatively focused, so must positive psychology be aware of the potential danger of polarization. Having said that, let us focus on happiness and what positive psychology has discovered, over the past few decades, about what makes us happy.

The concept of 'happiness'

Since the dawn of ancient civilization, humans have grappled with pinning down a clear and all encompassing definition of happiness (see, for example, Aristotle, *Nicomachean Ethics,* Book 1, Chapter 4). Although there is no consensus on the definition of 'wellbeing' (Snyder and Lopez, 2007), there are several synonyms used throughout the literature to describe it, such as happiness, self-actualization, contentment, adjustment, economic prosperity, quality of life and wellbeing. But what exactly is happiness and is it really the pursuit of positive psychology?

Think about it...

How do you define happiness? What is happiness for you? How do you know when you've found it? When you've lost it?

Subjective wellbeing (SWB)

As discussed in Chapter 1, establishing a scientific science of the concept of happiness has been a long road. In this section, we will focus on the hedonic concept of happiness as the attainment of subjective wellbeing (SWB). More specifically, SWB is defined as: satisfaction with life + high positive affect + low negative affect.

Life satisfaction encompasses the cognitive component of happiness when individuals rate the way their life turned out to be. Diener argues that it refers to discrepancy between the present situation and what is thought to be the ideal or deserved standard (Veenhoven, 1991). Affect refers to the emotional side of wellbeing, including moods and emotions associated with experiencing momentary events (Diener et al., 1999a). There needs to be a balance between the experiencing of positive and negative affect as well as an acknowledgement of the difference in frequency versus intensity of positive affect (Diener et al., 1991). Ultimately, people who report higher levels of SWB tend to demonstrate higher levels of creativity, increased task persistence, multitasking, being systematic, optimism, attending to relevant negative information; longevity, less vulnerability to illness, sociability, trust, helpfulness, and less hostility and less self-centredness (Diener, 2000).[1]

The role of pleasure

One of the criticisms of SWB is that it fixates too heavily on the experience of pleasure and positive affect, rather than what is meaningful (there will be more on this in the next chapter). On average, humans seek pleasure and try to avoid pain, due to activation of the brain's 'pleasure centre' (see the 'time out' section on the brain in Chapter 2).

RATS

James Olds and Peter Milner conducted an experiment where they placed an electrode into the hypothalamus of rats. When the rat pressed a bar, it would stimulate the electrode. Olds and Milner observed that the rats would press the bar up to 4000 times an hour, foregoing eating, sleeping and sexual behaviours and neglecting to care for themselves in a similar way to individuals with extreme addictions. The researchers believed they had found the brain's 'pleasure centre'. Since then, we know that the area they found (nucleus accumbens) is one of several areas related to wanting and needing a certain stimulus to the point where nothing else matters.

See Olds and Milner (1954) for the original article.

However, pleasure is not enough to make humans happy and fulfilled. Furthermore, when given the chance, individuals would rather exist in a real world, with the potential to experience both pleasure and pain, than a world that provides only pleasure and positive stimulation (Nozick, 1974).

Think about it…

Imagine a machine that was able to induce only positive experiences due to cutting-edge research completed by neuroscientists. You would not be able to tell that these experiences were not real. If you were given the choice would you choose the machine over real life?[2]

Measuring SWB

Subjective wellbeing encompasses how people evaluate their own lives in terms of affective and cognitive explanations (Diener, 2000) and there are multiple SWB scales (SWLS, PANAS). The majority of tools are single occasion, self-report tools such as the Satisfaction with Life Scale (SWLS) (Diener et al., 1985) and Subjective Happiness Scale (Lyubomirsky and Lepper, 1999; Lyubomirsky, 2008).[3] The scales mentioned have reported very high levels of validity and reliability (good internal consistency) and are sensitive to change in life circumstances. Furthermore, the tools converge with mood reports, expert ratings, experience sampling measures, reports of family and friends and smiling (Diener et al., 2002).

The scales used are itemized and involve a very short time frame. For example, the questions are very basic and non-situation specific. Furthermore, researchers argue that moods can have a heavy influence over how you determine your satisfaction with life at any given moment. However, Diener et al. argue that their research is not affected by the change in current mood and that life satisfaction is indeed stable enough to fight through the influence of a person's current mood.

Other methods of research into SWL and SWB include comparing in-person interviews with anonymous questionnaires in order to contain impression management (Diener, 2000). Experience Sampling Methods (ESM) has been employed in order to reduce memory biases. Finally, objective measurements (physiological markers) are used in tandem with self-reports, reducing subjective biases. The future of SWB measurement will rest on the reduction of questionnaires and cross-sectional surveys and the inclusion of more experience sampling or daily diary methods, qualitative descriptions, measures of cognitive and physiological aspects, as well as the use of longitudinal and experimental designs.

Major global studies

The increase in funding for major global polls has enabled scientists to collect data from 98 per cent of the world's population, from urban Manhattan to the remote plains of Kenya. The following polls/surveys have been around the longest and are currently the most influential and all encompassing:

1 *Gallup World Poll.* The most widely known global wellbeing poll, which boasts data from over 98 per cent of the world's population (see 'time out' below for a detailed review).

2 *World Database of Happiness.* This database contains information and results from nearly 30 years of scientific research on happiness across the globe.

3 *World Values Survey.* Since 1981, this survey has collected information on changing values within 97 countries around the world.

4 *Eurobarometer.* In Europe, the European Commission issued the Eurobarometer, which is used to measure citizens' perceptions of quality of life.

5 *European Social Survey (ESS).* Another European social survey, funded by the European Commission's framework programme, is the ESS, which aims to collect data from over 30 countries on their citizens' beliefs, attitudes and behaviours (including wellbeing). It is currently entering its fifth data collection period.

6 *LatinoBarometro.* In Latin America, the LatinoBarometro surveys over 400 million Latin Americans, from 18 countries, on several topics including trust in government and opinions (as cited in Buetnner, 2010).

time out

Gallup

George Gallup, the founder of what is now one of the world's leading poll companies, started his organization during the 1930s. From 1960 to 1980, the Gallup organization conducted extensive research into wellbeing. During the 1990s, the company began to look across the globe at satisfaction, until 2005, when they conducted a groundbreaking, unprecedented global study on wellbeing, representing over 98 per cent of the world's adult population in over 150 countries. Within these major global studies the following seven areas were targeted, including: 'Law and order, food and shelter, work, personal economy, personal health, citizen engagement and wellbeing' (Rath and Harter, 2010: 139). Wellbeing is separated into two categories: objective (GDP, health, employment, literacy, poverty) and subjective (evaluative – how they rate their own life – and experienced – what they experience in daily life).

Since then, Gallup has created the Wellbeing Finder, an instrument based on these initial findings. After several pilot studies, including qualitative and quantitative inquiries, they concluded that five elements were essential for overall wellbeing:

- career wellbeing;
- social wellbeing;
- financial wellbeing;
- physical wellbeing;
- community wellbeing.

They have also created a daily experience tracker, which can be used to help individuals track their 'experiencing self', thereby highlighting, in real terms, 'good' versus 'bad' days. From their research, they concluded that a good day includes ten circumstances, which are to be ranked on a scale of 1–10:

- feeling well rested;
- being treated with respect;
- smiling or laughing;
- learning or interested;
- enjoyment;
- physical pain;
- worry;
- sadness;
- distress;
- anger.

Although the new Wellbeing Finder needs further research to increase reliability and validity it is an interesting addition to Gallup's enormous database on happiness.

For more information see Rath and Harter (2010).

Who is happy?

Now that we are clear about how we are defining happiness within this chapter, we will move onto the data that we currently have on who is happy in the world. In reality, and from hundreds of thousands of data sets, it appears that most people are indeed happy (Myers, 2000). Although it is rare to be at the high end, the majority of people on Earth score in the 'somewhat satisfied set-point' (Diener and Diener, 1995: 653). This means that at any given time point, the majority of people view stimuli and circumstances as positive. Thus, a common assumption that most people view themselves as unhappy appears to be false (Myers, 2000). For example, most people (more than two-thirds) in most samples (across age, race, sex, measures) view themselves as 'above average' in happiness. The exceptions to this appear to be those that are 'hospitalized, alcoholics, newly incarcerated inmates, new therapy clients and students living under political suppression' (Myers, 2000).

Furthermore, the good news is that, as individuals, we have a lot of sway in whether or not we become happy. Researchers postulate that after genetics (50 per cent) (Tellegen et al., 1988) and life circumstances (10 per cent) we have control over approximately 40 per cent of our happiness levels (also called the '40 per cent solution') (Sheldon and Lyubomirsky, 2004, 2006, 2007, 2009; Lyubomirsky, 2006, 2008).

Happiest places on Earth

So which are the current happiest countries? Denmark, for example, has consistently scored within the highest ranking countries in happiness levels across the globe (8.0).

Rank	Country
1	Costa Rica
2	Denmark
3	Iceland
4	Switzerland
5	Finland
6	Mexico
7	Norway
8	Canada
9	Panama
10	Sweden

TABLE 3.1 Happiest places on Earth (World Database of Happiness, 2010)

time out

The sun

If you take a closer look at the table you will notice that the majority of the happiest countries are situated in the northern part of the hemisphere where there is not a lot of sun and there is limited light. This is interesting as research has shown that, when comparisons are made, people who live in colder climates also tend to have a higher suicide rate than those in warmer climates.

There are several explanations for this; for example, people in colder climates may be more diligent and open in reporting suicides. Another explanation is what scientists call the 'sun bonus'. A lack of sunshine can result in lower levels of vitamin D, which is directly related to serotonin in the brain. When people do not see light or sun for long periods of time they can experience seasonal affective disorder (SAD) or depression from the lack of sunlight. This may explain the correlation with suicide, as well as the findings that people who experience higher levels of sunshine and daylight hours experience a boost of happiness through their proximity to the equator.

Rank	Country
1	Zimbabwe
2	Armenia
3	Moldova
4	Belarus
5	Ukraine
6	Albania
7	Iraq
8	Bulgaria
9	Georgia
10	Russia

TABLE 3.2 Unhappiest places on earth (World Values Survey for 1995–2007)

The most recent polls showed that Costa Rica now holds the title as the happiest country in the world.

Five ways to wellbeing

Two major studies have recently revealed similar findings from their research endeavours. The Foresight Report (a collation of already completed pieces of research) and Gallup's most recent World Poll (150+ countries) suggest five necessary elements for wellbeing. This section will review these two reports before going into more detail on the specific facilitators of wellbeing.

The Foresight Report

The Foresight Report was conducted by the New Economics Foundation (NEF) to review all evidence-based research on ways to wellbeing. After reviewing over 400 pieces of wellbeing scientific research from around the world, Aked et al. (2008) suggested five consistent findings throughout the research that would increase wellbeing. Based on scientific evidence the five ways to wellbeing include:

- *Connect.* Research consistently shows that when we build connections with people around us, we experience higher levels of wellbeing as well as stronger resilience in the face of adversity. The report suggests identifying the influential and important people in your life and investing time and energy into building those relationships.
- *Be active.* As discussed in more detail within Chapter 9, an important part of wellbeing is taking care of the body as well as the mind. The NEF found that

activity is an important part of enhancing wellbeing. Simply moving the body can have a massive effect on your mood and cognitive functioning.

■ *Take notice.* Following from the exciting research on savouring, this element refers to research that demonstrates that 'stopping to smell the roses' actually can enhance our wellbeing (More on savouring in Chapter 8.)

■ *Keep learning.* By engaging the brain and challenging yourself to keep learning, you can enhance levels of wellbeing.

■ *Give.* As seen in results from random acts of kindness research, people experience high levels of wellbeing when they give something or their time to others.

Five essential elements for wellbeing

Based on new research from the Gallup organization, Rath and Harter (2010) reveal 'five essential elements for wellbeing'. Although they do not cover what may be morally important in life, these elements include, in order of importance:

■ Career wellbeing: this represents where you spend most of your time during the day.

■ Social wellbeing: this represents your relationships and experiences of love.

■ Financial wellbeing: this represents how well you can manage your financial situation.

■ Physical wellbeing: this represents your ability to have good health and energy.

■ Community wellbeing: this represents your role and participation within the community you live in.

The authors note that all five are essential and the pursuit of one over the others will hinder a person's wellbeing levels. The presence of all five is what distinguishes individuals who thrive from those who suffer. Harter and Rath state that approximately 66 per cent of us are doing well in at least one of the areas, however only 7 per cent are doing well in all five! Furthermore as you can see, the five elements are all things that are within a person's control.

So from two very different types of studies, and two very different types of results, what actually makes us happy? The next section will bring you through the wonderful work of SWB research, which will show you that what we think will bring us happiness does not always do so.

What makes us happy?

This section will review several proposed correlates and causes of happiness from the most recent polls (Gallup-Healthways Wellbeing Index and World Values Survey), including income, relationships and religion.

time out

The ladder of life

The Cantril Self-Anchoring Striving Scale (Cantril, 1965) has been included in several Gallup research initiatives, including Gallup's World Poll of more than 150 countries, representing more than 98 per cent of the world's population, and Gallup's in-depth daily poll of America's wellbeing (Gallup-Healthways Wellbeing Index – Harter and Gurley, 2008).

The Cantril Self-Anchoring Scale, developed by pioneering social researcher Dr Hadley Cantril, taps into happiness of the here and now (experiencing self) and the future (reflecting self).

When taking part, participants are asked the following:

Please imagine a ladder with steps numbered from zero at the bottom to 10 at the top similar to the one below (using a visual makes it easier to use cross-culturally, where language is a barrier).

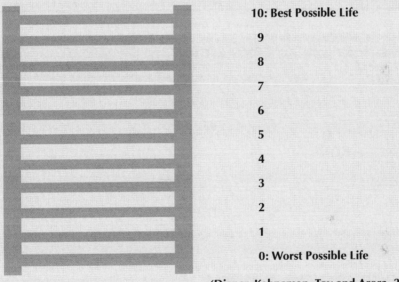

10: Best Possible Life

9

8

7

6

5

4

3

2

1

0: Worst Possible Life

(Diener, Kahneman, Tov and Arora, 2009)

The top of the ladder represents the best possible life for you and the bottom of the ladder represents the worst possible life for you.

On which step of the ladder would you say you personally feel you stand at this time (ladder-present)?

On which step do you think you will stand about five years from now (ladder-future)?

Scoring

Thriving: Individuals who score 7+ on their present life and 8+ on their future life are considered to be thriving. This means that they are experiencing high levels of wellbeing on a daily basis. Thrivers tend to report significantly fewer health problems, fewer sick days, less worry, stress, sadness and anger and more happiness, enjoyment, interest, and respect.

Struggling: Individuals who score 5 and 6 are considered 'struggling', meaning that they hold moderate views on their current and/or future life situations. People who are struggling tend to report more daily stress and worry and claim double the amount of sick days in comparison to their thriving peers.

Suffering: Individuals who score 4 and below are considered to be suffering, which means that they rate their life as very poor and do not see it changing in the future. Gallup have found that in comparison to their thriving peers, individuals who are suffering tend to lack satisfaction of basic needs and experience more physical pain, increased stress, worry, sadness and anger.

Think about it…

What do you think of the ladder of life? Is it a reliable tool to use when researching happiness? If not, why not? Where would **YOU** point to on the ladder of life?

Income and SWB

The verdict is in. The results have been counted and verified and the answer is . . . yes, money does buy happiness. At least a little bit. When reviewing the GDP of 132 countries, individuals who live in countries with high GDP such as Norway and the USA on average score higher on wellbeing measures than those living in countries with low GDP such as Togo and Bulgaria (Deaton, 2008). Replicated findings have confirmed this relationship between income and SWB in poor nations (Veenhoven, 1991; Diener and Diener, 1995; Schyns, 1998; Diener and Oishi, 2000). This seems to be more apparent when assessing one's life in general versus immediate affective experiences (Diener et al., 2009).

Think about it…

Bhutan, a tiny country in Asia, has rejected the concept of gross national product (GNP) as the measurement of its country's success, and introduced gross national happiness (GNH). Do you think this is a better way to measure a country's wealth?

In the Gallup World Poll (Kesebir and Diener, 2008) of 130+ nations, which was a representative sample of 96 per cent of the globe's population, there were striking disparities in health and consequences of income. Ultimately, income is linked to the satisfaction of basic biological needs (such as food and shelter) in poor nations, with social welfare programmes protecting against adverse effects of poverty in rich nations. Plus there is greater income inequality (variability) in poor nations. Income may also influence wellbeing because wealthier nations appear to have more human rights, lower crime, more democracy, more equality, more literacy, increased longevity and better health. However, countries with higher income tend to have more competitiveness, more materialism and less time for socializing and leisure.

FORBES

In 1985, Ed Diener and his colleagues had the fortunate opportunity to access 100 individuals on the *Forbes* list of richest Americans. An interesting survey asked several groups of people within several continents their rating of happiness. The results show that *Forbes* magazine's 'richest Americans' (net worth over $125 million) scored only slightly above (5.8) the random control group. Furthermore, 37 per cent of the rich list scored lower on happiness levels than the average American.

See Diener et al. (1985) for the original article.

The high income in these countries correlates significantly with lighter prison sentences for the same crimes, better physical and mental health, increased longevity, lower infant mortality, reduced risk of being the victim of violent crime, reduced likelihood of experiencing stressful life events, reduced likelihood of being diagnosed with DSM depression, greater chances of a child completing school and not being pregnant as a teenager and greater interpersonal trust. Furthermore, income tends to correlate modestly but significantly, even controlling for education, with marital status, occupation, employment, age and sex (Marks and Fleming, 1999; Tomes, 1986; Blanchflower, 2001; Blanchflower et al., 2001).

Interestingly, income is correlated with happiness in men, not women (Adelmann, 1987), and low personal income is related to depression for husbands, not wives (Ross and Huber, 1985). Low income is related to depression for single but not married women (Keith and Schafer, 1982) and people with high income are perceived as more intelligent and successful but also as more unfriendly and cold (see Diener and Biswas–Diener, 2008).

There are several disadvantages to having and maintaining higher levels of income such as spending more time at work and having less time for leisure and social relationships. Most importantly is the effect of 'the hedonic treadmill', which undermines happiness by forcing wealthy people to adapt to their conditions, raising expectations and desires, which makes it difficult for them to be happy with their current status. Ideally, research suggests that in order to maintain balanced levels of wellbeing, individuals must take home approximately $5000 (the equivalent of 3000 pounds) per month, anything more will do little to enhance happiness. Indeed, an extra $10,000 per annum will only bump up your happiness levels by approximately 2 per cent (Christakis and Fowler, 2009).

Think about it...

Does money make you happy? Based on evidence from multiple studies, Rath and Harter (2010) suggest five tips for enhancing 'financial wellbeing':

1 Be happy with what income you do have.
2 Live within these means.
3 Spend wisely and save wisely (by thinking long term as well as short term).
4 Spend on experiences and not just materials (experiences create memories that can then be savoured at a later date).
5 Spend your money on others and not just yourself.

Relationships and SWB

Friends and acquaintances

One of the greatest predictors and facilitators of SWB is social relationships. We need other human beings and we like being around them. Whether we are introverted or extraverted, spending time in social settings enhances our levels of wellbeing (Froh et al., 2007). More specifically, the Gallup-Healthways Wellbeing Index poll recently found that people need to spend six to seven hours per day in social settings, and up to nine if your job is stressful, to enhance or maintain wellbeing.

PEOPLE

Daniel Kahneman, a name you will be familiar with by now, conducted a study that employed the experience sampling method, which takes snapshots of people's happiness throughout their day. When people were buzzed, they were asked to write down what they were doing, who they were with and how happy they were. The results showed that people were happiest when they were with others and unhappiest when alone. The order of most to least happiness-inducing activities is:

> Socializing after work, relaxing, dinner, lunch, watching TV,
> socializing at work, talking on the phone at home, cooking, child
> care, housework, working, commuting from work, commuting to
> work (as cited in Buettner, 2010: 197).
>
> **See Kahneman et al. (2004) for the original article.**

It appears that happiness is contagious, meaning that people who interact on a daily basis with happy people, in small, large, direct or indirect networks, are happier (Fowler and Christakis, 2008). Not only do friends and wider social networks influence our SWB – they can influence our likelihood of engagement with detrimental health behaviours (such as smoking) (Fowler and Christakis, 2008 as cited in Rath and Harter, 2010).

Marriage and SWB

Good news for all soon to be or recently married couples. Chances are you are experiencing what scientists see as an acute rise in wellbeing. An interesting causal relationship has been found between happier people and likelihood of marriage, with happier people being more likely to get married and stay married while still reporting a happy marriage. Longitudinal research has recently shown, however, that after the initial one year 'honeymoon phase', individuals return to their previous levels of SWB. One caveat is that couples who cohabit tend to report less satisfaction than couples who are married.

Caveat: Children and wellbeing

Despite what society may have told us about children as an infinite source of joy, research demonstrates an opposite effect. Specifically, individuals who have children have lower scores on wellbeing measurement tools than those who do not. Furthermore, any additional children after the first born tend to reduce the wellbeing of parents involved.

The relationship between children and marital satisfaction appears to be curvilinear, with high levels of life satisfaction at the marriage ceremony, dropping significantly at the birth of the first child, followed by a continued drop throughout childhood and adolescence, where it hits bottom, and then retuning to higher levels after the children have left.

Work/employment and SWB

Work can have a tremendous effect on our overall wellbeing. Specifically, research has shown that how we perceive our job and our career orientation can further influence our happiness levels. Thankfully, it is not just doctors or nuns or what society feels as a 'meaningful' job that creates happiness. Indeed, manual labour hospital staff and janitors still report high levels of wellbeing in their work life. In fact, approximately one-third of employees in any sector or area of employment perceives work as a 'calling orientation'. So what is a 'calling orientation' and how does it differ from other types of jobs?

First of all, people who have a *job orientation* view their job in terms of a means to an end. The job equals money and is not important to their overall life. *A career orientation* (although a little more engaged) is concerned with building a career and such workers perceive the job they are in as a way to progress forward. Furthermore, these people are focused on the extrinsic rewards that can come with progressing in their career. Finally, a *calling orientation* is when workers are immersed healthily in what they do. They do the job not for the money or the fame but because they believe that it is worthy in its own right (Diener and Biswas-Diener, 2008).

Think about it…

What orientation did you adopt in your previous jobs? If you have had more than one, try and think about how it made you feel to start and end the day. If you dreaded getting up and heading to work, or felt relieved by the end of the day, you most likely had a job orientation.

Extensive research has been conducted on the relationships between happiness and success at work. The dangers of having a job orientation are that individuals who are simply waiting to punch out at the end of the day have higher levels of disengagement and stress and lower levels of reported happiness (except towards the end of the work day) (Rath and Harter, 2010). Since work is a place where we tend to spend over a third of our day, we must ensure that we create a place where we want to be, where we like to be and where we feel engaged (DeNeve and Cooper, 1998; Diener et al., 1999; Harter, 2009).

Researchers have found that certain personality characteristics are more predominant in certain occupational settings, and when personal and professional profiles are aligned, this can enhance satisfaction at work. Researchers have specifically looked at the interactions between the 'Big Five' and six occupations: teachers, managers, service workers, crafts persons, manufacturing (blue collar) and home workers (Winkelmann and Winkelmann, 2008). They found that a mismatch between personality profile and occupation led to reduced life satisfaction. Teachers scored the highest in life and job satisfaction, however the mix of personality traits in teachers explains some of this. It appears that the most important character trait for satisfaction with work is strength of vitality.

Think about it…

Do you like what you do each day? Harter and Rath (2010) state that only 20 per cent of us will respond with a resounding 'Yes' (p. 15).

Health and SWB

Diener and Biswas-Diener (2008: 33) separate the effects of SWB on our physical condition into three health categories: 'a) the likelihood a person will contract a specific illness; b) how long a person lives after contracting a life threatening illness and c) how long a person's lifespan is.' Within the first category, longitudinal research has shown that people who experience higher levels of positive emotions are protected from various illnesses including heart disease.

COLDS

Positive emotions may be the key to protecting yourself against those pesky winter colds. Sheldon Cohen, PhD, of Carnegie Mellon University, conducted a groundbreaking experiment on the beneficial effects of positive emotions on immune system functioning. For two consecutive weeks, 334 volunteers were assessed on their day-to-day experience of positive and negative emotions (vigour, wellbeing and calm; depression, anxiety and hostility). Once their data had been collected, the experimenters squirted a rhinovirus (otherwise known as the common cold) up participants' noses. The experimenters then kept the participants under observation for five days in a hotel specifically cleared for the experiment. The researchers were interested in whether or not the participants caught the cold, and to what degree they showed any symptoms. The results showed that individuals who experienced higher levels of positive emotions were more resistant and showed less severe symptoms than those that displayed less positive emotions. Thus, you could say a smile a day keeps the doctor away!

See Cohen et al. (2003) for the original article.

The second category, surviving after the diagnosis of a life-threatening illness, is slightly more complicated. When someone has balanced levels of positive emotions and optimism, their health can be positively influenced. However, when people adopt a 'positive viewpoint', which hinders the adoption of medical advice and treatment, high levels of happiness can be detrimental. Researchers argue this is because happier people are more likely to be too optimistic and delay seeking medical advice for potentially cancerous symptoms.

Finally, when defining health in terms of longevity, the research shows, quite simply, that happier people live longer (Rasmussen and Pressman, 2009).

PSYCHOLOGISTS

As a follow up from the famous nuns study, Sarah Pressman analysed the autobiographies of 96 famous psychologists. The results echoed the latter study, with psychologists who used more positive feeling words living, on average, six years longer than those that used more negative feeling words.

See Pressman and Cohen (2007) for the original article.

Religion and SWB

People who report themselves as being spiritual or religious tend to report slightly higher levels of wellbeing, in addition to higher scores on hope and optimism (Ciarrocchi et al., 2008; Diener and Biswas-Diener, 2008). But do all religions make us equally happy and, if so, what elements of religion? Is it the belief in organized religion or just a sense of spirituality? The belief in something higher? The concept of the afterlife? Attendance at religious ceremonies and adherence to religious practices? Research in America shows that people who identify with any of the above forms of 'religiosity' score mildly happier than those who do not. This effect is not present cross-culturally, however, and depends on the type of religion followed. Researchers expect that this is due to the unique elements found within different religious beliefs and their links to anxiety, guilt and oppression. Furthermore, religions that isolate and denigrate other religions and members outwith the community can cause unhappiness.

In order for a religion to enhance wellbeing, Diener and Biswas-Diener (2008) propose that the elements needed are:

- *Comforting beliefs* in what awaits us on the 'other side'.
- *Social support* from a community.
- *Connecting to something permanent and important* that can give comfort, meaning and a sense of identity.
- *Growing up religiously,* which may influence a solid upbringing with a clear set of values and morals to abide by.
- *Experience of rituals* that excite, amaze and involve the congregation and its followers.

Think about it...

If you were an atheist or agnostic, how could you adopt the principles of religion for a happier life?

Age, gender and education

Again, contrary to popular belief, scientists have found that elderly individuals are as happy as their younger counterparts. With regards to gender, there appears to be no significant differences between the happiness levels of men and women (Diener et al., 1999b; Nes et al., 2008). Finally, people who score high on wellbeing tend to have a higher educational attainment than those who score lower on the scales.

Think about it...

A re there any other correlates that you expected to be on the list (e.g. climate)?

Theories of SWB

So now that we know the potential correlates and the outcomes of SWB, why does it occur? We are still searching for answers as to what are the causes and/or consequences of wellbeing. Diener (1984) proposed two approaches to understanding causation within SWB research: *bottom up* and t*op down* causation. *Bottom up* approaches attempt to find which particular variables (genetics, personality plus demographics, age, sex, ethnicity, and so forth) cause SWB. *Top down* approaches attempt to understand SWB as producing certain outcomes (Headey et al., 1991).

Genetics and SWB

There appears to be a strong genetic influence on an individual's wellbeing. Indeed researchers have found predictive variability in life satisfaction according to personality traits (Magnus et al., 1993). *Dynamic equilibrium theory* states that personality determines baseline levels of emotional responses; events may affect us in the short term, however over time we eventually revert to our genetic set point (Headey and Wearing, 1989). Furthermore, people who are happy in their home life tend to be happy at work, thus displaying consistency across situations (work/leisure) (Diener and Larsen, 1984). Recently, set point theory has been contested by novel research findings (Headey, 2008; Headey et al., 2010). However, at the present time, set point theory tends to dominate the positive psychology discipline and underpins support for positive psychological interventions.

Epigenetics is the area of biological research that looks at the causal interactions between genes and the environment (Curley and Keverne, 2009: 347). More specifically, research has started to show that the environment can have an influence on gene expression and behaviour, especially in the mother–infant relationship during key developmental phases, thereby influencing 'brain development, behaviour as well as risk and resilience to health and disease.'

Adaptation theory

Humans have a unique evolutionary tendency to react strongly to recent events; however this diminishes over time (approximately 3 months). Following multiple studies, researchers have suggested that humans tend to have a natural happiness 'set point', which, following good and/or bad news/events, we tend to revert back to after approximately 3 months. This evolutionary adaptation process, hedonic adaptation theory (otherwise known as the 'hedonic treadmill') (Lykken and Tellegen, 1996) is linked to 'zero-sum theory', which posits that happy periods in our life are inevitably followed by negative periods, which cancel each other out, and thus any attempt to increase happiness will be unsuccessful.

LOTTERY

Do you play the lottery? If so, why? Do you believe it will make you happier? Unfortunately, Brickman's monumental longitudinal study on happiness among lottery winners suggests otherwise. Lottery winners who won amounts ranging from US$50,000 to 1 million were interviewed on basic demographic variables and questions pertaining to how their life had changed since winning. The lottery winners related everyday events as less pleasurable than the control groups and were no happier than they were before winning.

In relation to 11 paraplegics and 18 quadriplegics, the lottery winners scored the same on happiness levels. This does not mean that paraplegics were happy about their conditions. In fact, they tended to have a positive reflection on their past but a low satisfaction with everyday present life. Ultimately, this experiment supports the theory of hedonic adaptations, that bad or good, we have a natural set point that we will inevitably return to.[4]

See Brickman et al. (1978) for the original article.

The proposed antidote to this adaptation is *variety*, hence individuals must continually change their approach and happiness interventions in order to counteract any adaptation mechanisms (Tkach and Lyubomirsky, 2006). As reflected in the *hedonic adaptation prevention* (HAP) model (Lyubomirsky, in press), new research has shown that an individual's number of positive events directly affects the number of experienced positive emotions, which helps sustain wellbeing, all moderated by surprise and variety as well as intrinsic desire for change (Lyubomirsky et al., 2009).

Think about it…

Recall a time in your life when you were up for promotion, expecting an exciting event or bought a new item. How did you feel when this happened? How did you feel a week later? A month later? Reflect on the impact that moment has on you right now.

Daniel Gilbert (2007) focuses on the concept of *affective forecasting* and how this affects our ability to be happy. With the unique ability of humans to be able to think and imagine the future comes interesting and powerful consequences (Wasko and Pury, 2009). *Impact bias* is an evolutionary quirk that distorts our perception of the hedonic impact of future events. We may think that two outcomes, such as passing a test or failing a test, will have distinct intensity and durational differences on us; however, this rarely turns out to be true (Wasko and Pury, 2009).

TENURE

Linked to affective forecasting, Gilbert et al. (1998) conducted six studies that aimed to assess the discrepancy between how people forecast the impact of negative and positive news, as well as their subsequent emotions after achieving or failing to receive tenure. The results showed that those who had been denied tenure overpredicted how negative they would feel whereas assistant professors who were given tenure overpredicted how happy they would feel. For both groups, their long-term happiness level forecast was deemed accurate.

See Gilbert et al. (1998) for original article.

In fact, the only life experiences that have been found to have longer lasting negative impact on our happiness is the death of a spouse and long-term unemployment.[5] Bereavement is one of the most devastating life events and has a significant impact on individuals' wellbeing. Researchers propose that it takes approximately five to seven years to return to previous levels of wellbeing. The damaging effects of unemployment, on the other hand, are harder to recover from. In the same study, Clark et al. (2008) followed over 130,000 individuals over several decades. They found that men who were unemployed for a long period of time (more than one year) did not return to their previous levels of wellbeing.

Furthermore, according to Gilbert (2007) humans synthesize happiness. Natural happiness is what we feel when we get what we want; however, *synthetic happiness* is what we make when we don't get what we want. Gilbert argues that synthetic happiness is just as real and beneficial as the other type of happiness, and that perceptions of synthetic happiness as an inferior kind of happiness are incorrect. The reason we developed this evolutionary ability to synthesize happiness is argued to be due to the belief that we need to keep going and get what we want, otherwise we'd give up if we knew we would be just as happy as if we didn't.

Discrepancy theories

The 'American paradox' (Myers, 2000) refers to the phenomenon that, despite an increase in wealth across the globe over the past 50 years, happiness levels have stayed the same. There are several explanations for this. The first is the Relative Standards Model, which is reasonably well supported. Subjective wellbeing is primarily a function of comparison processes (social comparison, with past self, with internalized standards).

When we interact with others, we can't help but compare ourselves to them on many levels. Otherwise termed as *social comparison*, we can compare our situation, attractiveness and wealth to others either in an upward or downward spiral. Ultimately, we tend to seek out and interact with people who make us feel good about ourselves and not people who make us feel bad. Thus, our brand new designer handbag is only great until we see a bigger, more expensive and new season one on a friend. On the other hand, if we see a friend with a less expensive handbag, we will feel better about our status and ourselves.

Our personality may influence whether we use downward or upward social comparison and how we use it. The cancer patients that Kate has worked with use it in both ways, however in a positive way. They use upward social comparison when looking at cancer patients who have finished chemotherapy and think, 'someday that will be me'. Alternately, they will look around at fellow patients, some who are younger, with children, and think 'well at least I got it now, rather than when I was young, like them'. Thus, social comparison is only detrimental if you use it to negatively evaluate yourself with others.

Status anxiety and materialism have been linked to increased instances of depression and lowered SWB. Diener and Oishi (2000) found that placing high importance on money correlates inversely with life satisfaction (-0.53) whereas placing high value on love correlates positively with life satisfaction. Some scholars go even further and claim that materialistic attitudes can be equated to a virus called *affluenza* that causes dissatisfaction and worthlessness, crippling our lives. Although originally a metaphorical expression, affluenza seems to have its roots in rigorous research findings (James, 2007).

Think about it...

Taken from a well-known economic query (Solnick and Hemenway, 1998) to test the rationality of individuals and finance, please answer the following questions:

Would you rather earn $50,000 a year while other people make $25,000, or would you rather earn $100,000 a year while other people get $250,000? Assume for the moment that prices of goods and services will stay the same.

What did you say? Would it surprise you to know that the majority of people who are asked this question would prefer the first scenario? Why do you think this is?

Previous beliefs were that striving for material goods does not meet basic human needs (see SDT) and that materialistic goals may be unattainable. Furthermore, unhappiness and low social support might lead to compensatory materialism. However, an argument against the detrimental effects of materialism is that materialism is only bad if you can't afford it. Thus, those who report being higher on materialism with higher incomes report higher wellbeing (Crawford et al., 2002). As long as you live within your means and can afford what you like without the financial strain, materialism isn't as detrimental as previously believed.

Linked to discrepancy theory is the *paradox of choice* (Schwartz and Ward, 2004). As nations become richer and consumers become more demanding, our world is packed with choice, alternatives and variations to most everything for sale. Freedom of choice has now been replaced with the 'tyranny of freedom', where more choice isn't necessarily a good thing (Schwartz, 2000; Schwartz et al., 2002).

Think about it...

Can you recall a time when you wanted to buy a specific item, a new computer for example? How many choices were there? Did this make things easier or harder on your final decision?

An abundance of choice has lead to three leading problems for consumers and citizens of Western societies. These include:

- Information problems. We are swamped with information, which leaves us in a precarious position; how can we possibly gather all we need to know in order to make an educated choice?
- Error problems. If we are not able to access all information about all the possible choices, we are likely to make more errors of judgement.

■ Psychological problems. The stress and anxiety caused by excess choice and the above issues can create lowered levels of psychological wellbeing.

Of course, introducing choice is not necessarily the issue here; it is introducing too much choice that seems to affect one's levels of happiness.

JAMS

The supermarket is riddled with choice. We can have any type of food, any way we want it and packaged how we like it. However, the jams experiment showed that sometimes we can get too much of a good thing.

Taking place in an ordinary grocery store, researchers set up a stand to allow shoppers to taste test a selection of jams. The demonstration had two conditions. One had six types of jams, whereas the second had 24. The results of observation analysis showed that more shoppers stopped in front of the extensive-selection display of jams (60 per cent) than in front of the limited selection (40 per cent). Furthermore, the two stands experienced similar sampling statistics (1.5 flavours). However, when it came to actually choosing and purchasing a jam, shoppers who confronted the display of 24 jams were less likely to purchase any than when they encountered the display of six (3 per cent versus 30 per cent). Researchers suggest that too much choice can cause anxiety and decreased wellbeing.

See Iyengar and Lepper (2000) for the original article.

When it comes to decision-making, Schwartz has separated individuals into two categories: *satisficers* versus *maximizers*. Satisficers are individuals who are able to choose items that meet their minimum criteria and go for 'what's good enough'. Maximizers, on the other hand, are individuals who fixate on searching for all the possible options and look for the best possible choice. Accordingly, maximizers have a more difficult time making choices as they need to make sure they have covered all options.

Furthermore, researchers have identified that there are several pitfalls associated with being a maximizer including:

■ *Regret* at not getting the best choice or anticipating regret in the future.

■ *Opportunity costs.* Inevitably, when we choose one thing, we automatically reject the other. Each choice has a cost in itself.

■ *Escalation of expectations.* As the choices available to us rise, so do people's expectations.

■ *Self-blame.* Since we have so much choice available to us, we believe it is our own fault if things go wrong.

■ *Time.* The hours people spend sifting through the multitude of choice takes away from the time spent on more worthwhile pursuits.

There is some financial gain in being a maximizer (on average they obtain starting salaries $7000 higher than satisficers), however they are also unhappier, experiencing higher levels of regret, perfectionism, depression, upward social comparison and neuroticism.

Think about it...

What type of decision maker are you when it comes to choices? Do you like to research all the options before you make a final decision or do you tend to go for the option that suits what you need?

Goal theories and SWB

Everyone needs goals. Some researchers believe that, without them, we wouldn't be able to survive: 'Commitment to a set of goals provides a sense of personal agency and a sense of structure and meaning to daily life' (Diener et al., 1999: 284). Thus, happiness is the direct result of the process of attaining valued and self-congruent goals and it is the quality of the goals one chooses to pursue that influences wellbeing. Of course, this is culturally dependent; however, as long as people are engaged in meaningful goals and receive positive feedback in their attainment of the desired outcome, they are happy. Thus, as our mothers said, it's the journey, not the destination. We will talk about goal theory and goal setting in relation to wellbeing much more in Chapter 7.

AIM approach

Diener and Biswas-Diener (2008) propose an 'AIM approach' for creating a 'happy mindset'. According to Diener and Biswas-Diener, there are three basic components to a positive attitude and happy mindset that we need to engage: attention, interpretation and memory.

Attention refers to the ability of people to look at the entire picture when going through daily life – both the good and the bad. People who attend to only the negative will shut out the positives in life and live in what Diener and Biswas-Diener (2008: 188) term 'an ugly world'.

Interpretation refers to the tendency for humans to put together a story when all the facts are not yet presented. When people interpret events and situations in a negative light, it tends to spill over into their moods. According to Diener and Biswas-Diener (2008) there are six main destructive thinking patters that individuals tend to default to when interpreting events:

- *Awfulizing.* Exaggerating a negative event or person beyond what is objectively true.
- *Distress intolerance.* A perception that individuals adopt that tells them that they will not be able to recover or withstand potentially traumatic events.
- *Learned helplessness.* Stemming from Seligman's work, this is when people adopt a mentality that they have no control over their negative situations and give up.
- *Perfectionism.* Individuals who use this tend to fixate on the minute details and only accept excellence.
- *Negative self-fulfilling expectancies.* The phenomenon of eliciting negative responses from others via a person's previous communications with others.
- *Rejection goggles.* This is when people identify and fixate on rejection, even when it may not exist in the situation. (Adapted from Diener and Biswas-Diener, 2008: 193–4.)

Finally, *memory* relates to the large body of research showing that recalling and savouring past positive events and experiences leads to enhanced wellbeing.

COLONS

Nobel Prize winner Daniel Kahneman (1999) conceptualized the 'peak-end rule' or peak-end experience, where individuals judge their experiences on how they were at their peak (either pleasant or unpleasant) as well as how they ended. One slightly uncomfortable experiment demonstrating the peak-end rule involves several hundred participants and an intrusive colonoscopy. After finding contradictory reports on patients' actual experience and reported experience of colonoscopies, 652 patients were randomly assigned to either a control or experimental group. The control group simply went through the colonoscopy as planned. The intervention group, however, had the colonoscopy left in for an extra 60 seconds. Although leaving the apparatus in place for an additional minute was mildly discomforting it was less so than the actual procedure. Thus, ending on a mildly discomforting rather than painful note significantly affected the recollection of the entire procedure. This also supports the theory of duration neglect, as it is not the length of the occurrence that is important for recollection but how the event ends.

See Redelmeier et al. (2003) for the original article.

Overall, when we attend to positive things around us using clear rather than negatively biased interpretations of events and interactions, as well as engaging in positive reminiscence, we can set ourselves up to create a more positive attitude and happier existence.

Summary

There are several definitions of happiness, but that in most widespread use in research is 'subjective wellbeing' (SWB). Reflecting on the learning objectives, you should now understand SWB across cultures. More specifically:

- One of the reasons suggested as to why some humans are never satisfied is hedonic adaptation.
- The hedonic adaptation prevention model is currently being used to counteract this evolutionary tendency to revert back to our happiness set points.
- Subjective wellbeing is traditionally measured via self-report measurement tools, such as the SWLS, because happiness is a subjective phenomenon.
- Currently, there are several global happiness polls that enable us to look at countries' populations and their current happiness levels.
- Sometimes choice is not a good thing, especially if we tend to lean on the maximizing side.

Suggested Resources

http://www.gallup.com/home.aspx
   To find out more about the Gallup World Polls or to access books written by the organization, go this website.

http://news.bbc.co.uk/1/hi/programmes/happiness_formula/4771908.stm
   This link allows you to access some of the clips from the acclaimed BBC documentary, *The Happiness Formula,* featuring Ilona Boniwell.

http://internal.psychology.illinois.edu/~ediener/index.html
   This is an excellent website, allowing you access to free online journals regarding SWB, and new and innovative tools.

http://www.worldvaluessurvey.org/
   To track the world and its diverse and changing values, visit the world values survey website.

Further questions for you

1 Do you agree with the research findings on children and wellbeing? Honestly argue for or against these findings.

2 What would your life be like if you never had to worry about money?

3 What do you think is missing from the area of subjective wellbeing? Discuss.

Personal Development Interventions

The exercises presented below focus on identifying and enhancing your subjective wellbeing.

1 AIM approach

We would like you to try out Diener and Biswas-Diener's (2009) AIM approach at creating a positive attitude. Make sure you attempt each one!

Attention: tomorrow, make a concerted effort to attend to the positive experiences, events, people and environments around you. Write down what you witnessed and reflect.

Interpretation: challenge your interpretations. Refer to the list of six types of destructive thinking patterns and the next time you make a sweeping negative statement, reframe the sentence to use more constructive wording.

Memory: as you attend to the positives tomorrow, bank these memories so that you can reflect on them, savour them and replay them for future enjoyment.

2 Intensely positive experiences

Similar to the 'M' (memory) in the AIM approach, we would like you to take reminiscence one step further. We would like you to engage in writing about an intensely positive experience, such as wonder, happiness, ecstasy, love from graduation, family, children, vacations, etc. (Burton and King, 2004).

We would like you to think of an intensely positive experience and write about it for 15 minutes, for three consecutive days. Keep track of how you feel during, after and at the end of the week.

Measurement Tools

Satisfaction with Life Scale (SWLS)

(Diener et al., 1985)

Directions

Below are five statements with which you may agree or disagree. Using the 1–7 scale below, indicate your agreement with each item by placing the appropriate number on the line preceding that item. Please be open and honest in your responding.

1 = Strongly disagree
2 = Disagree
3 = Slightly disagree
4 = Neither agree or disagree
5 = Slightly agree
6 = Agree
7 = Strongly agree

_____ **1.** In most ways my life is close to my ideal.

_____ **2.** The conditions of my life are excellent.

_____ **3.** I am satisfied with life.

_____ **4.** So far I have gotten the important things I want in life.

_____ **5.** If I could live my life over, I would change almost nothing.

Scoring

Simply add your scores to attain one final score.

Interpretation

31–35 Extremely satisfied
26–30 Satisfied
21–25 Slightly satisfied
20 Neutral
15–19 Slightly dissatisfied
10–14 Dissatisfied
5–9 Extremely dissatisfied

Review

The SWLS is five questions on a 7-point Likert scale. It has high internal consistency (0.87) and good test–retest reliability (0.82) (over two months). Furthermore, the research shows us that it has strong correlations with other mental wellbeing measures (around 0.7) and between self-reported scores and experimenters.

Critiques of this test come from the confusion surrounding whether or not life satisfaction is a result of personality dispositions or current moods and current life circumstances. Pavot and Diener (2008) argue that it is the summation of both sets of factors and should be used in conjunction with more focused tools when assessing change. Furthermore, current mood has been shown to have little to no effect on our overall judgement of life satisfaction (bar long-term unemployment and widowhood) (Pavot and Diener, 2008).

Subjective Happiness Scale (SHS)

(Lyubomirsky and Lepper, 1999)

Directions

For each of the following statements and/or questions, please circle the point on the scale that you feel is most appropriate in describing you.

1 In general I consider myself

1	2	3	4	5	6	7
Not a very					**A very**	
happy person					**happy person**	

2 Compared to most of my peers, I consider myself

1	2	3	4	5	6	7
Less happy					**More happy**	

3 Some people are generally very happy. They enjoy life regardless of what is going on, getting the most out of everything. To what extent does this characterization describe you?

1	2	3	4	5	6	7
Not at all						**A great deal**

4 Some people are generally not very happy. Although they are not depressed, they never seem as happy as they might be. To what extent does this characterization describe you?

1	2	3	4	5	6	7
Not at all						**A great deal**

Scoring

Add together the four item scores. Item 4 is reverse coded, so that if you scored 1 give yourself 7. Then divide the total score by 4 to give a range of 1 to 7.

Interpretation

The world adult population scores, on average, between 4.5 and 5.5.

Review

This scale is even shorter than the SWLS, including only four items on a 7-point Likert scale. This scale does not explicitly discriminate between cognitive and affective dimensions, like the SWLS, however it does have good internal consistency of 0.79–0.96 (M = 0.86) as well as concurrent validity (0.7) with the SWLS and convergent validity with self-esteem, optimism and extraversion scales.

The Maximizing Scale

(Schwartz et al., 2002)

Directions

Below are twelve statements with which you may agree or disagree. These statements concern your past, present, or future. Using the 1–7 scale below, please indicate your agreement with each item by placing the appropriate number on the line preceding that item. Please be open and honest in your responding. The 7-point scale is:

1	2	3	4	5	6	7
Strongly disagree	Disagree	Slightly disagree	Neither agree nor disagree	Slightly agree	Agree	Strongly agree

_____ 1. Whenever I'm faced with a choice, I try to imagine what all the other possibilities are, even ones that aren't present at the moment.

_____ 2. No matter how satisfied I am with my job, it's only right for me to be on the lookout for better opportunities.

_____ 3. When I am in the car listening to the radio, I often check other stations to see if something better is playing, even if I am relatively satisfied with what I'm listening to.

_____ 4. When I watch TV, I channel surf, often scanning through the available options even while attempting to watch one programme.

_____ **5.** I treat relationships like clothing: I expect to try a lot on before finding the perfect fit.

_____ **6.** I often find it difficult to shop for a gift for a friend.

_____ **7.** Renting videos is really difficult. I'm always struggling to pick the best one.

_____ **8.** When shopping, I have a hard time finding clothing that I really love.

_____ **9.** I'm a big fan of lists that attempt to rank things (the best movies, the best singers, the best athletes, the best novels, etc.).

_____**10.** I find that writing is very difficult, even if it's just writing a letter to a friend, because it's so hard to word things just right. I often do several drafts of even simple things.

_____**11.** No matter what I do, I have the highest standards for myself. I never settle for second best.

_____**12.** I often fantasize about living in ways that are quite different from my actual life.

Scoring

Please add the items and average them to find your total score.

Interpretation

The authors consider people whose averaged score is higher than a 4 to be _maximizers._ If you scored higher than 5.5, you are classified as an 'extreme maximizer' (along with approximately 10 per cent of the population), however if you scored lower than 2.5, you are classified as an 'extreme satisficer' (again with approximately 10 per cent of the population). The rest fall between scores higher than 4.75 (approximately 33 per cent) and lower than 3.25 (approximately 33 per cent).

Review

Although undertaking this scale can be quite eye opening, researchers have begun to question whether or not this measurement tool is effective in measuring maximization, arguing that what Schwartz is measuring is not actually maximization in its truest from. Furthermore, there are issues surrounding the multidimensionality of the scale, whereas the concept should be placed on a unidimentional scale (Diab et al., 2008).

Notes

1 Thus criticisms of positive psychology and the pursuit of understanding happiness do not seem to stand in the research data. People who have higher SWB tend to be more altruistic and help others more – thus, positive psychology is not a self-centred, individualistic discipline.
2 Most people answer 'no', that they would prefer reality and glimpses of true happiness to a lifetime of simulated reality.
3 These tools are located for your convenience at the end of this chapter.
4 This study has recently been contested following the findings of another longitudinal research study on lottery winners with medium-sized wins (£1000–£120,000). Gardner and Oswald (2006) found that these winners had enhanced psychological health and wellbeing compared with controls (no wins) or smaller lottery winners (<£1000). All in all, the Brickman et al (1978) study is repeatedly mentioned throughout positive psychology, and it is a good one for you to know.
5 Divorce and chronic disability are close behind bereavement and unemployment in terms of their long-term negative effect on overall wellbeing (Lucas et al., 2003; Lucas, 2005, 2007).

CHAPTER 4

Eudaimonic Wellbeing

❖ LEARNING OBJECTIVES

Is happiness enough for a good life? Is merely feeling good an adequate measure of someone's quality of life? Do we really know what it means to be *subjectively well* when we assess someone's subjective wellbeing? This chapter will review some answers to these questions and introduce the notion of eudaimonic wellbeing, as well as some corresponding theories.

List of topics

- The definition and historical roots of eudaimonia.
- The concept of psychological wellbeing (PWB).
- The importance of meaning and purpose in life.
- The links between existential psychology and positive psychology.
- Positive death and meaning.
- The concept of flow and its characteristics.
- Self-determination theory (SDT).
- The three basic psychological needs.

MOCK ESSAY QUESTIONS

1 Compare and contrast the concepts of subjective and psychological wellbeing.

2 Based on our current knowledge of the subject, to what extent it is possible to arrive at a common definition of eudaimonic wellbeing?

3 'I would rather wake up unhappy than without meaning in my life.' Discuss.

The other type of happiness

As discussed in the previous chapter, there are two camps of thought about what makes people happy and/or experience wellbeing. The previous chapter discussed the concept of subjective wellbeing, which is a person's satisfaction with their life and the experience of positive affect and low negative affect. Ryan and Deci (2000) argue that SWB is simply a definition of hedonism and that the types of activities and goals theorized to promote wellbeing may be misleading. Vitterso (2004) criticized SWB for ignoring the complexity of philosophical conceptions of happiness and completely failing to explain the dimension of personal growth, while Ryff (1989) argued that there was a failure to answer the question of what it actually means to be well psychologically. Ultimately, the concepts of meaning and purpose, which appear to be very important for a balanced sense of wellbeing, are ignored (King and Napa, 1998; McGregor and Little, 1998).

'Eudaimonic wellbeing' argues that wellbeing lies in the actualization of human potential. Researchers within the eudaimonic framework argue that happiness and 'the good life' are not simply the experiences of feeling good. There has to be more to life than just pleasure and satisfaction. Eudaimonic wellbeing proposes that true happiness is found in the expression of virtue and doing what is worth doing. Thus, the realization of human potential is an ultimate goal (Aristotle). Individuals must therefore seek and pursue happiness through prudence (John Locke) and self-discipline (Epicurus). Eudaimonia is defined as fulfilling or realizing one's daimon or true nature. This occurs when people's life activities are most congruent with their deep values (Waterman, 1993) such as developing one's true self (Vitterso, 2004), engaging in activities for their own sake (Csikszentmihalyi, 2002) and belonging to and serving institutions larger than oneself (Huta et al., 2003).

Views differ, however, as to how the experiences of eudaimonic and hedonic wellbeing relate to each other. On the one hand, it may be that eudaimonic wellbeing always includes hedonic wellbeing to some extent, or that they are largely independent dimensions (Ryff, 1989), or that the experience of eudaimonic wellbeing can actively reduce hedonic wellbeing. On the other hand, Kashdan, Biswas-Diener and King (2008) consider the constructs and hence the experiences to be identical.

The question also arises as to whether eudaimonic wellbeing is a process or an outcome, or both. The prevailing discourse is to construct it as a state (for example, Kashdan et al., 2008; Waterman et al., 2008) but some researchers have suggested that it may be more appropriate to view it as a process (for example, Ryan et al., 2008; Vittersø et al., 2009).

Finally, researchers have started to look into whether there is a relationship between eudaimonic wellbeing and personality differences, or if eudaimonic wellbeing in itself can be seen as a personality trait. More specifically, research intends to discover whether there is there such a thing as a hedonic or eudaimonic orientation (Vittersø et al., 2009) that gives a greater propensity to experience eudaimonic wellbeing.

As Boniwell (2008) has pointed out, the area of eudaimonic wellbeing appears, at best, a mess. The next section will review the current alternative theoretical frameworks falling under the eudaimonic wellbeing umbrella.

Psychological wellbeing

The concept of PWB (Ryff and Keyes, 1995; Ryff and Singer, 2006) consists of six components: self-acceptance (positive evaluation of oneself and one's life), personal growth, purpose in life, positive relations with others, environmental mastery (the capacity to effectively manage one's life and environment) and autonomy. There is some empirical support for the six-factor model with moderate associations between two subscales of PWB (self-acceptance and environmental mastery) and SWB (the other dimensions correlated weakly or inconsistently with these indicators) (Ryff and Keyes, 1995). Ryff argues that this pattern demonstrates that traditional measures ignore the key aspects of wellbeing (Ryff, 1989). A number of researchers, however, are critical of these dimensions. Vitterso (2004) notes several findings suggesting that Ryff's six dimensions can be accounted for by two factors corresponding to hedonic and eudaimonic wellbeing.

Keyes et al. (2002) hypothesized that SWB and PWB, although conceptually related, are empirically distinct conceptions of wellbeing. Factor analysis of data from over 3000 respondents confirmed that SWB and PWB are two correlated but distinct factors and that they show a different pattern of relationships to demographic and personality variables.

Authentic happiness

Seligman (2002) argued that there are *three routes to happiness*: (1) the pleasant life, which enables high levels of positive emotion and gratification; (2) the good life, which enables constant absorption, engagement and 'flow'; and (3) the meaningful life, where one uses one's strengths in the service of something greater than oneself. The latter two fall under the umbrella of eudaimonia. The important thing to note from this area of research is that people who engage in hedonic, pleasant activities experience higher levels of positive affect in the short term; however eudaimonic pursuits may give meaning and value in the long term.

Flow

Think about it...

Have you ever started an assignment or essay only to find that five hours have gone by without you even noticing it? Have you ever played a football game, or a rugby match, or completed a dance routine, where you were so absorbed in what you were doing that you didn't notice anything or anyone else around you? And you played your best? This feeling of 'being in the zone' is what researchers describe as *flow*. Think about your experiences of flow as we go through the next section of the textbook.

Flow theory was created by Mihalyi Csikszentmihalyi after his fascination in the 1960s with artists and their unwavering concentration. He noticed that all rewards of painting came from painting itself – a theory now known as intrinsic motivation. During this time, researchers such as Maslow, Deci and Ryan began to look at why and how people were led to intrinsic behaviours (later, these same researchers would create what is now known as self-determination theory). However, Csikszentmihalyi wanted to go further and return to the subjective experience: How did flow actually feel? He entered into the realm of phenomenology, which focuses on the lived experience of psychological phenomena (Csikszentmihalyi, 1975, 1990, 2002; Smith and Eatough, 2006).

The main point here is that Csikszentmihalyi's early work was to focus on and understand what the lived experience was like when things were going well and when people were performing at their best. After several experiments across a range of participants (artists, dancers, rock climbers), Csikszentmihalyi noticed that 'a common set of structural characteristics was found to distinguish those patterns of action that produced flow from the rest of every day life' (Csikszentmihalyi and Csikszentmihalyi, 1988: 8).

Flow[1] is defined as 'the intense experiential involvement in moment-to-moment activity, which can be either physical or mental. Attention is fully invested in the task at hand and the person functions at her or his fullest capacity' (Csikszentmihalyi, 2009: 394). Flow has direct ties with consciousness and psychic energy where it is posited that when people feel *psychic entropy* (chaos and anxious thoughts) they will experience depression and stress. However, the attainment of *psychic negentropy* or *flow* (exclusion of any negative thought) is ideal for enhancing the experience's positive effect (Csikszentmihalyi, 2009).

Several conditions are needed to facilitate the flow experience. These include:

- Structured activity with clear goals and immediate feedback. This means that the activity must have rules and a clear outline in order to help orientate the person doing it. As we continue through the activity, we must be able to get a sense of feedback – a sense that we are on the right track towards the desired goal. Without feedback, confusion and consciousness will creep in.

- Balance of challenges versus skills. As the model of optimal experience (Figure 4.1) shows, in order to reach and maintain positioning within the flow channel, we must have a delicate balance between our skills level and the challenges at hand. If the challenge is too far above our current skill level, then this will produce anxiety. If it is too low, it will produce boredom. Furthermore, if a person has no skill and there is no challenge (such as TV watching) then they will exist in a channel of apathy.

- Complete concentration (merging of action and awareness). The activity must initiate a complete merger of the activity and all consciousness. All attention is within the activity and there is no room for consciousness. Also, you lose a sense of 'yourself' and become one with the activity you are completing. There is no time or room to be self-conscious. Attention is focused on the task at hand and on all task-relevant stimuli. Everything else but the activity is irrelevant at that point in time.

- Sense of control. This stems from the activity's ability to allow us to lose self-consciousness, thereby gaining a sense of control over what we are doing. This also ties in with the perception of skill versus challenge; thus if we perceive the skill and challenge to match, we will feel a better sense of control.

- Transformation of time. This element is the unique experience of where time speeds up, and before you know it, you've been engaging in the activity for hours when it felt like minutes. Or, as in dance, time can slow down, where a minute feels like hours, seconds like minutes. Basically, there is a definite distortion of time from the reality of the clock.

- Activity for the sake of activity (and a wish to repeat). This component refers to the activity's ability to make you want to do it all over again. No rewards, no external forces. Simply, you like doing it and want to repeat it.

- Finally, there is another potential facilitator of the flow experience and that is your personality. Perhaps you know someone who enjoys life and appears to be intrinsically led in his or her daily endeavours. They have skills that enable them to have an innate general curiosity in life, persistence, low self-centredness and an ability to be motivated by intrinsic rewards (Nakamura and Csikszentmihalyi, 2005). These people would be described as having an autotelic personality and are more susceptible to experiencing flow.

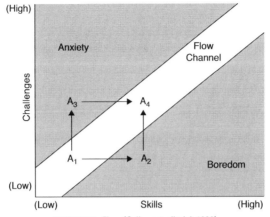

FIGURE 4.1 Flow (Csikszentmihalyi, 1990)

Demographics of flow

Are you in flow? This section will review who, when, where and with whom we are most likely to experience flow.

Who's in flow?

Much to our surprise, 10–15 per cent of the US and European populations have never experienced flow but 10–15 per cent of the same population report experiencing flow every day. Research has shown that we tend to experience flow in different measures and intensities throughout our life span.

Using the experience sampling method (ESM), Csikszentmihalyi and his colleagues have assessed real-time occurrences of flow in people from varied social demographics and countries.[2] The ESM (Csikszentmihalyi and Csikszentmihalyi, 1988) was created specifically for counteracting the detriments of conventional retrospective measurement within psychology. Now widely used in other areas of psychology, the ESM is a beeper that people are asked to carry for any length of time (usually a week). The beeper will randomly go off throughout the day and people are asked to answer a number of questions related to flow and the context they are in (work, leisure, alone, with friends, and so forth).

Csikszentmihalyi and Larson (1984) found that teenagers tend to feel their most happiest, strong and motivated when with friends, and the opposite when alone.

The activities in which we are most likely to experience flow are: sports and activity, dance participation, creative arts, sex, socializing, studying, listening to music, reading and paradoxically working. However, many other activities can produce the experience of flow (Csikszentmihalyi, 2002; Delle Fave and Massimini, 2004).

Activities that tend to inhibit flow (and induce apathy and boredom) include housework, watching TV and being idle.

Think about it...

Could the relationship between flow and the activities listed above be due to cultural influences? Research conducted in Iran, Romania, Nepal and several other countries contradict traditional Western findings with regards to housework, watching TV and raising children (Delle Fave and Massimini, 2004).

Benefits of flow

Ultimately, there are several consequences of attaining flow. Within the sport domain, athletes and coaches report peak performance and enhanced skill acquisition. Those who experience flow in play and leisure report increased positive emotions (after the fact). Education systems arranged in order to induce flow can bring about higher grades, levels of commitment and achievement in education within their students. Finally, occupational settings can experience greater engagement and leadership development.

Although there has been a lot of research done on flow, there are still a few avenues that are yet to be explored. For example, what about micro flow (those little spates of time that you appear to be in flow, albeit for seconds, not minutes)? What are the elements needed for this? How can we create it? Is it flow? Also, and importantly within the sport and occupational domains, is the concept of 'group flow', where people report being in flow in tandem with their fellow teammates. The dynamics between people and this phenomenon are yet to be fully understood.

Dangers of flow

In class, we get asked quite a lot whether flow is a morally good phenomenon. This is an interesting question that challenges the assumption that flow equals peak performance. The answer is that flow can be found in activities that are both morally good and bad (for example, gambling). Research has also demonstrated a potential to become addicted to flow-inducting activities (for instance, rock climbing, video game playing), where the activity becomes necessary for daily functioning (Csikszentmihalyi, 1992). Overall, engaging in flow-inducing activities that challenge and stretch you as a person, within reason, can have a tremendous positive affect on your overall wellbeing.

Applying flow theory

Flow does not just happen by chance (Csikszentmihalyi, 2002). Two approaches for applying flow have been suggested: 1) change environments to facilitate flow and 2) help others find flow (Csikszentmihalyi, 2009). Through the first facet, managers/workers can shape activity structures and environments to foster flow or obstruct it less (Whalen, 1999; Rathunde and Csikszentmihalyi, 2005; Emerson, 1998). Secondly, therapists can help assist individuals in finding flow, which in turn can lead to higher levels of performance and increased positive affect (Delle Fave and Massimimi, 2004; Csikszentmihalyi, 1993; Nakamura and Csikszentmihalyi, 2005). Therapists can also help clients identify activities that get him/her into flow, working together to increase the difficulty or complexity of these activities (ensuring that these are matched by growing skills). It is important for clinicians to encourage re-allocation of time away from apathetic activities (for example, TV) to flow-inducing activities.

Meaning and purpose in life

Throughout several areas of research and practice, the issue surrounding the meaning of life and meaning within life is essential to fulfilled individuals (Steger, 2009; Wong, 2009). Meaninglessness in life has been proposed to be akin to the existential fear of death. Researchers argue that when one is faced with meaninglessness, one can encounter several negative experiences. Thus, researchers would argue that the search for meaning and purpose is more relevant than the search for happiness (Wong, 2009). Researchers also argue that not only should we be measuring meaning in life but the structural properties of personal meaning systems, such as 'differentiation (how diverse the sources of meaning are), elaboration (how people construct their own links and connections between events to give life purpose) and coherence (how well do all the features fit together) measures' (Pöhlmann et al., 2006: 111). These measures enhance mental and physical health/wellbeing and predict life satisfaction (Pöhlmann et al., 2006).

A superb figurehead for both the positive psychology and existential areas, Frankl's work on meaning is still important today. His concept of 'will to meaning' proposed three benefits of living a meaningful life, including: creative, experiential and attitudinal value. Since Frankl's contribution, researchers have identified seven major sources of meaning, found cross-culturally, including: achievement, acceptance, relationship, intimacy, religion, self-transcendence and fairness.

King and Napa (1998) argued that it was a combination of both happiness (SWB = SWL, PA, NA) and meaning (such as connectedness, purpose and growth akin to eudaimonia) that created overall wellbeing. Furthermore, those who rate high on meaning have been found to be given the highest liking ratings in their samples.

McGregor and Little (1998) analysed a diverse set of mental health indicators and concluded that the concept of wellbeing should be regarded as consisting of two elements: happiness (satisfaction with life, positive affect, negative affect) and meaning (connectedness, purpose and growth). Compton et al. (1996) supported this combination, however they changed the second component to personal growth. Compton et al. (1996) identified two main factors out of 18 indicators of wellbeing, one representing happiness/SWB and the other personal growth. Measures of happiness/SWB related to a factor different from that of personal growth construct (e.g. maturity, self-actualization, hardiness, and openness to experience). The factors themselves were moderately correlated.

Developing a purpose in life and identifying reasons to live help mediate between stress, coping and suicidal behaviour (Mei-Chuan et al., 2007). Individuals who report enhanced levels of depression, hopelessness and suicidal thoughts are much more likely to use emotion-oriented coping strategies.

Avoidance coping strategies, when used in a healthy way, can be a positive approach to wellbeing, as they can channel negative thoughts into other area of life, thereby potentially creating reason for living (Mei-Chuan et al., 2007).

Self-determination theory (SDT)

Self-determination theory argues, like Maslow's hierarchy of needs, that there is an evolutionary adaptive function of three basic psychological needs. *Autonomy* is the tendency to self-regulate one's behaviour in accordance with personal volition (rather than external control). It is also the tendency to resist coercion, pressure, and control; to regulate one's behaviour in accordance with one's own needs (and situational affordances), which promotes better survival than organizing behaviour to meet external demands. Thus, autonomy is the volition and the desire to freely choose actions consistent with one's integrated sense of self; feeling that one is voluntarily engaging in a behaviour, regardless of whether the behaviour is dependent on others or not.

Competence is the tendency to be interested and open, to seek learning/mastery opportunities (promote acquisition of new skills). The need for competence manifests in early motor play, manipulation of objects, and exploration of surroundings. The tendency to experience satisfaction from learning for its own sake – and the tendency to explore and seek challenges. This need is shared to some degree with other mammals. Thus, competence is the ability to affect the environment and attain desired outcomes.

Relatedness is the tendency to feel connection and caring with group members (it promotes group cohesion and mutual protection). It is similar to Baumeister and Leary's 'need to belong' and overlaps with Bowlby's attachment need. This need can at times conflict with need for autonomy but normally it is complementary.

Besides the needs mentioned above (autonomy, competence and relatedness), are there any other basic needs that must be met for psychological wellbeing? We would argue, along with early humanistic psychologists, that physical thriving/health, or the feeling that one's basic biological needs are met, is essential to wellbeing. Furthermore, a sense of security, having a sense of order and predictability in one's life (Maslow), has also been put forth as a fundamental basic need (Sheldon et al., 2001).

Think about it...

Write a critical reflection on the similarities and differences of the following sectors of eudaimonic wellbeing:

1 PWB.
2 Authentic happiness.
3 Self-determination theory.
4 Flow and autotelic personality.

Which happiness do you subscribe to?

Existential psychology and positive psychology

Existential psychology focuses on 'human existence and the human drama of survival and flourishing' (Wong, 2009: 361). Traditionally, existential psychology has been deemed to be fixated on the darker side of human life (such as the view that happiness is derived from accepting suffering as the essence of the human condition) (Wong, 2009: 364) and overlooked within positive psychology research. Since the two areas of psychology focus on the same fundamental questions – what is a good life and what makes life worth living? (Wong, 2009: 361) – the separation appears ignorant and slightly dangerous.

A new wave of existential positive psychology aims to merge the two areas while endeavouring to find the answers to life's difficult questions (death, freedom, isolation, meaninglessness, identity and happiness). Existential psychology denotes that there are three types of mature happiness:

- authentic happiness (comes from being an authentic individual);
- eudaimonic happiness (comes from doing virtuous deeds); and
- chaironic happiness (a spiritual gift of happiness that is bestowed; it is independent of our abilities and circumstances especially within suffering).

Happiness is a process – not an end result, ongoing, and the result of forgoing self-interest and serving something higher than the self. What we like about this is that it acknowledges the importance of both negative and positive elements of human functioning that are essential for personal growth. Wong integrates the issue of identity crises and authenticity with the proposal that generational issues, via consumerism and capitalism, are crippling today's society in the search for 'the self'. Poignantly, Wong argues that when people are authentic, it doesn't always lead to happiness, just that they have to take the risk to be who they truly are.

Existential psychologists also accept that contentment can actually be a negative thing, leaving a void in a person's life with no goals or achievements left to strive for. Discontent has the potential for personal growth.

Ultimately, pursuing happiness may not be the aim of life; however, existential psychologists deem that by pursuing meaning and authenticity one will eventually achieve happiness. Like the perspective of Camus and May, Wong's duality hypothesis states that 'positives cannot exist apart from negatives and that authentic happiness grows from pain and suffering' (Wong, 2009: 364).

Death and positive psychology

Humans have developed the capacity to think, be conscious and anticipate the future. This powerful mechanism is also an anxiety-inducing mechanism that allows us to recognize that at some point we will die. However, even death, the most feared concept in human existence, is a potential avenue for growth and development. 'Positive death' or 'good dying' is proposed to have a link with the good life (Wong, 2009). Meaning management theory posits that death can have either a negative or positive effect on us, depending on how we view it. By embracing death, we can live more authentically, thereby enhancing the likelihood of self-actualization. Transforming death anxiety into a productive energy force is a positive viewpoint on a traditionally 'negative' component of the life process.

Researchers propose that there are three distinct attitudes towards death (our death attitude profile) including:

- neutral death acceptance, when one accepts that death is a part of life and attempts to live life to the fullest;
- approach acceptance, when one accepts that there is a an afterlife that will be pleasurable; and
- escape acceptance, which perceives death as the preferable option to a miserable life.

Terror management theory

Another theory linked to realization of death is terror management theory (TMT). This theory suggests there is an innate, biological need to survive and deals with the management of the evolutionary cognitive realization of inevitable death (Pyszczynski et al., 2002). The mortality salience hypothesis suggests that when people are reminded of the inevitability of death, their world view defence strengthens and they seek to conform to the accepted beliefs and behaviours of their culture (Harmon-Jones et al., 1997). Thus, a traumatic and life-threatening event, paired with the lifelong reminder of a person's close encounter with death (physical scars, deformity) creates a mortality salient environment. Such people will have a conscious reminder of the inevitability of their own death and, according to Pyszczynski et al. (2002), utilize proximal defences and distraction to defend themselves from death-related reminders.

Integrating hedonic and eudaimonic wellbeing

So how do we reconcile the debate within the field over what constitutes a good life: hedonic or eudaimonic wellbeing? We know that those who follow their eudaimonic pursuits score highly on satisfaction with life tools (Huta et al., 2003). However, increased scores on positive affect were strongly correlated with hedonic measures as were drive fulfilment and being relaxed and away from problems. Eudaimonic measures tend to correlate much better with growth, development, challenges and efforts (Waterman, 1993).

Criticisms of the hedonic paradigm stem from the lack of clarity on what types of positive affect are important for wellbeing. Is it Fredrickson's ten emotions? Should SWL be viewed as a component of hedonism? Satisfaction with life is an independent evaluative element and perhaps there needs to be a re-evaluation of the concept of hedonic wellbeing. For example, what do we really mean by happiness and wellbeing (Galati, Manzano and Sotgiu, 2006)?

Furthermore, within the eudaimonic paradigm, there is a lack of conceptual unity. (For example, what is being understood under personal growth? Is eudaimonic WB development/growth or transcendence/meaning? Or all of them?) Ultimately, the way forward includes the undertaking of exploratory research and to define and develop appropriate measures of eudaimonic WB. Qualitative approaches can offer intricacy and depth and capture complexity of phenomena. They can be extremely useful in mapping out the field, developing conceptual clarity and formulating an overarching framework. However, most existing studies have employed a top-down approach to data analysis. Furthermore, many studies focused on what lay people believe make them happy rather than exploring the meanings attributed to happiness.

Summary

Reflecting on the learning objectives you should now understand the concept of eudaimonic wellbeing. More specifically, you should know:

- Eudaimonia is defined as the area of happiness concerned with following the meaningful life and achieving actualization.
- Psychological wellbeing consists of six components considered to be neglected by the traditional hedonic paradigm.
- Meaning and purpose in life are essential for wellbeing.
- Purpose in life can reduce suicidal behaviours.
- Flow occurs when someone engages with an activity that is intrinsic and matches his or her skill level.
- Self-determination theory includes three psychological needs imperative for wellbeing: autonomy, competence and relatedness.

Suggested Resources

http://www.meaning.ca/
This website links you to Dr. Paul Wong and his meaning website. You will find all you need to know about existential and positive psychology as well as references to leading existential articles/books from across the decades.

http://qlrc.cgu.edu/about.htm
This is the Quality of Life Research Center, based at Claremont University, under the supervision of Mike Csikszentmihalyi. Use this for useful links regarding flow, optimal experience and general positive psychology.

Further questions for you

1 Should positive affect and the current version of the SWL scale be used as the outcome measures for studies of eudaimonic WB?
2 How should eudaimonic WB be defined?
3 Is flow always a good thing? What dangers can you think of?
4 Is flow the only optimal experience you can think of? List any additional experiences. You do not need to know the exact name for them.

Personal Development Interventions

1 Flow

Flow is a wonderful thing. Think about and write down three activities that you consistently experience flow in. This could be going to the gym, painting, socializing or reading, in fact any activity that meets Csikszentmihalyi's nine criteria for flow. Over the next week, try and incorporate at least one of these activities into your routine. Document how you felt immediately after the event. Continue to list and incorporate flow-inducing activities into your weekly agenda.

2 Meaning

You don't need a therapist or counsellor to help you find meaning in your life. Try and align your behaviours with your values and regulate the following throughout your daily life:

P urpose and life goals
U nderstanding the demands of each situation and life as a whole
R esponsible actions and reactions consistent with your purpose and
    understanding
E valuation of your life in order to ensure authenticity and efficacy

(PURE Model, adapted from Wong, 2009: 366)

Measurement Tools

Meaning in Life Questionnaire (MLQ)

(Steger et al., 2006)

Directions

Take a moment to think about what makes your life and existence feel important and significant to you. Respond to the following statements as truthfully and accurately as you can. Remember that these are very subjective questions and that there are no right or wrong answers. Please answer according to the scale below:

Absolutely Untrue	Mostly Untrue	Somewhat Untrue	Can't Say True or False	Somewhat True	Mostly True	Absolutely True
1	2	3	4	5	6	7

_____ **1.** I understand my life's meaning.

_____ **2.** I am looking for something that makes my life feel meaningful.

_____ **3.** I am always looking to find my life's purpose.

_____ **4.** My life has a clear sense of purpose.

_____ **5.** I have a good sense of what makes my life meaningful.

_____ **6.** I have discovered a satisfying life purpose.

_____ **7.** I am always searching for something that makes my life feel significant.

_____ **8.** I am seeking a purpose or mission for my life.

_____ **9.** My life has no clear purpose.

_____**10.** I am searching for meaning in my life.

Scoring

Presence = 1, 4, 5, 6, and 9 (reverse-coded).
Search = 2, 3, 7, 8, and 10.

Interpretation

Scores above 24 for both presence and search indicate life value and meaning.

If you scored above 24 on presence and below 24 on search implies that while you may feel that your life has value and meaning, you are not actively exploring that meaning at the present time. For further interpretations, please email Michael Steger at michael_f_steger@yahoo.com.

Review

Research on the MLQ has shown good reliability and test–retest stability. Presence is positively related to wellbeing, intrinsic religiosity, extraversion and agreeableness, and negatively related to anxiety and depression. The presence subscale positively correlates to multiple measures of wellbeing while negatively correlating with depression and anxiety.

The search subscale is positively correlated to scales such as neuroticism and depression and negatively correlated to well being. For a full review of both positive and negative correlates see www.ppc.sas.upenn.edu/ppquestionnaires.htm#MLQ.

Flourishing Scale

(**Diener et al., 2009**)

Directions

Below are eight statements with which you may agree or disagree. Indicate your response to each statement using the 1–7 scale below.

7 = Strongly agree
6 = Agree
5 = Slightly agree
4 = Mixed or neither agree nor disagree
3 = Slightly disagree
2 = Disagree
1 = Strongly disagree

____ **1.** I lead a purposeful and meaningful life.

____ **2.** My social relationships are supportive and rewarding.

____ **3.** I am engaged and interested in my daily activities.

____ **4.** I actively contribute to the happiness and wellbeing of others.

____ **5.** I am competent and capable in the activities that are important to me.

____ **6.** I am a good person and live a good life.

____ **7.** I am optimistic about my future.

____ **8.** People respect me.

Scoring

Add the responses, varying from 1 to 7, for all eight items.

Interpretation

The possible range of scores is from 8 (lowest possible) to 56 (highest possible). A high score represents a person with many psychological resources and strengths.

Review

This scale attempts to address the many variables proposed to coexist with human flourishing (for example, positive relationships, competence and meaning). Originally, the authors called the scale 'Psychological Wellbeing' but have since renamed it the Flourishing Scale to better reflect the items.

Flow Experience Questionnaire

(Csikszentmihalyi and Csikszentmihalyi, 1988: 195)

Directions

Please read the following and answer the questions below:

> My mind isn't wandering. I am not thinking of something else. I am totally involved in what I am doing. My body feels good. I don't seem to hear anything. The world seems to be cut off from me. I am less aware of myself and my problems.
>
> My consternation is like breathing. I never think of it. I am really oblivious to my surroundings after I really get going. I think that the phone could ring and the doorbell could ring or the house could burn down or something like that. When I start I really do shut out the whole world. Once I stop I can let it back in again.
>
> I am so involved in what I am doing. I don't see myself as separate from what I am doing.

Have you had experiences like those described in the three quotations?
How often have you had such experiences?
What were you doing when you had these experiences?
What started the experiences?
What kept them going?
What stopped them?

For these experiences, indicate the degree to which you agree or disagree with the following statements:

1	2	3	4	5	6	7	8
Strongly Disagree						**Strongly agree**	

_____ **1.** I get involved.

_____ **2.** I get anxious.

_____ **3.** I clearly know what I am supposed to do.

_____ **4.** I get direct clues as to how well I am doing.

_____ **5.** I feel I can handle the demands of the situation.

_____ **6.** I feel self-conscious.

_____ **7.** I get bored.

_____ **8.** I have to make an effort to keep my mind on what is happening.

_____ **9.** I would do it even if I didn't have to.

____**10.** I get distracted.

____**11.** Time passes more slowly or more quickly.

____**12.** I enjoy the experience and the use of my skills.

Scoring

The first section is analysed via qualitative analysis, whereas the second section is simply a summative score (reverse scoring for 2, 6, 7, 8, 10).

Interpretation

Within the second section, the higher the score, the higher the frequency of flow.

Review

The Flow Experience Questionnaire (Csikszentmihalyi and Csikszentmihalyi, 1988) consists of three vignettes with six questions and a Likert scale. However, present-day flow research primarily uses experience sampling methods to ensure accurate and immediate recollection of flow within everyday life.

Notes

1 Originally termed *autotelic experience.*
2 In 1997, the flow research lab boasted over 70,000 pages of ESM data (Csikszentmihalyi, 1997).

CHAPTER 5

Optimism, Explanatory Style and Hope

❖ LEARNING OBJECTIVES

People sometimes attribute miraculous powers to positive future-oriented thinking. To what degree is it really beneficial to have a positive, optimistic or hopeful outlook? Why and in which ways do optimism and hope confer their beneficial effects? This chapter discusses recent literature pertaining to optimism, hope, and related 'positive future-thinking' constructs.

List of topics

- Definitions of hope, optimism and explanatory style.
- A brief history of optimism.
- Differences and similarities between these constructs.
- Positive thinking and its effects on wellbeing.
- Defensive pessimism and positive illusions.
- Hope theory.

MOCK ESSAY QUESTIONS

1 Discuss the strengths and limitations of Snyder's cognitive formulation of hope.
2 Is seeing a glass as half full always beneficial?
3 Compare and contrast the theories of dispositional optimism and explanatory style.

History of optimism

Optimism has been described as a 'Velcro construct' (Peterson, 2006:119) as it has many correlates including happiness, health and achievement (Carver and Scheier, 2009). But what exactly is optimism and is it always good to 'look on the bright side of life?'

In the early days of philosophy and psychology, optimism was thought of as naivety or a superficial denial of suffering. Health practitioners regarded positive mental health as the absence of naïve optimistic illusions (optimism). Based in part on this logic, mental health experts, from the 1930s to the 1960s, often defined mental health as intact 'reality testing' such that the person holds only modest expectations about the future and has a more accurate or balanced view of the world (as reviewed in Peterson, 2000). However, since then, researchers have found mounting evidence to suggest that optimism isn't just a form of denial but a necessary component for resilient and happy individuals.

Of course, in psychology nothing is ever straightforward, thus within positive psychology there are two main schools of thought surrounding the definition and conceptualization of optimism: *dispositional optimism* and *explanatory style.*

Dispositional optimism (Scheier and Carver, 1987) is defined as a personality trait[1] relating to generalized outcome expectancies. Thus *optimists* are characterized by their broad expectancy that outcomes are likely to be positive whereas *pessimists* are characterized by the future anticipation of negative outcomes.

Leading researchers Scheier and Carver (2009) posit that optimism is tied into their self-regulatory model, which states that all human activity is based on goals. In order to reach our goals, we need to regulate our actions and behaviours. When experiencing hardship while trying to reach these goals, people who are optimists will continue and push through in order to reach their goal, whereas pessimistic people will be more likely to give up (Carver and Scheier, 1998).

The two main elements of dispositional optimism are the concepts of *expectancy* and *confidence*. Expectancy is the most crucial element as it has a direct link with expectancy value theories of motivation, which posit that all behaviour is a result of the desire to obtain a person's values or goals. Thus, in order to achieve the goal, it must have value and spark motivation to continue (Scheier and Carver, 2009).

Confidence, the second element, is highly influential on optimism. If confidence is high that the goal can be achieved, then the person is more likely to act. If there is doubt, then the person will disengage. Scheier and Carver (2009: 657) define optimism and pessimism as 'simply broader versions of confidence or doubt, operating to most situations in life rather than one or two.'

Psychologists measure dispositional optimism via the LOT-R, a short ten-item questionnaire that focuses on differentiating optimists from pessimists (Scheier, Carver and Bridges, 1994). We have included this measurement tool at the end of this chapter, so have a go and see what type of 'ist' you are!

Think about it...

Do you know anyone who is an 'eternal optimist' or a 'thundering pessimist'? Have they always been this way? Are you this way? Do you think you can learn to become more optimistic?

On the other hand, *attribution style (explanatory style)* (Seligman, 1998) refers to the way in which one explains the causes and influences of previous positive and negative events in order to create expectancies about the future. Research has shown that attributions for negative events are more important than those for positive events. Pessimists explain negative events by inferring internal, stable or global causes: The event was caused by myself (internal), by something that is chronic (stable), or by something that is pervasive and will affect other situations as well (global). Optimists explain negative events by inferring external, unstable or local causes: The event was caused by something/someone other than myself (external), by something that will probably not persist (unstable) or by something that is probably limited to this specific circumstance (local). Optimists adopt unstable, external (leaving one's self-esteem intact) and specific (depending on circumstances) explanations for bad events. Currently, literature has shown that the 'internal/external' component to explanatory style is not as important as stability and globality.

PRESIDENTS

Researchers in the US were interested in whether or not the optimistic content of a presidential candidate's speech could influence/affect the voting results. Peterson and his colleagues looked at speeches from 1900 to 1984 and found that individuals who used more optimistic wording (and less focus on the negative) won 85 per cent of the US presidential elections.

See Zullow et al. (1988) for the original article.

Psychologists measure attribution styles via the Attributional Style Questionnaire (ASQ), which presents vignettes (scenarios) to people, and they have to choose which of several explanations for the event seems most likely (some explanations being more internal, global, stable and so forth).

Think about it...

The *Pollyanna principle,* the name of which was taken from the protagonist in the classic novel *Pollyanna* (Porter, 1913), supposes that the subconscious human brain is wired to have a positivity bias towards situations and other people. How do we know this? Numerous studies have shown that the Pollyanna principle is more pervasive than we would believe. For example, people overestimate their interaction with positive more than they do with negative stimuli. Can you think of a time when this happened to you?

The main difference between the two schools of thought is that attributional style, based on Seligman's early work with learned helplessness as a model of depression (Abramson et al., 1978), recognizes optimism as a learned skill and not a stable personality trait. Seligman recommends monitoring your automatic thoughts and attitudes and disputing pessimistic explanations, which is similar to techniques used in cognitive behaviour therapy (CBT). The key to learned optimism is *reframing*. In order to achieve this, you must learn how to identify your beliefs about certain situations and recognize how these beliefs can have a detrimental effect on your emotions and subsequent behaviours.[2]

SELL, SELL, SELL

Optimistic attributional style has been associated with sales success. Researchers assessed an independent insurance company's sales persons on their optimistic explanatory style. Those sales persons who were in the top 10 per cent of scorers for optimistic explanatory styles sold 88 per cent more insurance than the bottom 10 per cent of scorers.

See Seligman and Schulman (1986) for the original article.

However, dispositional researchers have argued whether or not attribution style really is optimism. Attributional style is concerned with the question of *why* good and bad events happened whereas dispositional optimism focuses on what will probably happen in the future. Despite this difference, Peterson (2006) reports that the measurement tools for both schools of thought have similar correlates and have some levels of convergence.

time out

Learning optimism . . . learning your ABC's

The first step in learning your **ABC's** is to negotiate the acronym:

A dversity
B elief
C onsequence

Adversity: the straight, non-judgemental facts of the situation. For example: Who, what, when, where.

Belief: your immediate patterned belief (why it happened; what will happen next).

Consequence: your feelings and behaviours related to these beliefs.

Ultimately, when we identify our beliefs and recognize their effects on emotions and behaviours (beliefs cause consequences) we can challenge and change them to more productive thought patterns.

(Seligman, 1998)

Benefits of optimism

Over the past few decades, research has provided convincing evidence on the benefits of an optimistic outlook, especially within the areas of depression and stress, health and psychological trauma. We will go through the areas in more detail regarding the evidence to date.

Depression and stress

Optimists tend to experience less distress during adversity than pessimists, according to cross-sectional and prospective data reports (Carver and Scheier, 2009). Optimism does not simply mean that you lie down and wish for things to happen in a positive manner. Optimism predicts active coping with stress (for example, planning, social support seeking), whereas pessimism predicts avoidant coping (for example, distraction, denial). These differences in coping then tend to predict changes in psychological/physical adjustment. So, developing an optimistic trait might help lead to the engagement of active, constructive coping, such as acceptance, positive reframing and use of humour, whereas pessimism has been linked with disengagement and denial among breast cancer patients. Extreme forms of pessimism (hopelessness about the future) has also predicted an extreme form of disengagement coping, found to be moderated by the pathways dimension of hope (Lopes and Cunha, 2008).

With regards to depression, several studies have found that optimism prospectively predicts psychological and physical wellbeing (for example, perceived stress, depression, loneliness, social support) among college students, even when controlling for alternative predictors, such as self-esteem, locus of control and desire for control.

Optimism can also prospectively predict incidences and levels of postpartum depression, even when controlling for initial depression severity. Optimism is suggested to protect mothers against developing depression following the birth.

Optimism and health

Diseases that attack the immune system, such as cancer and HIV/AIDS, can show researchers objective markers with regards to self-reported optimism. For example, people who score higher on optimistic traits during early stage breast cancer diagnosis report higher levels of wellbeing. Furthermore, researchers have observed a correlation between pessimism scores and the prediction of early mortality among young patients with recurrent cancer. This correlation remained even after controlling for cancer site and symptom severity (Schulz and Mohamed, 2004).

There is also evidence to suggest that optimism is associated with living longer. Patients who engage in 'realistic acceptance' of the inevitability of death had a shorter survival time in a sample of 78 men with AIDS (Reed et al., 1994; reviewed in Taylor et al., 2000). In that study, those who scored high on 'realistic acceptance' died an average of 9 months earlier, even controlling for many other potential predictors of death such as AIDS-related symptoms, number of CD4 T-helper cells, medication, distress and overall health status. These researchers concluded that unrealistic optimism (or positive illusions) rather than realistic acceptance was actually a more effective predictor of survival. These findings fit with Taylor's general position that positive illusions can be beneficial when confronted with severe illness because such positive illusions help the person to find meaning even amidst extreme adversity (Taylor, 2009).

HEARTS

Before going into theatre, patients were asked to fill out a questionnaire regarding how optimistic they were about their upcoming coronary bypass surgery. Results showed that prior to surgery, optimists experienced less hostility and depression and greater relief, happiness, satisfaction with medical care, and perceived emotional support after surgery. Most interestingly, optimism significantly predicted rate of recovery, including behavioural milestones (sitting up in bed, walking) and staff member ratings. These effects remained 6 months post-surgery, and even 5 years later optimists were more likely to be working and less likely to be rehospitalized. On objective measures of physical health, optimistic patients were less likely to develop problematic enzymes and heart problems than pessimists. Pessimists were also more likely to suffer a heart attack during surgery even when controlling for relevant disease parameters.

See Scheier et al. (1989) for original article.

One way in which optimism appears to mediate these effects is the facilitation of positive affect, because optimism is associated with positive affect. It may be the interaction between these factors such as good mood and immune system functioning that mediates the effect. Furthermore, optimistic patients with HIV practised better health habits than their more pessimistic counterparts (better health behaviours in general: more medication compliance, less smoking/drinking, better diet, more exercising, fewer casual sexual partners, and so forth). Optimists tend to be unrealistically optimistic about their ability to control their own health but this can lead them to persist with health-promoting behaviours such as eating lower fat food, taking vitamins, enrolling on a cardiac rehabilitation programme (Scheier and Carver, 2009).

Overall, researchers in optimism would argue that optimists are not simply people who stick their heads in the sand and ignore threats to their wellbeing. For example, they attend to health warnings and usually discover potentially serious problems earlier rather than later. Pessimists, on the other hand, are far more likely to anticipate disaster – and as a result are more likely to give up.

Think about it...

Researchers suggest we can experience 'big optimism', which focuses on generic, more grand positive expectations, or 'little optimism', which focuses on more immediate and specific positive experiences. Can you give an example of each? (Peterson, 2006)

Optimism as positive illusions

Positive illusions (Taylor, 1989) are predicated on the belief that most people are biased towards viewing themselves in an optimistic way – thus they see their past behaviour, personal attributes and themselves in an enhanced light; they have an unrealistic sense of personal control and they have an unfounded sense of optimism that the future will be better than the facts suggest. Like positive illusions, self-deceptive strategies (Taylor and Brown, 1988, 1994) are used to manage 'negative information' (limited control over an unpredictable world, our future is bleak; losses and death). These arguments have some backing following research that shows that we are not good at accurately identifying reality. Chapter 6 will discuss the benefits of positive illusions with regards to illness, health and survival.

Optimism and locus of control

What is it about control that makes us happy? This section will review the concepts of locus of control and perceived control. Perceived control relates to a person's self-assessment of their ability to exert control, which interestingly, we humans frequently overestimate. Thompson proposes that there are three main strategies of maintaining control:

- changing to the goals that are reachable in the current situation;
- creating new avenues for control; or
- accepting current circumstances (Thompson, 2002).

PLANTS

L anger and Rodin, both Yale Professors, argued that nursing homes are decision-free environments for those who live there. They conducted a study that gave patients some control over small decisions in their lives. The researchers split the members of the nursing home into two groups: the responsibility-induced group (RI) and the control group. At a floor meeting, the RI residents were told they had choices on the arrangement of furniture, visiting hours, entertainment and they were given a small plant to care for. The other group (control group) had a floor meeting where they were told that the nurses would take care of their every need, what entertainment to expect, what visiting hours were set, how room layouts are arranged and that nurses would care for their plants. They tested the floors on several pre-post measures and the RI group reported better moods, enhanced alertness and were more active. However, the disturbing results came 15 months after the intervention was finished. Pre-intervention, the nursing home reported a 25 per cent mortality rate in any 15 month period. This time, they found that the participants who were in the RI group had a 50 per cent lower mortality rate than the control group (15 per cent versus 30 per cent). The difference in mortality between groups as well as to previous baseline measures was believed to be the result of giving control and choice to the participants.

See Langer and Rodin (1976) for the original article.

Locus of control (LOC) was developed as a concept in 1966 by Rotter and since then has been examined by many researchers against hundreds of diverse dependent variables. People with a strong internal locus of control believe that the responsibility for whether or not they succeed ultimately lies with themselves. Internals believe that success or failure is due to their own efforts. Externals, on the other hand, believe that the reinforcers in life are controlled by luck, chance, or powerful others. Therefore, they see little impact of their own efforts on the amount of reinforcement they receive.

Researchers have been studying whether or not LOC was a stable personality dimension, however it is now agreed that LOC is not a fixed personality trait and can vary according to situation.

Rotter (1966) challenged the oversimplified conceptualization of LOC that implied that internality is associated only with positive consequences, whilst externality is associated only with negative consequences. Rotter argued for the unidimensionality of the locus of control scale, whilst acknowledging the presence of some subfactors. A substantial body of research, however, supports the multidimensional characteristics of the majority of locus of control scales, varying from two to three factors with several subfactors.

There appear to be several benefits of adopting an internal LOC. For example, internals are more likely to work for achievements, to tolerate delays in rewards and to plan for long-term goals, whereas externals are more likely to lower their goals. Internals are better at tolerating anxiety, but are also more guilt prone. Internals benefit more from social support and are more likely to prefer games based on skill, while externals prefer games based on chance or luck.

Although the research findings are inconclusive there is some link between LOC and increased exercise, weight control, breast examination, alcohol consumption, both in alcoholic and non-alcoholic populations, and delay in gratification (in children but not in adults).

This concept is also important in relation to education. Internal locus of control is related to higher academic achievement, with internals earning somewhat better grades and tending to work harder. This includes spending more time on homework, as well as studying longer for tests (Findley and Cooper, 1983).

Think about it…

How is it possible that both internal locus of control and optimistic explanatory style for bad events contribute to functioning? (Tip: consider the internality dimension.) How would you work on increasing internal locus of control and self-efficacy, bearing in mind the difference between these two concepts?

Defensive pessimism

So, with all the positive evidence behind it, is optimism always a good thing? Well, as these data are based on averages, some evidence suggests that optimism can be detrimental in certain circumstances and for certain individuals.

While on holiday, we came to the realization that we were, plain and simple, defensive pessimists. And furthermore – we liked it. So what, if any, are the benefits of being a defensive pessimist? Well, thankfully, yes there are.

Defensive pessimism is based on the ability to think of, and plan, for the worst-case scenario of a situation; hence defensive pessimists like to be prepared and cover all angles. It is a cognitive strategy to set low expectations for upcoming performance, despite having performed well in previous similar situations (Norem and Cantor, 1986). This thinking style has been found to cushion the potential blow of failure, motivate reflection and rehearsal, and used as a strategy to 'harness' anxiety for motivation. Defensive pessimists set their sights unrealistically low and think about how to solve potential problems in advance of a daunting task (Held, 2004).

Trying to change defensive pessimists into optimists is counterproductive (and vice versa) but positive psychologists try to explain away the benefits of defensive pessimism. In fact, defensive pessimists tend to be more anxious and deliver poorer performance if they are 'not allowed' to engage in pessimistic rehearsal. This is opposite to optimists, who are more anxious if they are 'made to think about' possible failure.

Defensive pessimists have also been found to show significant increases in self-esteem and satisfaction over time, perform better academically, form more supportive friendship networks and make more progress on their personal goals than equally anxious students who do not use defensive pessimism (Norem and Chang, 2002).

Unrealistic optimism

Unrealistic optimism or wishful thinking can have negative consequences on individuals. They tend to perceive risk as lower than average. There tends to be an optimistic bias in risk perception, with optimists viewing themselves below average for such occurrences as cancer, heart disease, failure and heartbreak (Peterson and Deavila, 1995; Peterson and Vaidya, 2001). Furthermore, in the case of serious traumatic events (such as death, fire, flood or violent rape) optimists may not be well prepared (although optimists might be better equipped to rebuild than pessimists).

Thus, engaging in blind optimism may be unhealthy for long-term physical and psychological wellbeing. Introducing positive realism or *flexible optimism* into your thinking will allow you to avoid 'wishful thinking', whilst realistically assessing the likelihood of positive and negative outcomes in any given situation.

Think about it...

Is it better to think things are going to turn out well, and avoid worrying? Or should we expect the worst, and not be disappointed? Which is more valuable in our lives: do we want to know the truth, even when that makes us unhappy? Or is it sometimes better to look on the bright side, despite the evidence?

The three 'selves' in optimism: self-confidence, self-esteem and self-efficacy

The three 'selves' (self-confidence, self-esteem and self-efficacy) are used interchangeably within everyday linguistic life. So what exactly are these concepts and how do they relate to optimism and wellbeing?

Think about it...

When you think of yourself and your qualities, do you tend to think in a more abstract or detailed perspective? Researchers have found that how we perceive ourselves has a significant impact on our overall wellbeing (Lucas et al., 1996). More importantly, research shows that happier people report thinking about themselves with a higher level of abstraction then less happy individuals (Updegraff and Suh, 2007).

The most notorious of the three is *self-confidence*. Self-confidence has had some nastier, narcissistic connotations, inducing an inflated sense of self being among them. Carol Craig, founder of the Centre for Confidence and Wellbeing in Glasgow, Scotland, researches Scotland's 'crisis of confidence' and attempts to enhance levels of confidence in schoolchildren. Typically, confidence can be thought of as: 'being certain in your own abilities . . . and about having trust in people, plans or the future' (Craig, 2007: 2). As discussed earlier in the chapter, confidence in the self and the situation is important for perseverance towards goals.

Self-efficacy, on the other hand, is 'the belief a person has that they can reach their goals or a desired outcome' (Bandura, 1997). If you are one of the many who become confused by the concept of the 'selves' we would suggest thinking of self-efficacy as 'the power of I can'. Simply put, it is the expectation that one can master a situation, and produce a positive outcome based on beliefs about our personal competence or effectiveness in a given area. Ultimately, self-efficacy is a person's belief about his or her chances of successfully accomplishing a specific task (Maddux, 2009a).

Self-reflection is one of the core features of agency and is expressed in the concept of self-efficacy. Self-efficacy beliefs provide the foundation for human motivation, wellbeing, and personal accomplishment. This is because unless people believe that their actions can produce the outcomes they desire, they have little incentive to act or to persevere in the face of difficulties.

People's level of motivation, affective states and actions are based more on what they believe than on what is objectively true. For this reason, how people behave and their accomplishments can often be better predicted by the beliefs they hold about their capabilities than by what they are actually capable of accomplishing. People who regard themselves as highly efficacious act, think, and feel differently from those who perceive themselves as inefficacious. They produce their own future, rather than simply foretell it.

It is important to note that self-efficacy is not a perceived skill; it is what individuals believe they can do with their skills under certain conditions. Self-efficacy beliefs are not predictions of behaviour (what I can rather than what I will do), nor are they causal attributions. Furthermore, self-efficacy is not the same as self-concept or self-esteem, although it can contribute to them. Self-efficacy is not a motive, drive, or need for control. Self-efficacy beliefs are not outcome expectancies but a belief that I can perform the behaviour that produces the outcome. Finally, self-efficacy is not a personality trait; it is domain and situation specific.

So where does self-efficacy come from? Bandura (1977, 1986, 1997) posits that self-efficacy derives from our mastery/performance experiences, our own direct attempts at control (most powerful source). It can also be developed through vicarious experiences, watching someone else's accomplishments and behaviours. The closer you identify with the model, the greater the impact on self-efficacy. We can also develop self-efficacy by verbal persuasion, which is encouragement from outside sources meant to increase efficacy. Maddux (2002) suggests that we can develop self-efficacy via *imaginal experiences*, which is imagining ourselves or others behaving effectively in hypothetical situations.

time out

Social cognitive theory

Conceptualized by eminent psychologist Albert Bandura, self-efficacy derived from his work in social cognitive theory (Gomez, 2009). Social cognitive theory consists of personal factors in the form of cognition, affect, and biological events; behaviour and environmental influences which create interactions that result in a *triadic reciprocality*. Social cognitive theory differs from biological and behaviourist theories as it views people as self-organizing, proactive, self-reflecting and self-regulating. Individuals are agents proactively engaged in their own development and can make things happen by their actions (Lent and Hackett, 2009).

Observational learning is another component of SCT discovered via a set of well-known experiments, called the 'Bobo doll' studies. Bandura showed that children (aged 3 to 6) would change their behaviour by simply watching others. Bandura and his colleagues also demonstrated that viewing aggression by cartoon characters produced more aggressive behaviour than viewing live or filmed aggressive behaviour by adults. Additionally, they demonstrated that having children view pro-social behaviour could reduce displays of aggressive behaviour (Bandura et al., 1961; Bandura, 1977, 1986).

Implications of self-efficacy

People with high levels of self-efficacy demonstrate a high quality of functioning, resilience to adversity and reduced vulnerability to stress and depression (Maddux, 2002), such that low self-efficacy expectancies are an important feature of depression, dysfunctional anxiety and avoidant behaviour.

Self-efficacy is critical to the adoption and success of healthy behaviour changes including exercise, diet, stress management, safe sex, smoking cessation, overcoming alcohol abuse and compliance with treatment regimes. Furthermore, research has shown that self-efficacy affects the body's physiological response to stress, including the immune system whilst also playing a part in the activation of catecholamines and endorphins (Maddux, 2002).

When people have high levels of self-efficacy, they tend to engage more with goal setting and self-regulation, influencing choices of goal-directed activities, expenditure of effort, persistence in the face of challenges and obstacles. Since people who regard themselves as efficacious attribute their failures to insufficient effort, they tend to try more things and pick themselves back up again.

Collective efficacy (Maddux, 2002) is defined as a group's shared belief in its conjoint capabilities to organize and execute the courses of action required to produce given levels of attainment. It involves identifying the abilities of others and harnessing these to accomplish a common goal. High levels of collective efficacy have been linked to marital satisfaction, athletic team success in competitions, academic achievement of pupils and group brainstorming among teams.

Think about it...

School performance is improved and efficacy is increased when students adopt short-term goals, learn specific learning strategies, and receive rewards based on engagement and not just achievement. Write down your short-term academic goals and reward yourself for your engagement with the material once you've hit those targets.

But can we really distinguish self-efficacy from other related constructs? Judge et al. (2002) conducted four studies to determine the discriminant validity of self-esteem, neuroticism, locus of control and generalized self-efficacy. The measures of all four traits were strongly related, with a single factor explaining the relationships among the four constructs, thus these constructs may be markers of a higher order construct.

In conclusion, self-efficacy impacts the choices we make, the effort we put forth/level of motivation, how we feel about ourselves, others, the task and how long we persist when we confront obstacles (especially in the face of failure).

Self-esteem

Over the decades, there have been several definitions proposed for the concept of *self-esteem*. For example, Rosenberg (1965) defined self-esteem (also known as self-appraisal) as the 'totality of the individual's thoughts and feelings with reference to himself as an object.' Today, we would define self-esteem as 'the disposition to experience oneself as competent to cope with the basic challenges of life and as worthy of happiness' (Hewitt, 2009).

There have also been several proposed types of self-esteem such as:

- global and specific (Rosenberg et al., 1995);
- trait and state (Crocker and Wolfe, 2001);
- contingent and true (Deci and Ryan, 1995);
- explicit and implicit (Karpinski and Steinberg, 2006).

We need to distinguish between being conceited, narcissistic and defensive on the one hand, and accepting oneself with an accurate appreciation of one's strengths and worth on the other. The effects of self-esteem are often enmeshed with other, correlated variables such as high subjective wellbeing, low neuroticism and high optimism.

Individuals with high levels of self-esteem tend to report greater perseverance in situations where they consider themselves likely to succeed. They also tend to self-report higher levels of intelligence and happiness. Low levels of self-esteem have been linked to several negative outcomes such as depression in times of low stress, smoking in young women and increased bulimia risk, body dissatisfaction and perfectionism, and a tendency to experiment with drugs/alcohol (also sexual initiative) and aggression.

However, high levels of self-esteem aren't always a good thing. People who score high but have unstable self-esteem tend to be particularly prone to anger and aggression. They appear confident and secure but in reality are highly sensitive to evaluative feedback. To protect themselves from ego challenges they become angry and deny the legitimacy of the perceived injustice.

Think about it...

Write a character sketch of yourself, but in the third person, as it might be written by a friend who knows you well. Reflect on both your positive and negative characteristics. (Branden, 1994)

Models of self-esteem

According to the *sociometer model* of self-esteem, self-esteem generally correlates strongly with whether one believes that one is included or excluded by other people (Leary et al., 1995). Children and adolescents who feel more accepted by their parents have higher levels of self-esteem (Litovsky and Dusek, 1985). Low self-esteem and depression often follow social exclusion (for example, divorce, relationship breakups, failing to be admitted into a group, not being accepted by one's peer group). Hence, aggression among low self-esteem individuals can be better explained by social rejection than low self-esteem per se. Children who are ostracized are more hostile, aggressive, and disruptive (and have lower self-esteem).

The *terror management model* of self-esteem perceives self-esteem as a function to shelter people from deeply rooted anxiety inherent in the human condition (Goldenberg and Shackelford, 2005; Pyszczynski et al., 2004). Self-esteem is a protective shield designed to control the potential for terror that results from awareness of the horrifying possibility that we humans are merely transient animals groping to survive in a meaningless universe, destined only to die and decay. However, Deci and Ryan (2000) would argue against this, claiming people typically engage with life; that is, they seek challenges, connections, authentic meaning, and significance, not because they are trying to avoid the scent of death but because they are healthy and alive.

It is probably misguided to assume that interventions aimed at boosting self-esteem will produce positive outcomes. High self-esteem is often a product rather than a cause of high competence/good performance. High self-esteem can also sometimes be illusory and lead people to conclude that they are doing better than they are.

Think about it...

How are your levels of self-esteem? Researchers would argue that merely reciting boosters or affirmations is likely to result in an inflated sense of worth. Thus, to boost self-esteem, try and engage in realistic and accurate self-appraisal, reflect on your meaningful accomplishments and situations where you have overcome adversities.

Hope

Hope is defined as the determination to achieve goals (agency) plus the belief that many pathways can be generated. *Agency* is the belief that one can begin and sustain movement along the envisioned pathway towards a given goal. Agency thoughts serve to motivate the person. *Pathways* thinking reflects an individual's perceived ability to formulate plausible goal routes (Snyder, 2002). This explanation of hope is very different from the dictionary definition of 'hope' (positive expectation, desire, longing).

Hope is thought to energize goal-directed striving, particularly when the attainability of goals is at least somewhat in doubt and when the goal is viewed as very important (similar to all expectancy-value theories). People with high levels of hope often set more difficult goals, but are more likely to achieve them. They probably break the goals down into smaller subgoals. This is used in CBT where therapists facilitate both agency thoughts (efficacy thoughts) and pathways thoughts (breaking down complex goals into achievable steps). Remoralization, the facilitation of hope, is the common pathway in therapy.

High scores on hope correlate with self-esteem, positive emotions, effective coping, academic achievement, and physical health (reviewed in Peterson, 2000; Snyder, 2002). Hope also buffers against interfering, self-deprecatory thoughts and negative emotions and is critical for psychological health. People who are hopeful focus more on the prevention of diseases (for example, through exercising); they have higher levels of success in their performance and academic achievement.

Overall, the explanatory style model of optimism and Snyder's hope model suggest that we can change to a greater extent than the dispositional model of optimism. Explanatory style explains most of the mechanism through which we are optimistic. It is also least focused on the future and all models have cognitive and emotional elements, and all address motivation. Its focus on causality and how goals can be achieved is similar in concept to agency within hope theory.

Future research should focus on clarifying the structure of optimism. Are optimism and pessimism direct opposites of each other along the same continuum? Does having one automatically mean you cannot have the other? Recent research suggests that the polarization is not as clear-cut as this and whether or not optimism is the opposite of pessimism, or two distinct constructs still remains a question today (Scheier and Carver, 2009).

More research is needed to understand the developmental antecedents of optimism, especially within a child environment. Research has shown that there is a clear link between childhood socioeconomic status and later optimism, even if the adult's socioeconomic status changes. So what is it about the early environment that is so crucial for optimism development? Parent transmission (modelling, teaching coping styles) is an important topic for future research, as is the development of interventions targeted at increasing optimism, both in early and adult life (Scheier and Carver, 2009: 663).

Summary

Reflecting on the learning objectives you should now understand the concept of optimism, explanatory style and hope. More specifically, you should know:

- Definitions of hope, optimism and explanatory style.
- That until the last few decades, optimism was seen as a deficit, rather than a good thing.
- The main difference between the two concepts of optimism involves the argument between trait versus learned ability.
- There are many health benefits from engaging in optimistic thinking as well as positive illusions.
- Pessimism isn't always a bad thing (for example, defensive pessimism).
- Hope theory posits that people need agency and pathways to experience hope.

Suggested Resources

http://www.apple.com/downloads/macosx/home_learning/ optimismformentalhealth.html
Engage with technology and download the following mood monitor application link from Apple's 'home learning' section. Alternatively, check out ITunesU for free psychology lecture downloads.

http://c.r.snyder.socialpsychology.org/
Leading positive psychologist Richard Snyder tragically passed away in January 2006. Thanks to colleagues of his at the Social Psychology Network, you can access his profile with links to his work at the above address.

Further questions for you

1 Which type of 'IST' are you? An optimist? A pessimistic? A defensive pessimist?
2 Which theory of optimism do you relate to? Why?
3 Is it better to think things are going to turn out well, and avoid worrying? Or should we expect the worst and not be disappointed?
4 Is hope always a good thing?

Personal Development Interventions

1 Cultivating optimism
One of the ways that we can start to build and cultivate optimism is by engaging in the Best Possible Selves exercise (Sheldon and Lyubomirsky, 2006). This exercise requires you to sit, undisturbed, in your favourite writing space, alone from the madding crowd. You are asked to do this exercise, for 20 minutes, for three consecutive days.

Think about your life in the future. Imagine that everything has gone as well as it possibly could. You have worked hard and succeeded at accomplishing all of your life goals. Think of this as the realization of all of your life dreams. Now, write about what you imagined.

Now reflect on your future goals and then list several ways that you could achieve them. These larger goals can be broken down into smaller, more achievable subgoals. Keep motivating yourself to pursue your goals and reframe any obstacles you meet as challenges to be overcome (adapted from Boniwell, 2008: 23).

2 Increasing self-esteem

This exercise is designed to help enhance your self-esteem. Based on Nathan Branden's sentence-completion exercise, you are asked to conduct the following exercise for the next week. If you relate to this task check out Branden's 31-week self-esteem programme in his book, the *Six Pillars of Self-esteem* (Branden, 1994).

For this task, we would like to you to set aside 2–3 minutes in the morning before you head off to your daily routine and when you are alone, complete the following sentences. Make sure you do them quickly, without thinking too much and try and come up with no less than six endings and no more than 10.

If I bring more awareness to my life today . . .
If I take more responsibility for my choices and actions today . . .
If I pay more attention to how I deal with people today . . .
If I boost my energy level by 5 per cent today . . .

At the end of the week, reflect on the endings and try and see what patterns emerge. Once you have done this, complete the following:
If any of what I wrote this week is true, it might be helpful if I . . .

(Branden, 1994: 310–11)

Measurement Tools

Life Orientation-Revised (LOT-R)

(Scheier et al., 1994)

Directions

Please be as honest and accurate as you can throughout. Try not to let your response to one statement influence your responses to other statements. There are no 'correct' or 'incorrect' answers. Answer according to your own feelings, rather than how you think 'most people' would answer.

4 = I agree a lot
3 = I agree a little
2 = I neither agree nor disagree
1 = I disagree a little
0 = I disagree a lot

_____ **1.** In uncertain times, I usually expect the best.

_____ **2.** It's easy for me to relax.

_____ **3.** If something can go wrong for me, it will.

_____ **4.** I'm always optimistic about my future.

_____ **5.** I enjoy my friends a lot.

_____ **6.** It's important for me to keep busy.

_____ **7.** I hardly ever expect things to go my way.

_____ **8.** I don't get upset too easily.

_____ **9.** I rarely count on good things happening to me.

_____**10.** Overall, I expect more good things to happen to me than bad.

Scoring

Items 2, 5, 6, and 8 are fillers and therefore should be excluded. Please add the scores for the remaining items to calculate your final score.

Interpretation

There are no 'cut-offs' for optimism or pessimism. Higher scores reflect higher levels of optimism.

Review

The LOT-R is a revised version of the original LOT, which focused on differentiating optimists from pessimists. The newer version includes more explicit items regarding an individual's prediction about the future. This test is quick, easy to use and good for research purposes, hence many studies have used this scale.

Generalized Self-efficacy Scale (GSE)

(Schwarzer and Jerusalem, 1995)

Directions

Below are ten statements about yourself, which may or may not be true. Using the 1–4 scale below, please indicate your agreement with each item by placing the appropriate number on the line preceding that item. Please be open and honest in your responding.

1	2	3	4
Not at all true	**Hardly true**	**Moderately true**	**Exactly true**

____ 1. I can always manage to solve difficult problems if I try hard enough.

____ 2. If someone opposes me, I can find the means and ways to get what I want.

____ 3. It is easy for me to stick to my aims and accomplish my goals.

____ 4. I am confident that I could deal efficiently with unexpected events.

____ 5. Thanks to my resourcefulness, I know how to handle unforeseen situations.

____ 6. I can solve most problems if I invest the necessary effort.

____ 7. I can remain calm when facing difficulties because I can rely on my coping abilities.

____ 8. When I am confronted with a problem, I can usually find several solutions.

____ 9. If I am in trouble, I can usually think of a solution.

____10. I can usually handle whatever comes my way.

Scoring

Please add the item scores together and divide by the number of items to calculate your final score.

Interpretation

Overall scores can range from 10 to 40 points, with an average score of 29. There is no cutoff; however, you can work out where you fall in relation to the group/median.

To see where you score in relation to others, there is an international data set as an SPSS SAV file that includes about 18,000 respondents, available for free download at: http://www.fu-berlin.de/gesund/gesu_engl/world_zip.htm.

Review

This scale has been translated into 30 languages and is based on very large amounts of data.

Notes

1 Research into genetic factors and optimism demonstrates that 25–30 per cent of the variability is due to genetics.

2 We will look at the ABC technique in more detail in Chapter 7.

CHAPTER 6

Resilience, Post-traumatic Growth and Positive Ageing

❖ LEARNING OBJECTIVES

Stress, limitations, challenging situations, loss, significant life changes like getting older and even death are inevitable parts of being human. Although on the surface, these issues sound like nemeses of positive psychology, some researchers argue that, instead of ignoring them, positive psychology should study how managing them can contribute to a life well lived. This chapter will focus on the topics of resilience and growth as well as how to embrace ageing with a positive perspective.

List of topics

- Three proposed psychological responses to trauma.
- Definition of resilience and its proposed facilitators.
- Sense of coherence and its effects on health and wellbeing.

- The phenomenon of post-traumatic growth (PTG).
- Wisdom and its place in the developmental process.
- Components to positive ageing.

MOCK ESSAY QUESTIONS

1 'That which does not kill us makes us stronger.' Discuss.
2 Critically discuss the role of sense of coherence in facilitating well-functioning.
3 Critically evaluate available research evidence that ageing can be associated with positive outcomes.

Stress versus trauma

We all know that prolonged, stressful living can cause havoc on our physical, emotional and psychological wellbeing. However, research suggests that stress can sometimes be good when it is offered in small and infrequent doses. Intermittent stress, or tight allostasis (Charney, 2004) is important to keep us prepared for future stressors. Furthermore, the experience of adversity/stressors, if not chronic, can equip a person with what is known as 'psychological preparedness' or a sort of 'stress inoculation', enabling the individual to become stronger in the face of future stressors (Janoff-Bulman, 1992, 2004; Tedeschi, Park, and Calhoun, 1998).

Trauma, however, is the 'unexpected'. It is an occurrence that is 'out of the ordinary; creates long lasting problems and substantially interrupts personal narrative' (Tedeschi and Calhoun, 1995, 2006). Thus, there is an intense sense of 'before and after'. There is debate however as to what constitutes a traumatic event. In the example of cancer diagnosis, is it finding the lump? The diagnosis? The hair loss? The breast loss? As you can see, there are multiple stressors and traumas following each traumatic event and a re-definition of 'trauma' may be needed within the literature (Hefferon et al., 2008, 2010).

When individuals are faced with trauma or unintentional change, there are three proposed psychological responses: (1) Succumbing to the stressor (also referred to as post-traumatic stress disorder or PTSD);[1] (2) resilience and or recovery; and (3) post-traumatic growth. The common belief is that after trauma such as the diagnosis of an illness, a person becomes severely stressed. In actuality, research shows that only 5 per cent to 35 per cent succumb to this negative way of thinking (Kangas et al., 2002; Cordova, 2008). Positive psychology asks: 'what about the other 65 per cent to 95 per cent? What happens to them?' This will be discussed later in the chapter.

Resilience

Resilience is a multi-definitional construct. We define it here as 'the flexibility in response to changing situational demands, and the ability to bounce back from negative emotional experiences' (Tugade et al., 2004: 1169). However, some researchers see resilience as more multifaceted than this. Lepore and Revenson (2006) separate resilience into recovery, resistance and reconfiguration. Recovery is simply the return back to baseline levels of functioning, whereas resistance is when a person shows no signs of disturbance (low distress) following a traumatic event (Lepore and Revenson, 2006). Finally, reconfiguration is when people return to homeostasis in a different formation: they have changed (either positively or negatively) from their traumatic experience. This last element of resilience has many similarities with post-traumatic growth (PTG), which will be discussed in detail in the next section.

Think about it...

Think of a time when you:

- overcame a difficult period of time;
- bounced back from a tough situation;
- got through a difficult time with relative ease;
- challenged yourself and went out of your 'comfort zone'.

(Adapted from Reivich and Shatte, 2002)

What are the components of resilience?

The next section will review the major components that have been identified throughout decades of research as facilitators of resilient individuals. These include: (1) reframing; (2) experience of positive emotions; (3) participation in physical activity; (4) trusted social support; (5) the use of personal and authentic strengths; and, of course, (5) optimism.

One of the first questions we are usually asked in class is 'who is resilient and who is not?' The second question is 'why?' A ground breaking study conducted by Werner and Smith in the 1970s–1980s identified several risk factors associated with non-resilient individuals. After following a cohort of babies from birth to mid life, they concluded that individuals who had the following risk factors were more likely to succumb that those who did not: low birth weight, low socio-economic status (SES), low maternal education and an unstable family structure (for example divorce or abuse) (Werner, 1993, 1996).

The good news is that, despite these risk factors, anyone can 'retrain' to become more resilient. As previously mentioned, one of the biggest obstacles to healthy psychological function is negative/pessimistic ruminative thought. One of the main pathways to a more resilient self is changing negative or pessimistic thinking patterns and developing an *optimistic explanatory style* (Reivich and Shatte, 2002; Seligman, 2002). Based on the popular method from cognitive behavioural therapy (Beck, 1976), research has shown that when we are faced with a challenging situation, employing the *ABCDE* technique, where A = Adversity (the issue or event); B = Beliefs (automatic pessimistic beliefs about the event); C = Consequences (of holding that belief); D = Disputation (your conscious arguments against your pessimistic belief); and E = Energization (what you feel when you've disputed your B effectively), can increase resilience and decrease depression levels (Gillham et al., 1995, 2007). Since pessimistic rumination is the precursor and the maintainer of depression (Papageorgiou and Wells, 2003), this technique is imperative for challenging destructive thoughts and creating more resilient individuals.

When faced with a difficult situation, individuals tend to engage in one of several 'thinking traps', such as 'jumping to conclusions; tunnel vision; magnifying the negative and minimizing the positive; personalizing or externalizing blame; over generalizing small setbacks; engaging in mind reading and using unhelpful emotional reasoning.' (For a full review, see Reivich and Shatte, 2002: 95–122.) Individuals need to identify which thinking traps they tend to succumb to and then construct a more realistic view of the adversity.

time out

Community resilience interventions

There are several resilience programmes in progress throughout the world; one of the most notable is the Penn Resilience Programme (PRP). This was developed based on the work of resilience experts Reivich and Shatte and Seligman's work on learned optimism. The approach takes on a very cognitive behavioural slant and focuses on teaching students, at a young age, to identify pervasive negative/pessimistic thinking and test/challenge these thoughts. The programme runs over 18–24 one hour sessions on the main principles found to increase resilience and wellbeing topic matters. The results so far are promising, with two year follow ups showing that intervention groups have less depression, higher wellbeing, and increased grades. Originally only in the US, the Penn Resilience programme has been adapted to the UK system and trials are currently underway in the Midlands and North of England.

Resilience and the body

After the slaughter of six million people in the Holocaust, the survivors and those left behind have shown tremendous resilience (low PTSD) and growth in the face of adversity. Not only have we seen psychological growth but research has shown that, even all these decades later, survivors from the prison camps show significant physical health functioning (salutogenic) versus illness-inducing (pathogenic) outcomes (Cassel and Suedfeld, 2006). Disclosure to others, marital history and religious observance have been proposed as mediators to both positive and negative long-term consequences (Lev-Wiesel and Amir, 2003).

Salutogenesis is implicitly linked to *sense of coherence (SOC)*. Antonovsky (1979) originally developed SOC in an attempt to understand why some people are less likely to be affected by stressful environments than others. At the point of its discovery, SOC represented a departure from a pathological perspective dominant in medical and social sciences. SOC is defined as:

> 66 a global orientation that expresses the extent to which one has a persuasive, enduring though dynamic feeling of confidence that (1) the stimuli deriving from one's internal and external environments in the course of living are structured, predictable, and explicable; (2) the resources are available to one to meet the demands posed by these stimuli; (3) these demands are challenges, worthy of investment and engagement'.
>
> *– (Antanovsky, 1987: 19)* 99

In other words, to what extent one is confident that internal and external environments are predictable and there is a high probability that life situations will work out as well as can be expected.

- *Comprehensibility* refers to a person's insight into their achievement and difficulties. We can hardly judge whether appropriate resources are at our disposal to cope with a task unless we believe that we have some understanding of its nature. Seeing and confronting stimuli as making sense in that they will be expected or if unexpected they will be ordered or explicable.

- *Manageability* refers to a high probability that things will work out as well as can be reasonably expected; the extent to which someone perceives that the resources at their disposal are adequate to meet the demands posed by the stimuli that are bombarding them. Manageability has some similarity to Bandura's concept of self-efficacy. Of course, this element is not sufficient on its own, as cognitive and motivational components are no less essential.

■ *Meaningfulness* refers to the motivational belief that it makes emotional sense to cope, that, though life may have its pains, one wishes to go on. People have areas of their life that they care about and that make sense to them. Thus, people with a weak SOC give little indication that anything in life seems to matter particularly to them.

So how does one accrue a SOC? Researchers would argue that a SOC usually develops by around age 30. The more one's experiences are characterized by consistency, participation in shaping outcome, and balance of stimuli (rather than overload or underlay), the more one is likely to see the world as coherent. Antonovsky believed the SOC remains relatively stable as long as 'radical and enduring changes in one's life situation' do not occur (Antonovsky and Sagy, 2001). Some studies appear to confirm this, although in one large study, SOC was significantly lower in the youngest age group and increased with age.

It is possible to conceive SOC as a personality characteristic or coping style (Antonovsky and Sagy, 2001). SOC is a rich concept and includes the elements of hardiness, self-efficacy and locus of control (Linley, 2003). It is, however, seen as more universally meaningful than the constructs mentioned above (Antonovsky, 1993). There exists substantial empirical and theoretical support for its nature as a unitary construct (Antanovsky, 1987, 1993).

Sense of coherence has been linked to high associations with wellbeing and life satisfaction, reduced fatigue and loneliness. Some research has found significant negative correlations with anxiety and depression; moreover a strong SOC protects against depression, predicts low suicidal thoughts in depressed patients and predicts lower (30 per cent) mortality from all causes (Antonovsky, 1993).

Furthermore, low SOC predicts musculoskeletal symptoms (neck, shoulder, and low-back) in later life and is a predictor of response to pain-management programmes for chronic pain sufferers. It is linked to pain levels in cancer patients. In arthritis patients, lower SOC is linked to pain levels, as well as greater difficulty in performing daily activities and general health (Antonovsky, 1993, adapted from Boniwell, 2008).

Coping styles

Lazarus and Folkman's transactional model of stress appraisal is the most widely known and used model within coping research. Coping is defined as 'constantly changing cognitive and behavioural efforts to manage specific external and/or internal demands that are appraised to be taxing or exceeding the resources of the person', (Lazarus and Folkman, 1984, as cited in Cheavens and Dreer, 2009: 233).

Primary appraisal is the extent to which individuals perceive their situation to be threatening. Secondary appraisal is an individual's perception of whether or not they have the resources available to them to deal with the stressor.

There are two main coping strategies that individuals use when faced with stressful or adverse situations. *Problem-focused coping* is when people identify the stressor and take active steps to engage with and tackle the issues at hand. *Emotion-focused coping* is when individuals tend to focus on dealing with the emotions surrounding the situation, rather than attempting to change or deal with the situation. Emotion-focused coping tends to consist of turning to others and seeking social support. This type of coping includes avoidance, which is when an individual ignores the situation at hand and avoids any interaction with solving the issue (Collins et al., 1990; Urcuyo et al., 2005; Thornton and Perez, 2006).

Earlier research posited that problem-focused coping was the better form of coping; however, newer research shows that emotion-focused coping can indeed have positive consequences. For example, avoidance was once seen as a negative copping strategy although we now know that, in the short term, engaging in healthy distractions can be a good thing for people who have experienced significant trauma (Reynolds and Kee Hean, 2007).

The next section will move away from resilience or returning to 'normal' levels of functioning, and look at the phenomenon of post-traumatic growth, or thriving following adverse events.

A common theme throughout humanity is the notion of self-sacrifice and suffering for a greater good (Jimenez, 2009). Indeed, Judaeo-Christian religions are based on the sacrifice of one man's life for all humankind. Thus, an implication of divinity through suffering is apparent with rewards of immaterial kinds in the afterlife awaiting those that suffer on Earth now. Suffering for self-actualization is present within the philosophical and psychological literature, with an emphasis on meaning and development of the self (authenticity) via adversity (Kierkegaard, Nietzsche, May, Yalom).

Although there are sections of academia that look into the 'use of trauma' as a way to better the self, there is a field of study within positive psychology that looks at how, through dealing with (and not the direct result of) trauma, a person can become better, stronger and operate at higher levels of functioning than which existed before the traumatic event occured. Previously studied under the terminologies of benefit finding, positive changes, growth from adversity, thriving, and psychological growth (Tennen and Affleck, 2004; Lechner, 2009), this phenomenon is now known as post-traumatic growth (PTG). Post-traumatic growth has been found to exist within samples of survivors from 'war, bereavement, breast cancer, mastectomy, bone marrow disease, heart attack, rheumatoid arthritis, spinal chord injury, MS, shipping disaster, tornado, plane crash, rape, childhood sexual assault, incest, shooting, HIV, infertility, chemical dependency, military combat and bombing' (Joseph et al., 2005: 263–4; Ai et al., 2007).

Viktor Frankl

For those of you who have read the wonderful and powerful book *'Man's Search for Meaning'*, you will be well aware of the name Viktor Frankl (Frankl, 1963). Frankl was an Austrian psychiatrist who was imprisoned in Theresienstadt, Auschwitz and Turkheim during the years 1942–5. Throughout his incomprehensible ordeal in the Nazi concentration camps, Frankl lost his wife and family. During his incarceration, Frankl watched his fellow inmates to discover a theory of survival and human drive: the will to meaning. Frankl proposed that those who had a will to meaning, those that had something to live for, even in the direst circumstances, survived. Frankl's theory was later translated into a form of psychotherapy, entitled logotherapy, with the main school still in operation in Vienna. His story and theories are a triumph to the human spirit and a testament to his belief that when everything is taken away from someone, they still have the ability to choose their reactions.

Post-traumatic growth is currently divided into five domains (Calhoun and Tedeschi, 2004):[2]

- The first domain is *personal strength* (or perceived changes in self). This is when trauma survivors report becoming stronger, deeper, more authentic, confident, open, empathetic, creative, more alive, mature, humanitarian, special, humble, and the list goes on. Many describe themselves as a 'better person' now that they have undergone this wake up call.

- The second domain is *relating to others*, where people report becoming closer with their immediate and extended families. People report that friendships bind tighter and that people who were acquaintances/strangers/neighbours before the event, become prominent positive features in their daily life. Camaraderie and friendship among survivors of the same trauma is common. A downside of this is that many trauma survivors report that some friends go missing and are not supportive during their adversity. Although painful at the time, people report that this is a bonus as it allows them to identify their true friends and spend time (which is so much more precious) with those that count.

- The third domain encompasses *appreciation for life* (or increased existential awareness). As one would expect, many people undergo a change in life philosophy. When trauma highlights our vulnerability and the fact that we are not invincible, we start to reflect on deeper issues such as mortality, spirituality, the meaning of and purpose in life, and so forth. Many survivors report that the trauma allowed them to 'see clearly', to understand what matters in life and allowed them to make changes to their priorities, from how and with whom they decide to spend their day with, to the importance of nature, health, life, importance (or unimportance) of physical appearance and monetary goods.

- The fourth domain, *new possibilities,* covers the desire of individuals to change their life goals, re-enrol in schooling to learn a new subject, gain a degree or obtain new skills. Overall, they have a keen focus on the 'here and now' with a new appreciation of life and their time here on Earth.

- The fifth domain is *spiritual change* where people may decide to return to their previous (or alternative) faith. They begin to actively participate (attend church, pray) and their belief in a higher being is strengthened via gratitude to that being.

Examples of post-traumatic growth

In order to materialize the concept of growth, we've chosen some quotes that truly resonate with us as researchers in the area. One is from the well known cyclist, Lance Armstrong who, after battling three types of cancer and given a negative prognosis went on to win the Tour de France seven times and maintains the world record to this day. The other is from a former female cancer patient that Kate worked with who recounted her experience of cancer and growing from the experience:

> Without the illness I would never have been forced to re-evaluate my life and my career. I know if I had not had cancer, I would not have won the Tour de France.
>
> – (Lance Armstrong)

> And it's . . . and I feel my life's better! I know it sounds crazy (laughs), but I feel the quality of my life is better because (sniffles) I've prioritized (sniffles) and I know what matters.
>
> – (Brenda, cancer survivor)

Criticisms of PTG

One of the major criticisms of PTG is whether or not it truly exists. Some researchers believe that what trauma survivors are actually experiencing is a form of cognitive dissonance (Festinger et al., 1956, 2008) or positive illusion (Taylor, 1989). Both protect the individual from the overwhelming confusion and devastation of the trauma. Cognitive dissonance is psychological reasoning in which reality is actually so different from what one believes that in order to understand, the person rationalizes the occurrence in order to maintain equilibrium within the psyche. Thus, for someone who loses a loved one, accepting the death is too much for one person to bear so the individual creates or rationalizes the death in order to keep going (Festinger et al., 1956, 2008).

Positive illusions, on the other hand, can actually be good for us. Like cognitive dissonance, people create positive illusions about their traumatic situation in order to rationalize and move on. Again, if someone is diagnosed with cancer, they can create positive illusions that the experience taught them something, in order to comprehend the trauma has not happened in vain. These theories postulate that we can't have trauma happen for no reason; humans need to find a reason for it, otherwise it would be too hard to comprehend.

Furthermore, criticisms have come in the form of the *tyranny of positive thinking* (Held, 2004). Thus, not only are people required to recover, but they now have the added pressure to find something positive out of the experience as well. This can cause an overwhelming sense of pressure, depression and disappointment in the self if positivity is not found immediately or at all. Ultimately, PTG does not push this but rather highlights that alongside deep sadness, hurt and distress, people (but not all) can find something beneficial out of their struggle with adversity. Simply knowing that this is possible can have a profound positive effect on current trauma survivors. It must be made clear that not everyone can achieve PTG, and that this is OK.

Whether or not PTG is actually real, the argument appears counterproductive, as it is simply the subjective sense of being bettered (Thornton, 2002: 162). If there is no obvious psychopathology, and no detriment to anyone, and it appears to be beneficial on both psychological and physical levels, then researchers within the domain believe that it is important to study it in its own right. Furthermore, if PTG is simply an illusion or a socially desirable bias, the critics have not yet created measurement tools or agreed upon definitions for identifying illusions or distortions (Calhoun and Tedeschi, 2008).

What's the point of it?

Thus, whether or not PTG is 'real' in an objective positivistic sense, there appears to be genuine, objective markers that show that the presence of PTG is indeed beneficial on several fronts. First of all, survivors of traumatic events, who experience PTG in the immediate aftermath of tragedy, tend to report and show improved psychological adjustment, improved health, longer life and an improved quality of life (QOL). Although small in number, longitudinal studies (Tennen and Affleck, 2002) have shown that benefit finding after a loss of a loved one predicted lower levels of distress 13 months later and this has been extended to lower levels of occurrence of PTSD three years following a traumatic event. One of the most powerful findings to date was by Affleck et al. (1987), who reported that heart attack patients who found benefits immediately after their first attack had reduced reoccurrence and morbidity statistics eight years after the attack.

Post-traumatic growth and benefit finding do not need to occur only in those that have had seismic, one-off events. Individuals with arthritis with higher levels of benefit finding were more likely to report lower levels of pain severity and activity limitations.

For terminal patients, those that score higher on PTG measurements have been found to live longer than their lower scoring peers, with objective records of greater immune system functioning (Bower et al., 1998; Milam, 2004; Dunigan et al., 2007).

Post-traumatic growth facilitators

One of the biggest questions for PTG researchers is that of who is more likely to experience PTG. Unfortunately, there are no definite personality or circumstance factors that will guarantee PTG occurrence. The research has shown correlations between variables and higher scores on PTG tools; however the results are quite mixed. People who are more wealthy, educated and younger tend to experience higher levels of growth. This could be for several reasons. First of all, people who are higher in SES tend to be more educated and therefore have less financial worries after trauma. Thus, someone who struggles day-to-day with financial worries, when diagnosed with cancer, has the added stress of providing for their family, as well as the time and physical toll of chemotherapy.

With regards to the existence of PTG personalities, the evidence is not clear cut and although certain personality traits such as optimism and extraversion tend to appear (Antoni et al., 2001) there are similar numbers of studies suggesting otherwise. This is a good thing we think, as it means that anyone is capable of experiencing this phenomenon. Not surprisingly, researchers have suggested that people who experience more positive emotions will be better equipped to deal with adversity (broaden and build) as well as experience PTG (Linley and Joseph, 2004). Again, certain personalities are more prone to experiencing higher levels of positive emotions, thus personality may play a factor within this facilitator.

Time and type

Again, PTG researchers are currently trying to understand whether time and the objective severity of a trauma matter in the attainment and valence of growth. This is not easy. For example, objectively, stage 3 cancer is worse than stage 1; however, depending on the individual, stage 1 might be enough to shatter their previous beliefs and send them into a pit of despair. The person with stage 3 may have had several earlier traumas that prepared them for this and thus not experience PTG due to their current levels of resilience. Indeed, those that are more resilient may not experience higher levels of growth. This is reasoned because they may not see the trauma as 'traumatic' due to the fact that they are resilient in the face of adversity.

Furthermore, in terms of time since severity, researchers believe that there needs to be enough time to contemplate the tragedy and work through the survivor's cognitive beliefs before it can be incorporated; however, research has shown that those who are able to report immediate benefits have lower levels of stress several months/years later. It appears that the reaction and attainment of growth is quite individual (Cordova et al., 2001; Weiss, 2004).

Social support

The presence of social support (Cadell et al., 2003) is one of the most important facilitators we know within PTG research. Currently, researchers are looking at the effects of and participation in group-based therapies (Cordova, 2008; Lechner, Stoelb, and Antoni, 2008) in the facilitation of growth due to this repetitive finding (Sabiston et al., 2007; Hefferon et al., 2008; Lechner et al., 2008).

Coping styles

PTG is not coping, however there are links with coping styles and PTG (Urcuyo, Boyers, Carver, and Antoni, 2005). For example, people who use approach focused coping (active and problem focused coping) are able to engage in positive reappraisal, acceptance, seeking social support and contemplating reason for the tragedy. Furthermore, emotional approach coping is highly beneficial as greater emotional expression in the immediate aftermath has been linked to PTG. Despite the beneficial effects of approach-oriented coping, the use of avoidance coping can be beneficial depending on the individual, the trauma and the length of use. As discussed earlier, escape, avoidance and healthy distraction can be quite necessary when dealing with trauma. As long as they are not ongoing and the only form of coping, they can be used to enhance PTG. Overall, the use of dynamic coping is ideal for the experience of PTG to exist.

How do we measure it?

The majority of PTG research is measured through quantitative assessment. The major tools include the Stress Related Growth Scale (SRGS) (Park et al., 1996), the Post-traumatic Growth Inventory (PTGI) (Tedeschi and Calhoun, 1996), the Benefit Finding Scale (BFS) (Antoni et al., 2001) and the Changes in Outlook Questionnaire (Joseph et al., 1993). The tools tend to ask questions surrounding cognitive shifts in thinking since and related to the trauma. For example, within the PTGI (Tedeschi and Calhoun, 1996), individuals are asked to think about the trauma they experienced and respond to the following questions on a Likert scale from 0 (I did not change as a result of the event I described above) to 5 (I changed to a very great degree as a result of the event I described above):[3]

1 My priorities about what is important in life   0   1   2   3   4   5
2 An appreciation for the value of my own life   0   1   2   3   4   5
3 I developed new interests   0   1   2   3   4   5
4 A feeling of self-reliance   0   1   2   3   4   5
5 A better understanding of spiritual matters   0   1   2   3   4   5

The tools mentioned above have very high internal consistency and reliability. Since quantitative measurement tools are numerically restrictive and can lack access to the entire phenomenon, we also use qualitative research strategies, which allow the participant to speak freely about the phenomenon in their own words. The data are typically accessed via semi-structured interviews, written responses, focus groups and/or diaries.

How does PTG happen?

There are several leading models of PTG, including: shattered assumptions theory (Janoff-Bulman, 1992), organismic valuing theory (Joseph and Linley, 2005) and the transformational model (Tedeschi and Calhoun, 2006). *Shattered assumptions theory* assumes that we all have an inner world in which we harbour fundamental assumptions of a sense of safety and security. Trauma occurs when these assumptions are tested and our sense of security is 'shattered'. Post-traumatic growth is the process of rebuilding around the traumatic experience and thus acknowledging the trauma in a non-anxious way.

Organismic valuing theory of growth through adversity (Joseph and Linley, 2008) is a person-centred approach. This theory assumes that a person must overcome obstacles in their social environment and not necessarily their pre- or post-trauma personality in order to obtain PTG. Known as the c*ompletion tendency*, a person must incorporate the trauma into their world-view via accommodation or assimilation. *Assimilation* is when individuals keep their old world-view and initiate self-blame. Hence there is no reordering of their previous schemas. *Accommodation*, on the other hand, modifies pre-existing schemas in order to accommodate the new information. A person can do this in one of two ways: either positively or negatively. Negative accommodation leaves a person susceptible to depression and helplessness, whereas positive accommodation leads to growth (Joseph and Linley, 2008).

This theory goes beyond discussing outcomes and attempts to clarify the cognitive processes following trauma (assimilation, positive accommodation and negative accommodation). Furthermore, it attempts to explain the reasoning for why people can become more vulnerable and not resilient in the aftermath of crisis (Joseph and Linley, 2008). Thus, by assimilating the trauma into their cognitive functioning, the person returns to baseline with feelings of being more vulnerable to future traumas. A person can experience accommodation and assimilation within differing components of the self-structure; a person is not limited to either/or.

The transformational model (Tedeschi and Calhoun, 1995) is the most complete and widely used model of growth. It posits that PTG is the result of excessive rumination (or cognitive processing) following a seismic event (Tedeschi and Calhoun, 2003). Following the seismic event, the person is presented with challenges (for example, management of emotional distress). A person must then engage in managing excessive rumination in three stages. Firstly, one experiences automatic and intrusive thoughts; over time, individuals will learn to manage these automatic thoughts until they engage in what is called 'deliberate rumination'. Throughout their grappling with these thoughts, they are engaged in self-disclosure as they attempt to reduce emotional distress. By doing so, they commence their disengaging from previous goals, resulting in changed schemas and narrative development. Once these processes have been completed, the person is able to achieve PTG in addition to wisdom or 'preparedness'. Importantly, this model acknowledges that distress can co-exist alongside PTG (Tedeschi and Calhoun, 2008).

Think about it…

Have you personally experienced PTG or has someone close to you? Have you seen it modelled? What were the mechanisms that brought you to experience growth? Which model do you relate to?

Post-traumatic growth in therapeutic settings

It is only recently that PTG has been incorporated into the therapeutic environment. Ultimately, since not everyone is able to achieve PTG, it would be dangerous to enforce the attainment of PTG on a recent trauma survivor. Tedeschi and Calhoun (2008) suggested several steps for therapists to engage in when working with a client who may be on the path to discovering some form of PTG. Ultimately, they warn that a therapist must not use PTG as a sign of their intervention working. It is not the be all and end all, and to force this is detrimental to the client's wellbeing.

In conclusion, when tragedy strikes, there are three main *psychological responses* to trauma. Resilience is important for protective and reactive functions. PTG is a real phenomenon, which has real physical and psychological benefits.

Wisdom

One of the proposed benefits of surviving a traumatic experience is the attainment of wisdom (Tedeschi and Calhoun, 1995; Haidt, 2006). But what is wisdom? What makes a wise judgement (or a wise action) different from an unwise one? Are we only wise once we have reached old age? The VIA strengths approach defines wisdom as

66 the ability to take stock of life in large terms, in ways that make sense to oneself and others. Perspective is the product of knowledge and experience, but it is more than the accumulation of information. It is the coordination of this information and its deliberate use to improve wellbeing. In a social context, perspective allows the individual to listen to others, to evaluate what they say, and then to offer good (sage) advice. Directions back to the interstate do not qualify as wisdom, unless the highway is the metaphorical route to the life well-lived.
– *(Peterson and Seligman, 2004)* 99

> ## Think about it...
>
> Can you give an example of someone you consider wise? Why is this? List their wise attributes and reflect upon them.

However, there are many approaches to wisdom within the psychology discipline. For example, developmental psychologist Erik Erickson noted wisdom as the final stage of personality development (60 years and up). Piaget called wisdom the product of the final stage of cognitive development; the application of dialectical thinking to solving complex problems. There is one other main model of wisdom, Sternberg's *balance theory of wisdom,* which we will now discuss in more detail.

Leading wisdom researcher, Robert Sternberg, conceptualized wisdom as a balance between practical intelligence and tacit knowledge applied to solving problems to achieve the greater good for all (Sternberg, 2009). In order to achieve wisdom one must balance several competing interests such as intrapersonal (your own), interpersonal (others) and extrapersonal (communities and environment) conditions. Furthermore, when faced with a certain situation we can respond in one of three ways: (1) we can *adapt* to it; (2) we can *shape it* so the situation adapts to us; or (3) we can *select* to change our environment to something more advantageous to our needs. Overall, Sternberg's Balance Theory of Wisdom posits that wisdom comes from solving problems while also taking other people into account, using multiple response strategies and aiming for the result to serve the common good of all.

According to researchers within this area, wisdom has little to do with age, with levels of wisdom levelling into young adulthood. It is experience and the amassed encounters with life complexities that create wisdom (Baltes et al., 1995).

> ## Think about it...
>
> What prevents us from thinking and acting in a wise manner?
>
> What ways can you think of that would help to increase wisdom in action?

Positive ageing

Leading ageing researcher, George Vaillant, proposed that researchers should be concerned with the focus 'to add more life to years, not just years to life' (Vaillant, 2004: 561). This is an ever-increasing issue as our world life expectancy grows year on year (Table 6.1). Since 1990, there has been a global reduction of infant mortality by 50 per cent, highlighting the shift in population growth and extensions of life.

Not only are populations rising – they are getting older. The WHO's mass global survey places a global leap in life expectancy. Whilst there is less than a 1 per cent chance of living until 100 (Guralink, as cited in Buettner, 2010: 257), the most recent figures from 2007 show that, on average, males and females can expect to live 4 years longer than was previously predicted in 1990 (Table 6.1).

Year	1990	2000	2007	Healthy LE
Males	62	64	66	59
Females	66	68	70	

TABLE 6.1 WHO Global Life Expectancy

Within the UK, on average, men and women can expect to live up to 78 and 80 respectively, with healthy and disease-free living until age 72 (Table 6.2).

Country	1990	2000	2008	Combined HLE
UK (M/F)	73/75	75/78	78/80	72
USA (M/F)	72/79	74/80	76/81	70
Canada (M/F)	74/80	77/82	79/83	73
Japan (M/F)	76/82	78/85	79/86	76
Sierre Leone (M/F)	38/44	37/45	48/50	35

TABLE 6.2 WHO Global Life Expectancy for selected countries

There are several implications of living longer – one in particular, is retirement. Statutory retirement at 65 and the state pension were introduced when the average length of life was around 50. Since then, and due to tough economic times, countries like France are extending the retirement/pension age as their population grows older. Since the average length of life is now around 80, the post-retirement period may occupy a quarter of our life!

Possible solutions to the retirement paradox have included (adapted from Boniwell, 2008):

■ creating age-friendly work environments and valuing diversity;
■ continuing career development and introducing phased retirement schemes;
■ enhancing and enabling a better work–life balance before retirement.

Any way we look at it, the human race is living longer and the majority of us can look forward to a long and healthy old age. Our chances of extended physical and mental health can be further improved by the lifestyle choices we make.

Ageing well

There are several negative myths about the ageing process that lead society to begrudge and fear this inevitable and natural process (Lupien and Wan, 2004). Two of the most important myths include (1) loss of neurons and (2) irreversible deterioration of cognitive abilities. However, this is certainly not the case. Modifying lifestyle habits can prevent the deterioration of cognitive functioning. Numerous studies have found that higher levels of physical, mental or social activity reduce risk of cognitive impairment or dementia five or more years later. Furthermore, research has found links between age of dementia onset and strength of social ties.

Think about it...

What do you think are the key ingredients for healthy ageing? How important do you rate:

- diet;
- exercise;
- genetics;
- family environment;
- wealth?

How to age 'healthily'

From a longitudinal study spanning several decades, Vaillant and his colleagues discovered six factors that **do not** predict healthy ageing (Vaillant, 200). These include:

- ancestral longevity;
- cholesterol level at 50;
- parental social class;
- warm childhood environment (stability of parental marriage, parental death in childhood, family cohesion);
- stable childhood temperament (rated by parents); and
- stress.

These findings were in direct contradiction of what research believed to be major determinants of whether or not a person aged healthily. Interestingly, factors that did predict healthy ageing (Vaillant, 2004) included:

■ not being a heavy smoker or stopping smoking young (by about the age of 45);

■ mature adaptive defences;

■ absence of alcohol abuse (moderate drinking is perfectly fine);

■ healthy weight;

■ stable marriage;

■ exercise (burning more than 500 kilocalories per week);

■ years of education (the more, the better).

The good news is that the list of predictive healthy ageing factors includes many aspects that are under our own control.

Benefits of ageing

One major benefit of ageing is the significant reduction in depressive episodes and anxiety disorders, with the prevalence of common mental disorders dropping around statutory retirement age (Carstensen and Charles, 2002; Vaillant et al., 2006). Older adults tend to experience fewer negative emotions but a similar number of positive emotions and develop greater emotional complexity (for example, joy and sadness can be intermixed at the same moment).

Studies show that with age comes more contentment and the formation of deeper and closer bonds with people, thereby deriving more satisfaction from relationships. As with PTG, time becomes more meaningful and older people select contacts more carefully and strategically. Older people tend to have an intact memory for emotionally important material and an increased ability to see interpersonal problems from multiple perspectives.

So in order to engage in successful ageing, Lupien and Wan (2004) offer several tips: (1) engage with life and maintain activities that are personally meaningful to you; (2) create environments where you are able to feel in control and able to make choices; (3) maintain a positive attitude (associated with good memory, longevity, good health, wellbeing and a will to live); and (4) always believe that you can keep learning and remember.

STEREOTYPES

Becca Levy and colleagues at Yale University have conducted a series of experiments comparing the effects of positive and negative age stereotypes on memory, numerical ability, self-confidence and cardiovascular responses to stress (Levy, 1996, 2009). They used positive (wise, astute, enlightened, sage)

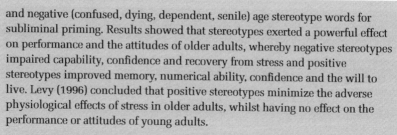

and negative (confused, dying, dependent, senile) age stereotype words for subliminal priming. Results showed that stereotypes exerted a powerful effect on performance and the attitudes of older adults, whereby negative stereotypes impaired capability, confidence and recovery from stress and positive stereotypes improved memory, numerical ability, confidence and the will to live. Levy (1996) concluded that positive stereotypes minimize the adverse physiological effects of stress in older adults, whilst having no effect on the performance or attitudes of young adults.

See Levy (1996) for the original article.

Living longer

Adopting positive attitudes has been linked to increased longevity, such that positive self-perceptions held at 50 years of age can add up to 7.5 years of life (Levy et al., 2000, 2002) regardless of gender, socioeconomic status, loneliness and health. In addition, the will to live is an important influence on longevity.

In conclusion, people are living longer, healthier, more productive lives and social structures and social attitudes lag behind the new realities of ageing. Thus, research shows that negative age stereotypes are outdated and dangerous, impairing performance, confidence and physiological functions. Positive attitudes to ageing reflect the new reality and reinforce health and capability. Encouraging positive attitudes is a matter of urgency as is communicating the benefits of age and the ways of improving functioning through exercise and activity. This can all contribute to creating a positive ageing culture.

Summary

Reflecting on the learning objectives you should now understand the concept of resilience, post-traumatic growth and positive ageing. More specifically, you should know:

- There are three main psychological responses to trauma: succumbing, resilience and post-traumatic growth.
- Resilience can be defined in several ways.
- A sense of coherence is important for wellbeing.
- There are five main components within post-traumatic growth (PTG).
- Wisdom and its place in the developmental process.
- The human race is getting older, but we can enhance wellbeing by positive ageing.

Suggested Resources

www.lancearmstrong.com
> For an inspirational example of thriving in the face of adversity, see how Lance Armstrong describes his past battles with cancer.

http://www.logotherapyinstitute.org/index.htm
> At the official Logotherapy website you can find links to Victor Frankl's biography to learn more about this fascinating man.

http://www.ppc.sas.upenn.edu/armyresiliencetraining.htm
> See how the University of Pennsylvania, under the supervision of Professor Seligman, are initiating resilience training with the US Army.

http://adultdev.bwh.harvard.edu/training.html
> A growing area in the field of positive psychology, you can access information on training courses and/or internships to work within adult development lab.

Further questions for you

1 When it comes to resilience, whom should we be targeting? Children or adults? Vulnerable populations or 'normal' functioning populations?

2 'That which does not kill us makes us stronger.' What do you think of Nietzsche's quote?

3 What do you think about PTG? Is it real? Does it matter?

4 How do you intend to 'age well'?

Personal Development Interventions

1 Expressive writing

As demonstrated by the powerful work on expressive writing by Texan Professor James Pennebaker (1997, 2004), you can try, if you feel you are ready, to engage in expressive writing. Pennebaker has shown that writing can organize thoughts and emotions and help find meaning in tragic experiences. If you have experienced an adversity, and would like to try the following exercise, then please do so. However, if the tragedy is too raw, then you are advised to wait until you are emotionally ready to take part.

You are asked to choose and then write about a painful, distressing experience in detail. Please take the next 15–30 minutes to write anything about this specific traumatic experience. You are then asked to continue for three consecutive days. You may choose to write about the same experience or another one if you wish.

Measurement Tools

Changes in Outlook Questionnaire (CiOQ)

(Joseph et al., 1993)

Directions

Printed below are some statements about your current thoughts and feelings following the event you described above. Please read each one and indicate, by circling one of the numbers beside each statement, how much you agree or disagree with it at the present time using the following scale:

1	2	3	4	5	6
Strongly disagree	Disagree a little	Disagree	Agree a little	Agree	Strongly agree

1. I don't look forward to the future anymore.   1 2 3 4 5 6
2. My life has no meaning anymore.   1 2 3 4 5 6
3. I no longer feel able to cope with things.   1 2 3 4 5 6
4. I don't take life for granted anymore.   1 2 3 4 5 6
5. I value my relationships much more now.   1 2 3 4 5 6
6. I feel more experienced about life now.   1 2 3 4 5 6
7. I do not worry about death at all anymore.   1 2 3 4 5 6
8. I live everyday to the full now.   1 2 3 4 5 6
9. I fear death very much now.   1 2 3 4 5 6
10. I look upon each day as a bonus.   1 2 3 4 5 6
11. I feel as if something bad is just waiting around the corner to happen.   1 2 3 4 5 6
12. I am a more understanding and tolerant person now.   1 2 3 4 5 6
13. I have a greater faith in human nature now.   1 2 3 4 5 6
14. I no longer take people or things for granted.   1 2 3 4 5 6
15. I desperately wish I could turn back the clock to before it happened.   1 2 3 4 5 6
16. I sometimes think it's not worth being a good person.   1 2 3 4 5 6

17. I have very little trust in other people now.	1	2	3	4	5	6
18. I feel very much as if I'm in limbo.	1	2	3	4	5	6
19. I have very little trust in myself now.	1	2	3	4	5	6
20. I feel harder towards other people.	1	2	3	4	5	6
21. I am less tolerant of others now.	1	2	3	4	5	6
22. I am much less able to communicate with other people.	1	2	3	4	5	6
23. I value other people more now.	1	2	3	4	5	6
24. I am more determined to succeed in life now.	1	2	3	4	5	6
25. Nothing makes me happy anymore.	1	2	3	4	5	6
26. I feel as if I'm dead from the neck downwards.	1	2	3	4	5	6

Scoring

The scale is simply a summative score. Please reverse score the following items: 1, 2, 3, 4, 9, 11, 16, 17, 18, 19, 20, 21, 22, 25, 26.

Interpretation

Scores can range from 26 to 150. A higher score indicates greater levels of change.

Review

Currently the CiOQ and the PTGI are the most used tools within PTG research. The CiOQ is a retrospective self-report measurement tool that assesses positive and negative change following trauma. The measurement tools and methodologies for assessing PTG have come under scrutiny in the past few years (Ford, Tennen and Albert, 2008) and the field must create less fallible modes of inquiry (Linley and Joseph, 2009).

Notes

1 PTSD is characterized as the hyper-arousal of the autonomic nervous system (as discussed previously) where individuals are exposed to the constant re-experiencing of the trauma and the need to avoid all things associated with trauma (Rothschild, 2000).
2 Although the authors would argue there are several more domains which are specific to each trauma endured (see Hefferon et al., 2008, 2009, 2010).
3 For the full 21-item PTGI scale, please contact the original authors

CHAPTER 7

Values, Motivation and Goal Theories

❖ LEARNING OBJECTIVES

This chapter focuses on the relevance of motivation and goal theories for understanding optimal adjustment and wellbeing. This includes, for example, differences in wellbeing between people who are intrinsically versus extrinsically motivated. Some of these researchers have examined whether it is psychologically better to strive for wealth and fame versus meaning and personal growth. This chapter will also reflect upon the role of values and time perspectives in motivation and goal achievement.

List of topics

- The importance of goals and goal setting.
- The role that values play in our decision making.
- Intrinsic versus extrinsic motivation theories.
- Self-determination theory continuum.
- Psychological needs (autonomy, competence and relatedness).
- Time perspective and time use.

MOCK ESSAY QUESTIONS

1 Critically discuss the importance of psychological need satisfaction for intrinsic motivation.

2 Discuss the contribution of self-determination theory to our understanding of human motivation.

3 Drawing on available research evidence, compare and contrast different time perspective profiles with reference to wellbeing (broadly defined).

Goals

Goal theorists argue that human subjective wellbeing cannot be explained purely in terms of either objective external conditions or stable internal traits. They claim that it depends on the human ability to reflect, to choose a direction in life, to form intentions and to direct oneself towards a certain path or goal (Schmuck and Sheldon, 2001).

Life goals (also called core goals, personal striving, personal projects, life tasks, future aspiration) are motivational objectives by which we direct our lives. They are deemed long-term goals as they direct someone's life for an extended period of time. When we consciously attempt to understand our goals, why we are pursuing them and if they match our values, we can enhance our wellbeing (Sheldon et al., 2010).

Goals and making lists of short-term and life goals are important for our wellbeing and even daily survival (Cantor and Sanderson, 1999). People make lists for many reasons; however, research has shown that goals are important for several reasons. First, goals give us a sense of purpose, a reason for being. We would be lost without goals. It is also the actual progression towards the goal and not necessarily the attainment of the goal that creates wellbeing (the journey not the destination) (Brunstein, 1993). Furthermore, goals add structure and meaning to our daily life, helping us learn how to manage our time. Thus, as we go through our day and meet smaller subgoals, we can enhance our self-esteem and self-efficacy (Carver and Scheier, 1990, as cited in Lyubomirsky, 2008). For example, people with aspirations and dreams that are in progress or achievable and are personally meaningful, are happier than those that do not have them.

Within *goal theory* there are two research traditions: (1) focus on the process of goal pursuit (how well an individual is doing) and (2) focus on the content and quality of life goals (what and why). The process of goal pursuit was discussed in Chapter 2 (linked with positive emotions); therefore we will now focus on the second element of goal theory.

Content-related goal theories focus on the following aspects of goals:

■ *What* goals are pursued – for example, personal growth or money? Love or attractiveness?

- *Why* goals are pursued – for example, because I want to or because I have to?
- *How congruent* one's activities are with one's values? For example, value-as-a-moderator model.

What goals are descended from Fromm's (1976) 'having orientation' (obtaining wealth and status) versus 'being orientation' (self-actualization). Other researchers have also defined the same concepts in several ways, for example: self-focused versus others-focused goals (Salmela-Aro et al., 2001); extrinsic (financial success, image, fame) versus intrinsic aspirations (personal growth, relationships, community involvement (Kasser and Ryan, 2001); self-enhancement versus materialist values (Schmuck, 2001).

Think about it…

Do you have a 'bucket list'? These tend to be lists that are done under the assumption that there is a race against death. This could be a death that is imminent or a 'to do-list' before you die. Either way, there is an implicit challenge against time and mortality. Furthermore, 'bucket lists' or 'life lists' can be lists that are set 'to do' before a specific or momentous change in a person's life (for example, turning 50, getting married, having a baby). Again, there is a challenge to achieve against the clock. Take a moment to reflect and write your own bucket list.

Remember, not all goals are equal. Lyubomirksy (2008) argues that goals need to be:

- *Intrinsic* (do it for the sake of doing it) versus extrinsic (do it for the sake of something else – feeling driven by something other than pure motivation, such as work and money). If we engage with and enhance intrinsic motivation, we can become more authentic and self-fulfilled (Deci and Ryan, 2000; Schmuck et al., 2000).
- *Authentic/self-concordant:* the goals match our values, which are our deep-set beliefs. These can change and they form the basis of why we do what we do. Values help us prioritize. Value as a moderator model: not the content but the congruence between the person's values and their goals (Oishi et al., 1999).
- *Approach oriented:* do something rather than avoid something.
- *Harmonious:* sometimes goals can be conflicting – try to maintain harmonious goals that complement rather than contradict each other (Oishi and Diener, 2001).
- *Flexible and appropriate:* change with age and time.
- *Activity goals:* joining a club, volunteering, new experience and new opportunities.

Goals are linked with *challenge*. When challenges match our skill levels or just push/stretch us a little beyond what we are used to, we can enter into the psychological domain of flow. Flow is the total absorption in the task that leads to an engaged life and enhanced positive emotions (see page 79 for more information).

So when making a life list choose wisely and make sure your list includes all the above. If you stay flexible you will be open to more opportunities.

Motivation and self-determination theory

G oals link heavily with self-determination theory (SDT) (Chapter 4). Self-determination theory is a positive psychology theory of motivation, which posits that humans strive to be self-governed, where their behaviour is 'volitional, intentional and self-caused or self-initiated' (Wehmeyer and Little, 2009: 869). Originally, Ryan and Deci wanted to understand the conditions that promote intrinsic motivation. Over the decades, they concluded that the social environment has a powerful influence in promoting intrinsically healthy, self-determined development and satisfying our three basic needs (autonomy, relatedness and competence). When intrinsically motivated, people *want* to engage in the activity; they need no external prompts, promises, or threats to initiate action. Being intrinsically motivated also enhances wellbeing, engagement and success. Extrinsic actions, on the other hand, offer a reward separable from the behaviour itself.

Think about it...

I n general, are your goals more extrinsic versus intrinsically based? Does it depend on the goal? Write down your current goals and reflect on whether you are striving for intrinsic versus extrinsic rewards.

Of course, we can't be intrinsically motivated all the time. Especially as we get older, we need to do or are told to do things that we would otherwise not choose to do (homework, housework, and so forth). What happens then? Ryan and Deci's self-determination continuum (Figure 7.1) tackles this conundrum, proposing six types of motivations applicable in the quest for becoming self-determined. The first type is *amotivation* – when an individual has absolutely no motivation to do what is asked and will most likely not do it. The next stage is *external regulation*, where one is not self-determined and controlled by external forces. This individual will most likely do what is asked because someone is 'making them do it'. *Introjected regulation* occurs when someone is motivated to do something based on guilt if they do not do it. This is more an internalized 'ought to, should do' rather than a 'want to' type of motivation.

Identified regulation is the starting point for increasing self-determination. This is when we are motivated by the knowledge that the goal is personally meaningful and valuable. The actions are carried out because we recognize that it is in our best interest. *Integrated regulation* is evident when we engage in a goal that we find consistent with who we are, yet there is still some outcome at the end. The activity is not done for the sheer sake of it. Finally, *intrinsic regulation* is when we engage in a goal or activity that is fully intrinsic and done because it is interesting in itself. Deci and Ryan (2000) argue that although we can't be intrinsically motivated all the time, the further to the right end of the continuum we are, the greater levels of autonomy we will begin to feel.

Think about it…

What activities do you have to do that you feel are governed by extrinsic motivation? In order to enhance your intrinsic motivation and move towards achieving integrated regulation, try to enhance your autonomy, competence or relatedness. For example, if your activity is studying, looking at the entire textbook can be daunting. Separate it into sections, creating smaller subgoals. Each time you finish a section, and achieve your subgoal, you will move towards building your levels of competence and thus move towards becoming more intrinsically motivated.

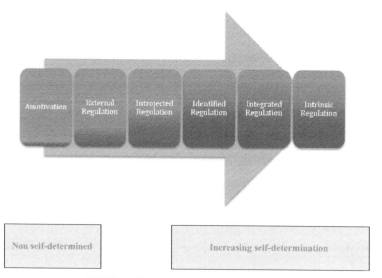

FIGURE 7.1 The process of organismic integration

Benefits of being self-determined

There are several benefits of promoting autonomous versus controlled behaviour. For example, actions that are autonomous and thereby have an internal locus of causality have been found to promote greater creativity (Amabile, 1983a, b); cognitive flexibility and depth of processing (Grolnick and Ryan, 1987a; 1987b); higher self-esteem (Ryan and Grolnick, 1986); enhanced positive emotions (Garbarino, 1975); satisfaction and trust (Deci et al., 1989) as well as physical and psychological wellbeing (Langer and Rodin, 1976). Furthermore, people who perceive their actions as autonomously regulated tend to enjoy and achieve higher levels of satisfaction from school, increased behavioural persistence, effective performance, better mental and physical health (Miserandino, 1996; Black and Deci, 2000; Deci and Ryan, 2000).

Individuals who report having identified regulation in religious attendance, relationship status, weight loss and addiction programmes, are associated with better mental health, better adjustment, better attendance, better weight loss maintenance and increased positive affect. Not surprisingly, external and introjected motivation reduced wellbeing and success in all three cases (Ryan et al., 1995; Williams et al., 1996).

Children of parents who use a controlling versus autonomy-supportive parenting style have been found to be less likely to be intrinsically interested in play. Researchers propose that controlling parenting styles spoil children's fun and interest in play. Ultimately, a lack of basic need satisfaction (for example, cold, controlling parenting) can lead to the development of extrinsic need substitutes. Adolescents with mothers who were rated as cold and non-nurturing were more oriented towards compensatory aspirations (wealth) and the emotional coldness of mother at the age four has been linked to predicted extrinsic aspirations 12 years later (Kasser et al., 1995).

Think about it...

Intrinsically motivated behaviours have internal locus of causality (feeling self-determined). So what would happen if we were to introduce extrinsic rewards for the same activity? For example, what if we said that we would give you £5 for reading the rest of this book chapter, when you already intrinsically enjoy reading it?[1] Research has found that the activity would feel controlled by external rewards, your intrinsic motivation would decrease and the activity would be pursued less when the reward is withdrawn. The implication of this is: don't turn play into work by conveying that the activity should only be done for external rewards.

The quickest way to undermine motivation is to threaten negative consequences, conduct surveillance and evaluation of performance and introduce deadlines. But wait a minute . . . doesn't this look like the entire education system? Unfortunately, it does. However, if parents, teachers and other figures of authority want to facilitate intrinsic motivation they can adopt several methods. First of all, providing choice is an excellent way to engage the fundamental need of autonomy. Secondly, they can provide positive informational feedback that acknowledges competence and is not viewed as controlling. Finally, fostering secure relatedness provides a secure base of a warm/caring relationship that encourages safe exploration of the environment.

Values

We will now shift to look at congruence of values and goal pursuit in the attainment of wellbeing. Values are different from needs in that they are ideas that are dear to us and that implicitly or explicitly govern our lives. Similar to emotions, researchers have identified a list of 10 universal values (Schwartz, 1994; Schwartz and Sagiv, 1995). These include:

- power;
- achievement;
- hedonism;
- stimulation;
- self-direction;
- universalism;
- benevolence;
- tradition;
- conformity;
- security.

The value-as-a-moderator model predicts that people gain a sense of satisfaction out of activities and goals congruent with their values (Oishi et al., 1999). Furthermore, research suggests that when people engage in activities that are congruent with their goals, they will derive a sense of satisfaction from their day, regardless of whether or not they are extrinsic values (such as power) or intrinsic values (for example, benevolence or self-direction). People exhibit more intense positive and negative affect in response to daily events if these events are coherent with their personal strivings (Emmons, 1991; Brunstein et al., 1998; Oishi et al., 1999).

Finally, Sheldon and Kasser (1995) have researched whether or not *congruence* and *coherence* are essential for personality integration. *Vertical coherence* refers to the consistency between lower and higher levels of goals. *Horizontal coherence* involves consistency between goals at the same level. Lastly, *congruence* refers to the pursuit of goals for self-determined reasons and through intrinsic motivation. Both congruence and vertical coherence have emerged as predictors of various wellbeing outcomes. Thus, research shows that you must try to maintain harmonious goals that complement rather than contradict each other (Oishi and Diener, 2001).

Failing to reach our goals

If the pursuit of goals is so fundamental for wellbeing, why do people so often fail to pursue goals that are important to them? Many reasons have been proposed for this. It is often simply due to logistical reasons, as we need to put our effort into less important but more immediate goals (Ford and Nichols, 1991). Furthermore, finding and maintaining that passion and desire can be difficult over sustained periods of time, thus sometimes we just 'run out of steam'. Finally, research has shown that when people follow 'the wrong goals' (for example, money, fame and other extrinsic goals), they tend to disengage with them sooner and give up. Thus, choosing the right goals, maintaining passion (by reminding yourself of the importance of the immediate drudgery for future success) and making time for your valued goals is important for successful outcomes and wellbeing. Interestingly, writing goals down and discussing with others makes us more likely to commit (Lyubomirsky, 2008).

The next section will focus on an important influence on goal attainment and motivation: *time*. The next section will also explain how the perspective we take on time can have a massive impact on our overall wellbeing.

Time

Time. It is the one thing that we can't buy, we can't make, or sell and in today's world, we often come across the problem of time crunch. The area of 'time research' focuses on time perspective and time use as important contributors to wellbeing.

There appears to be a dual nature of time: time as an objective phenomenon (geographical, 'clock' time) versus time as an internal phenomenon (psychological time, time as it is processed by the human mind, subjective time, the inner time of the mind, lived time). From an objective perspective, time is an infinitely large container for all events. *Time perspective* is defined as an individual's cognitive way of relating to the psychological concepts of past, present and future. Thus, *subjective time use* is a person's own perceived representation of his or her own time use. Individuals are proposed to have a *time personality* with dimensions including punctuality, planning, leisure-time awareness, impatience, and time congruity. *Time urgency* refers to time-urgent individuals who are more time aware, chronically hurried, trying to fulfil their ambitions, quite efficient, prioritizing tasks and using deadlines as measures of time remaining (Boniwell, 2008).

A time perspective (TP) can also be thought of as a preferential direction of our thoughts towards the past, present or future, which exerts a dynamic influence on our experience, motivation, thinking and several aspects of behaviour (De Volder, 1979). The formation of a TP is influenced by many factors learned in the process of socialization, including cultural and religious background, education, belonging to a particular social class and family modelling.

Although situational forces, such as inflation, being on vacation or under survival stresses, can affect TP, it can also be seen as a relatively stable dispositional characteristic. Zimbardo's theory of time perspective proposes that there are five factors:

- *Future time perspective (TP)*. This is when an individual tends to work for future rewards, engages in delayed gratification and is often linked with success (for original articles, see Mischel, 1970, 1978; De Volder and Lens, 1982; Mischel, Shoda, and Rodriguez, 1989; Shoda, Mischel, and Peake, 1990). A focus on the future is fundamental to wellbeing and positive functioning (Wessman and Ricks, 1966; Kahana and Kahana, 1983; Kazakina, 1999; Wills, Sandy, and Yaeger, 2001). Bohart (1993) proposes that the ability of humans to be future oriented is fundamental for human development because it allows the sense of possibility of being agentic, of taking responsibility and of making choices. Furthermore, future time perspective, and especially possession of long-term goals, positively correlated with virtually all aspects of wellbeing, especially a meaningful life, social self-efficacy, and realism/persistence (Zaleski et al., 2001).

- *Present hedonistic TP*. This is when individuals exhibit little concern for the consequences of their actions. Their behaviour is determined by physical needs, emotions, strong situational stimuli and social input. This TP risks giving in to temptations, leading to addictions, accidents and injuries, and academic and career failure.

- *Present fatalistic TP.* This is when an individual is characteristically hopeless, with a belief that outside forces control one's life (for example, spiritual or governmental forces).

- *Past positive TP.* This is when we have a warm, pleasurable, often sentimental and nostalgic view of our past. We maintain relationships with family and friends, continue traditions and history and hold a continuity of self over time. Furthermore, past positive TP has been linked to higher levels of meaning and satisfaction with life (Foret and Steger, 2004).

- *Past negative TP.* This is when an individual focuses on previous personal experiences that were aversive or noxious.

Researchers have found that there is a strong tie between the TP you adopt and your wellbeing. For example TP has been found to be related to many attitudes, values and status variables, such as: educational achievement, health, sleep and dreaming patterns and romantic partner choices (Zimbardo and Boyd, 1999). Furthermore, TP is indicative of choice of food, health choices, parental marital state, desire to spend time with friends and perceived time pressure (Zimbardo and Boyd, 1999). Time perspective is also predictive for a wide range of behaviours, including risky driving, delinquency and unsafe sexual behaviours (Zimbardo et al., 1997) as well as substance and alcohol abuse (Keough et al., 1999).

Time perspective even predicts the extent to which unemployed people living in shelters use their time constructively to seek jobs (future oriented), or waste time watching TV and engaging in other non-instrumental activities and avoidant coping strategies (present oriented) (Epel et al., 1999). Researchers have found significantly shorter time horizons in pathological versus social gamblers (Hodgins and Engel, 2002).

Time perspective has been shown to be related to culture. Protestant nations tend to be more future oriented than Catholic nations. Within countries, those living in southern regions tend to be more present oriented than those in northern regions. Cultures with a more individualistic focus tend to be more future-oriented than do those emphasizing collectivism. Western ways of life have become predominantly goal focused and future oriented.

Balanced time perspective

Ideally, researchers would suggest adopting a balanced time perspective where 'the past, present and future components blend and flexibly engage, depending on a situation's demands and our needs and values' (Zimbardo, 2002: 62). People with a balanced time perspective are capable of operating within a temporal mode appropriate to the situation in which they find themselves.

Think about it...

Try to understand your TP profile and evaluate whether your dominant TP is serving you well. Remember that a future TP does not have all the answers. Make sure you pay attention to past negative TP. Try to work on the development of a balanced TP.

Time use

We know that how we perceive time can have an influence on our overall wellbeing; however, does this hold for how we manage and use our time? There is no apparent relationship between objective time use (amount of time) and global wellbeing but there is a relationship between activity time allocation and experienced happiness and a relationship between satisfaction with time use and wellbeing (Hafstrom and Paynter,

1991; Pentland et al., 1998). Higher income is associated with higher life satisfaction but it is not related to happiness in the moment, because people with greater income tend to devote relatively more time to work, commuting, compulsory non-work activities (shopping and childcare) and active leisure, and less of their time to passive leisure pursuits. Work, commuting and compulsory activities are associated with higher tension and stress.

In 2007, the very first review of empirically based time-management literature looked at 35 papers published between 1954 and 2005 on time management, time use, time and structuring on academic and work performance (Claessens et al., 2007). The effects of time-management programmes (based on eight studies) showed mixed results with regard to self-reported engagement in time management behaviours and performance improvement; however, time-management programmes provided positive supervisor ratings in one study and increases in feelings of control of time. The effects of time management (self-perceptions) was also found to improve college grades but had no effect on job performance.

Think about it...

Focus on psychological aspects of time use (congruence, responsibility, anxiety) but do not become overly enthusiastic about time management tricks (planning, clearing, organizers). Remember, knowing *why* can make an activity worthwhile. It's important to achieve something on a daily basis.

Summary

Reflecting on the learning objectives you should now understand the concepts of goals, motivation and values. More specifically, you should know:

- Goals are important to our sense of wellbeing.
- It is the what, why and congruence of these goals that can enhance or inhibit our wellbeing.
- Motivation to continue goals must be developed into intrinsically motivated goals to enhance wellbeing.
- Self-determination theory employs the organismic integration model, which suggests that as well as moving from one end of the scale to the other, we become more self-determined and authentic.
- There are five main time perspectives, which have been linked to higher and lower levels of wellbeing.

Suggested Resources

http://www.worldvaluessurvey.org/
This is the most comprehensive, up to date survey regarding value changes across the globe. The WVS is currently undertaking new research for 2010–2011.

Further questions for you

1 What makes you achieve your goals? Do you have any that you would like to achieve in the next month? Year? 5 years?

2 What values do you relate to and why do they influence your daily life and the decisions you make?

3 Are you time-spent? Do you constantly find that you run out of time to finish papers, study or socialize? What are the reasons for this? Where might you be able to save time?

Personal Development Interventions

1 Values
Integrity has been associated with increased levels of happiness (Branden, 1994). Values and behaviour need to match for happiness. Make a list of the activities that you find most pleasurable and meaningful – that make you happy. Place beside it how much time you spend per week/month engaging in those activities. Does the maths reflect harmony between your values and your behaviour? Take a look in the mirror – are you living your life the way you really want to?

2 Intrinsic motivation
For the next week, we would like you to try to increase your intrinsic motivation, when it comes to studying for exams. Make sure you give yourself as many choices as possible (for example, when to study and for how long to study). Once you've made these choices, reflect on how you feel about them. Do they differ from how other people choose to study? By increasing your choice selection, you will enhance your level of autonomy, thereby hopefully moving towards the self-determined end of the SDT continuum.

Measurement Tools

Self-Determination Scale (SDS)

(Sheldon and Deci, 1995)

Directions

Please read the pairs of statements, one pair at a time, and think about which statement within the pair seems more true to you at this point in your life. Indicate the degree to which statement A feels true, relative to the degree that statement B feels true, on the 5-point scale shown after each pair of statements. If statement A feels completely true and statement B feels completely untrue, the appropriate response would be 1. If the two statements are equally true, the appropriate response would be a 3. And so on.

1 A. I always feel like I choose the things I do.
 B. I sometimes feel that it's not really me choosing the things I do.

Only A feels true   1   2   3   4   5   **Only B feels true**

2 A. My emotions sometimes seem alien to me.
 B. My emotions always seem to belong to me.

Only A feels true   1   2   3   4   5   **Only B feels true**

3 A. I choose to do what I have to do.
 B. I do what I have to, but I don't feel like it is really my choice.

Only A feels true   1   2   3   4   5   **Only B feels true**

4 A. I feel that I am rarely myself.
 B. I feel like I am always completely myself.

Only A feels true   1   2   3   4   5   **Only B feels true**

5 A. I do what I do because it interests me.
 B. I do what I do because I have to.

Only A feels true   1   2   3   4   5   **Only B feels true**

6 A. When I accomplish something, I often feel it wasn't really me who did it.
 B. When I accomplish something, I always feel it's me who did it.

Only A feels true   1   2   3   4   5   **Only B feels true**

7 A. I am free to do whatever I decide to do.
   B. What I do is often not what I'd choose to do.

Only A feels true   1   2   3   4   5   **Only B feels true**

8 A. My body sometimes feels like a stranger to me.
   B. My body always feels like me.

Only A feels true   1   2   3   4   5   **Only B feels true**

9 A. I feel pretty free to do whatever I choose to.
   B. I often do things that I don't choose to do.

Only A feels true   1   2   3   4   5   **Only B feels true**

10 A. Sometimes I look into the mirror and see a stranger.
    B. When I look into the mirror I see myself.

Only A feels true   1   2   3   4   5   **Only B feels true**

Scoring

Items 1, 3, 5, 7, 9 need to be reverse scored. Calculate the scores for the Awareness of Self subscale (items 2, 4, 6, 8, 10) and the Perceived Choice subscale (items 1, 3, 5, 7, 9) by averaging the item scores for the five items within each subscale.

Interpretation

The subscales can either be used separately or they can be combined into an overall SDS score. Higher scores indicate a higher level of self-determination.

Review

This scale is a short, easy-to-administer test that assesses self-determination levels.

Note

1 Which, of course, we will not do.

CHAPTER 8

Positive Psychological Interventions

❖ LEARNING OBJECTIVES

In psychology theory is just half of the puzzle. We need to know how the topics we research can be used to help people change to become happier, more fulfilled and flourish.

This chapter will review recent research on positive psychology interventions (PPIs) and how we can begin to change our behaviours.

List of topics

- Mindsets.
- Transtheoretical model of change.
- Grit and perseverance.
- Self-regulation to keep the change going.

- Evaluating interventions.
- Positive psychology interventions.
- Gratitude.

MOCK ESSAY QUESTIONS

1 Grit explains academic achievement over and above our IQ. Discuss.

2 What are some of the concrete interventions by which positive psychologists might try to enhance wellbeing and what is the evidence that such procedures are effective?

3 Critically discuss the contribution of the mindset theory to our understanding of change processes.

Positive psychological interventions (PPIs)

First comes the change

Think about your role models when you were a child. Or, even better, who are your role models now? Chances are your role models were/are people who have achieved something in an area of life that you find admirable. So how do these people become so good at what they do? Are they born like that? Or do they develop, with hard work, into the achievers we eventually come to know. And, if they develop through hard work, what is it that keeps them going through the difficult times. Researcher Carol Dweck would argue that 'the view you adopt for yourself profoundly affects the way you lead your life' (Dweck, 2006: 6). This view is also known, in the research world, as your *mindset*.

Mindset is defined as how you perceive basic abilities and qualities such as intelligence, parenting, business, relationships, musicality and creativity. There are two types of mindsets: the fixed and growth mindset. The *fixed mindset* believes that qualities are carved in stone. They are either present naturally or not at all, therefore you are either good at maths or not; you can play sports or you can't. Things must come naturally to people with a fixed mindset or else they perceive the ability to be out of their grasp. People with a fixed mindset tend to focus more on success as winning and achieving, rather than about developing as a person. People with a *growth mindset,* on the other hand, believe that with experience, effort and engagement, people can grow! Thus, our abilities are not carved in stone and, although we may be born differing in talents, these talents can be developed over time.

You may find that you have tendencies in different areas and that is normal. For example, you may have a fixed mindset when it comes to maths but hold a growth mindset when it comes to learning an instrument. However, we may have a natural tendency to lean towards one of the two mindsets. Also, if you like your mindset, then you don't have to change it. This section is about highlighting that there are differences and that adopting a growth mindset has several beneficial consequences for happiness, satisfaction and performance success in the long run.

Understanding mindsets

So what do these mindsets look like when they are in action? The first difference relates to how each mindset views goals: either *performance oriented* or *learning oriented*. Someone with a fixed mindset views goals in terms of a successful outcome. For the fixed mindset, the goal is validation from others and achievement. They believe that potential can be measured (for example low marks equals not smart). Unfortunately for this mindset, both success and failure cause anxiety because the person now has to keep up the standard they have created and becomes afraid of failure. The growth mindset, on the other hand, focuses on *learning goals*, where the focus is on mastery and competence and not simply winning. The growth mindset recognizes that scores and marks reflect how people are doing *now* and do not measure a person's potential. People who have a growth mindset have been found to increase their performance and enjoyment of skills and tasks, as well as decrease negative emotion.

Think about it…

Have you ever been hampered by a fixed mindset? Where and when does this usually occur?

Why mindsets matter

So, why does it matter whether or not we see things through a fixed or growth mindset? Well, researchers argue that when people come up against tough times, the type of mindset they default to will either enable or hinder them in attaining their desired goal. This process involves how a mindset responds to setbacks, views effort in tackling the situation and how they eventually develop strategies to overcome their difficulties. Let's take a closer look at the fixed mindset.

When we harbour a fixed mindset and are confronted with a difficult situation, we tend to elicit a 'helpless response'. This means that when faced with failure or challenge, people with a fixed mindset do not pay attention to learning information. They can get depressed, become de-energized and lose self-esteem. They also denigrate their abilities and under-represent past successes and over-represent failures. Ultimately they explain the cause of events as something stable about them.

Also, 'effort' is akin to a curse word to the fixed mindset. Those with a fixed mindset view effort as a reflection of low ability because hard work and effort means they were never really good at it anyway. Simply put, effort equals a lack of ability. Since the fixed mindset is so against effort, they move on to develop strategies that hinder any progression from their current status. Fixed mindsets continue to use the wrong strategy when faced with a problem. When this eventually doesn't work, they then disengage from the problem and, finally, they give up.

Now let's take a closer look at how the growth mindset responds to adversity or challenging situations. They tend to use a 'mastery response', which enables them to pay attention to learning information. The growth mindset tries out new ways of doing things, as they are not afraid of failing in the process. When faced with tests that are impossible to pass they will factor in other reasons for their lack of success and not blame their ability (for example, this test was beyond my ability for now). To the growth mindset, effort is a good word! It views effort as a necessary part of success and tries harder when faced with a setback. Simply put, effort equals success. Finally, the strategies the growth mindset uses are focused on generating other ways of doing things. Thus, if one route doesn't work they will try others. They tend to think 'outside of the box'. Thus, as you can see, there are several benefits of adopting a growth mindset, especially in the face of challenge and setbacks.

Where do mindsets come from?

Dweck (2006) argues that mindsets are socially constructed and are therefore learned within the home and classroom environments. The development of mindsets is influenced by the messages we pick up, especially in relation to praise. Praise, as demonstrated by several large experiments, can have a detrimental impact on children. Of course, good feedback is important and constructive criticism is necessary to develop and learn. Praise is not a villain – however, praising for effort and process, rather than outcome, will help the person become more motivated to persevere and ultimately become more resilient.

*[handwritten annotation: learned beliefs *]*

PRAISE

Mueller and Dweck (1998) performed an experiment to make one of the strongest cases for the 'perils of praise'. It can get a bit confusing, so try and follow along.

Children in late grade school and kindergarten were given a first series of easy problems to solve. Following completion, children were offered one of three types of praise:

Intelligence praise – 'You must be really smart!'
Process praise – 'You must have worked really hard!'
Factual praise – 'You got 8 out of 10 right. Well done!'

The students were then, on purpose, given a set of much harder problems to solve (beyond their comprehension level). No matter what they scored, they were all told that they got 5 out of 10. The students that were given the *intelligence praise* attributed their failure to the fact that they 'weren't good enough'. They reported that their fun declined significantly and when asked if they would like to take the games home to practise, the

▶ future likelihood of them playing the game again declined significantly. This was directly in opposition to the results of the *process praise* group. These students attributed their low mark to the fact that they 'didn't work hard enough'. They also reported having the same amount of fun as the first set and were more likely to take the games home with them.

The next stage of the experiment asked all students to choose their next task. They had to choose between one that would challenge them or one that was designed for them not to fail. They were also offered the choice to receive a new set of challenges or to receive a review of how they scored in relation to other students. Finally, they were asked to write to a student in another state and tell that student how they did on the problem-solving tasks. As you may already guess, the intelligent praise group chose the problem that was easy, they chose to see where they fit in relation to others, and in the letter task over 40 per cent lied! In contrast, the process praise group chose their next problem designed on learning more and when they were asked to tell others how they did only 1.3 per cent lied!

The interesting results came when the researchers reviewed the real scores for each group. Remember how we said that the first set was easy. Well most did well on those (all equal at baseline). Of course, the students all did worse on the second set because the problems were for a few levels higher than where they were. However, on the third set, the problems were readjusted to be the same level of difficulty as the first set (easy). Theoretically, they all should have done better. But this didn't happen. The process praise group did significantly better on the easy problem tasks in the third set than the intelligent praise group.

See Mueller and Dweck (1998) for the original article.

Summary of mindsets

Dweck and colleagues (Bempechat, 1983; Dweck et al., 1995) argue that we, as parents, teachers or any figurehead in a child's life, need to tune into the messages we are sending and praise for strategies, effort and process rather than the final outcome. We can also try and be a role model to others, showing that we are not fixed, but can grow!

Positive change

After we have worked through perceptions of abilities, how do people actually change and can they change long term? For any of us who have decided (usually around 1 January) to take on lifestyle change, you will know how hard it is to maintain that alteration.

The first question we need to ask ourselves is whether or not we are actually ready for change. James Prochaska and his colleagues at the University of Rhode Island have done fantastic work in the area of negative behaviour changes. Specifically, they have documented decades of research on how people give up unhelpful behaviours such as smoking, drinking, tanning and unhealthy diets. Prochaska was mainly interested in why and how people change of their own volition. His work has had a significant impact on addiction research and he continues to produce evidence to explain such complex human behaviours (Prochaska and DiClemente, 1984; Prochaska et al., 1992, 1994; Prochaska and Velicer, 1996).

Prochaska's transtheoretical model (TTM) of change contains five stages of change, including:

- pre-contemplation;
- contemplation;
- preparation;
- action;
- maintenance.

Within these stages, there are processes of change that can help us move from one stage to another. The processes include: consciousness raising, counterconditioning, dramatic relief, environmental re-evaluation, helping relationships, reinforcement management, self-liberation, self-re-evaluation, social liberation, and stimulus control.

As we progress through the stages, we shift how we think and feel. At first, we consider the costs versus benefits of change, creating a *decisional balance*. The TTM predicts that when in the pre-contemplation stage, the cons are more salient than the pros. The decisional balance will be reversed as the person gradually moves through the stages (Prochaska et al., 1994). So how then do we change for good? And is this even possible? Prochaska posits that it takes, on average, five attempts at the model before someone reaches long-term maintenance (termination). Of course, termination means different things for different maladaptive behaviours; however, it is usually the absence of the negative behaviour for six months plus a day (Prochaska and Prochaska, 2009).

We recognize that the TTM is not the only model available to help us try to understand behaviour change – others include, for example, the *theory of reasoned action* (TRA) (Ajzen and Fishbein, 1980) and the *theory of planned behaviour* (Ajzen, 1988, 1991) – there is huge support for the TTM model within unhealthy behaviour change research (for example, smoking, alcohol and dieting).

Keep the change going. . .

So once we have changed our behaviours, how do we keep it up? There is a family of closely related concepts, (1) self-discipline, (2) grit and (3) self-regulation, which we believe are important for understanding how and why people persevere with lifestyle changes. *Perseverance* is especially important when we are looking at making people happier. Perseverance is defined as 'the intentional continuation or re-application of effort towards a goal despite a temptation to quit' (Pury, 2009: 678). Thus, we can persevere in terms of how long we stick at a project or how many times we attempt to change.

Self-discipline and grit

We all know it's good for us, and it's good to have plenty of it, but how often do we work on enhancing our grit and self-discipline? Indeed, self-discipline is frequently within the bottom five strengths in global polls (Peterson, 2006). Critics have argued that positive psychology offers too readily the ability to give into impulses; that in order to be happy, we need to give up some things in life (Van Deurzen, 2009). In response to this, you just have to read the research on grit, self-discipline, delayed gratification and self-regulation (all done by researchers within the realm of positive psychology), which shows links between these impulse control mechanisms and wellbeing.

We will define grit as 'perseverance and passion for long term goals' and *self-discipline* as 'the ability to choose successfully among conflicting impulses.' Research has continued to show that scoring high on assessment tools pertaining to these concepts can predict final grades, school attendance, test score achievement, selection into competitive high-school programmes, hours doing homework and hours spent watching TV better than IQ in teenagers. Thus, many teenagers do not reach their intellectual potential based on failure to exercise self-discipline and not their overall intelligence levels (Duckworth and Seligman, 2005, 2006).

MARSHMALLOWS

Imagine you are a kid again. You are invited into a room and told to sit down. In front of you is a nice, sweet, fluffy marshmallow just waiting to be eaten. Except there's a catch. The experimenter says that you can either have this one marshmallow now, or wait and receive two. It's up to you. What would you do? Take the one right away, or wait patiently in order to receive a second marshmallow? In the 1970s, Walter Mischel, a professor at Stanford University, found that not many children were able to delay gratification (approximately 30 per cent), as demonstrated by the famous marshmallow experiment. Years later, Mischel recontacted the 650+ participants (then teenagers) and found a link between the children's early ability to resist temptation and success in later life. Specifically, children who were unable to resist the marshmallow (less than 30 seconds) had increased behavioural problems, lower academic achievements and problems maintaining social relationships. On the other hand, those that were able to resist had significantly higher academic achievement scores (SATs).

See Mischel and Ebbesen (1970), Mischel (1978), Mischel et al. (1989) and Shoda et al. (1990) for the original articles.

Self-regulation

Self-regulation (SR) is defined as 'the process by which we can seek to have control over our thoughts, feelings and impulses.' Scoring high on measurements of SR demonstrates increased flexibility and adaptability to circumstances as it enables people to adjust their actions to a remarkably broad range of social and situational demands. Self-regulation also allows us to change ourselves to live up to social standards and facilitates our interaction with the outside world (Maddux, 2009b).

So what do we need to attain SR? There are several ingredients needed for the acquisition and maintenance of SR. These include:

- *Standards.* In order to initiate SR, you need clear, well-defined standards. If the standards that you are trying to aspire to are ambiguous, inconsistent or conflicting then you will have severe difficulty in engaging in self-regulation. Carver and Scheier (1982, 1998) proposed their feedback loop model to understand goal-directed SR maintenance. First of all, a person performs a test by comparing it to the standard. If the person falls short of the standard, SR requires some operation to be initiated to change the self in order to bring it up to what it should be.

- *Monitoring.* We must be able to monitor and keep track of our progression to the goal, and monitoring must be done in a positive and not destructive fashion (Kirchenbaum, 1984).

- *Strength/willpower.* Self-regulation appears to depend on limited resources that operate like energy and can become temporarily depleted (ego depletion). Studies have shown that there may be links to blood glucose (the brain's principal source of fuel) as an important component of SR. Results show that acts of self-control (SR) consume large amounts of glucose, resulting in lower levels in the bloodstream (Gailliot and Baumeister, 2007; Gailliot et al., 2007).

- *Motivation.* Above all, even if the standards are clear, monitoring is fully effective and resources are abundant, we may still fail to self-regulate if we do not care or have no motivation to reach the goal.

Ego depletion

Baumeister, a leading researcher on the topic area, has completed several studies in order to understand the complex behaviour of SR (Baumeister et al., 1998, 2000; Baumeister, 2003). It appears that when people engage in a task that requires effort, and then engage in an SR-depleting exercise, their ability to self-regulate weakens (Vohs et al., 2008). Thus, SR is impeded by depletion. Some traits manifest themselves more strongly in depleted people and, when SR stops, these inner differences may emerge with a vengeance – for example, alcohol, restrained eating, prejudices, sexual infidelity and poor self-presentation.

So what can we do about the nasty effects of ego depletion? Research shows that SR is actually like a muscle and can be built up. The more we work it, the stronger it gets (Baumeister et al., 2006). Performing non-taxing exercises (for example, food diaries, monitoring posture, following a budget) can help build SR and spill over into other areas of our life. Self-regulation is a core capacity, therefore used in one area it may spill over into other areas such as healthy eating, study habits, chores completion, alcohol, tobacco and caffeine consumption, emotional control and financial budgeting.

Thus, developing grit, engaging in delayed gratification and enhancing self-regulatory practices can have an immense impact on our ability to persevere and achieve our goals.

Think about it…

How self-regulated are you? Try building up your SR muscles. For the next week, write down everything you spend, to the last penny.

Positive psychological interventions = PPI's *

The next section reviews how we positive psychologists evaluate whether or not interventions have worked from both a qualitative and quantitative perspective. Do mental wellbeing interventions work? Well yes, actually, and quite significantly! Sin and Lyubomirsky's (2009) meta-analysis demonstrated that in a sample of 4000+, both normal and depressed populations benefited from participation in PPIs. There were, however, several important factors for impact. Depression status influenced results, with those reporting higher levels of depression at baseline reporting the greatest impact. Also, as found in other studies, people who self-selected for the studies had higher levels of improved wellbeing. The age of participants was also influential, with younger ones experiencing more benefits. Whether the PPIs were delivered in individual or group therapy or self-administered had an impact, with individual therapy having greatest impact. Finally, PPIs that were longer than four weeks, but shorter than 12 weeks tended to have better results.

Qualitatively evaluating PPIs

Evaluating PPIs is a very complex, time-consuming and expensive endeavour. There is also a very large difference between evaluating a large-scale versus small-scale study. In a perfect world, all interventions would use proper assessment tools and neat research designs. They would recruit appropriate sample sizes and conduct proper statistical analyses with everyone on the research team having the relevant education. In reality, however, we may not have access to hundreds of participants or to data-analysis software (such as SPSS). We may not have access to or knowledge of statistics or the money to buy in people to analyse statistics. However we still want to know if it worked, by how much, for whom, what worked best and what didn't.

One major criticism of positive psychology, from a European perspective, is that it has fixated itself on the 'scientific method' and less on using methodologies that enable researchers to access the entire human participant.

Accessing the person as a whole falls under the realm of qualitative methodology. Conducting this type of research is an important piece of the jigsaw that can give us information we would never obtain from quantitative inquiry alone. Researchers and students can use structured, semi-structured or unstructured interviews to collect data on the experiences of the PPIs. It is best to use qualitative enquiry for small sample sizes as it focuses on in-depth, exploratory analysis of interventions (Robson, 2004). Questions should be open, non-directive and focus on one concept at a time. Try not to use double negatives, use 'what' or 'how' instead. Examples of intervention evaluation questions could be:

What was your experience of the programme?
What was your favourite part of the programme? Least favourite?
What would you change about it?
Would you recommend this programme to others? (Why or why not?)

Furthermore, you can use a data-collection technique called the focus group. Focus groups access people whose 'voices' are not traditionally heard and researchers therefore evaluate the findings through the eyes of the people that the research is about. A quote from Fine and Gordon sums up the benefits of a focus group situation:

> If you really want to know either of us, do not put us in a laboratory, or hand us a survey, or even interview us separately alone in our homes. Watch me with my women friends, my son, his father, my niece, or my mother and you will see what feels most authentic to me.
> *– (Fine and Gordon, 1989, as cited in Wilkinson, 1998)*

If you decide that this is the most appropriate method for you, make sure that you allow two hours – you don't want to be tied for time. You need to think about whether or not you will use one group once or several focus groups on several different occasions, which allows you to get a range of viewpoints. In terms of size, you need to be wary of too many participants versus too little. Focus groups tend to range from 2–12, although the norm tends to be 4–8. One of the biggest issues with this type of data collection is the breach in confidentiality, since people will be talking about their experiences, in front of others. Moderators need to ensure that all individuals are aware of what confidentiality means and that the participants agree not to break it.

To start the focus group, the moderator should explain the purpose and objectives of the session. They are allowed to prompt discussion by posing questions from an already created and edited list. Moderators must try to enable participation by all members and appear non-judgemental.

Analysing the data

There are several types of analysis you can use with your data set. One in particular is content analysis, which commences with a list of predetermined themes or key words (objectives). The researcher then searches for matching words and records frequency, with a higher number of instances equalling a higher importance. This technique can be used to work with qualitative or quantitative data.

Another type of analysis is *thematic analysis* (TA). An umbrella term until 2006, TA is the most common method of analysis used by novices. One of the reasons students and researchers like this approach is that it does not stem from an underlying philosophical theory and is therefore used a lot by researchers with no real affinity to qualitative methods; although if the researcher does identify with a theory, this needs to be stated clearly and followed.

Thematic analysis is the analysis of textual material, which looks for major themes, beyond surface-level description. It attempts to organize text into coherent sections. By following three major steps – transcription, theme identification and analytic effort – you can ensure that you undertake a proper qualitative approach (Braun and Clarke, 2006).

The transcription process ranges from superficial/simple transcription to more in-depth (literal or Jefferson). You must try to do the transcription yourself as this will get you closer to the data.

When beginning the analysis, make sure you read through the scripts and become familiar with the text. You can highlight and code based on very detailed line-by-line coding, to see broader overarching themes. Ultimately, the further you take the analysis, the better the analysis – it's all about *refinement.* The key in the write-up is to (1) be transparent, (2) clearly display results and (3) write the report demonstrating these themes and appropriate quotes.

There are several issues with TA. Accounts on 'how to' are scarce and actual methods tend to be neglected in report write-ups. Furthermore, it does not demand intensely close detailed analysis. Finally, you must make sure you go beyond simple labelling – themes need to cover the entire data set.

For more information on qualitative inquiry (for example, interpretative phenomenological analysis, conversational analysis, grounded theory) please see:

Willig, C. (2008) *Introducing Qualitative Research in Psychology*. Philadelphia: Open University Press.
Smith, J., Flowers, P. and Larkin, M. (2009) *Interpretative Phenomenological Analysis: Theory, Method and Research.* London: Sage Publications.

What are positive psychology interventions?

As with psychology in general, the application of theory is paramount to thoroughly understanding any phenomenon. The next section of the chapter will focus on PPIs and how they differ from 'normal' interventions. We will review the mounting major evidence-based interventions and try exercises along the way. As we came to realize, it is important to try them out in order to understand the impact that they can have.

Why do we need positive interventions?

Remember the 40 per cent solution? This theory is predicated on the basis that although 50 per cent of our happiness levels may be determined by genes and 10 per cent by circumstances, we still have a hefty 40 per cent to work with – hence the interventions.

Definition of PPIs

The clearest and latest definition of positive psychology interventions comes from the meta-analysis by Sin and Lyubomirsky, who defined PPIs as:

> 66 Treatment methods or intentional activities that aim to cultivate positive feelings, behaviours or cognitions . . . Programs, interventions, or treatments aimed at fixing, remedying, or healing something that is pathological or deficient – as opposed to building strengths – do not fit the definition of a PPI.
>
> – *(Sin and Lyubomirsky, 2009: 468).* 99

Although this definition appears divisive, it enables researchers to conceptualize the differences between PPIs and 'psychology as usual' interventions.

Think about it...

What is YOUR definition of a positive psychology intervention?

What makes it different from mainstream psychology interventions?
Who should they be used on?
When should we employ them?

Birth of the first PPI

Michael Fordyce (1977) was one of the pioneers in implementing positive psychological intervention programmes. In fact, he piloted several experimental conditions over several years, on hundreds of college students, to create his programme, *14 Basic Happiness Principles* (Fordyce, 1981, 1983). The theoretical underpinning of the programme is that, if people can try and enhance these 14 characteristics found in very happy people, they too will become happy. The 14 principles include:

- be more active and keep busy;
- spend more time socializing;
- be productive at meaningful work;
- get better organized and plan things out;
- stop worrying;
- lower your expectations and aspirations;
- develop positive, optimistic thinking;
- get present oriented;
- work on a healthy personality;
- develop an outgoing, social personality;
- be yourself;
- eliminate negative feelings and problems;
- close relationships are the number one source of happiness;
- value happiness.

For further information, see Fordyce (1981). Since Fordyce's work, some of these principles have been upheld via scientific research. Unfortunately, Fordyce's work has been overlooked by many new 'positive psychologists' and a return to the beginning is necessary to paint the whole picture of intervention research.

PPIs in the noughties

So just how many PPIs are there? Seligman et al.'s (2005) review of the literature yielded over 100. Using the definition mentioned above, Sin and Lyubomirsky (2009) found 51. Finally, in her well documented book *The How of Happiness,* Lyubomirsky (2008) proposed that there are 12 mechanisms that underpin PPIs with enough validation behind them to count as appropriate for use. To this day, however, only a few positive interventions have been empirically tested compared to the number of interventions that exist. Positive psychology needs controlled lab setting investigations on specific interventions as well as longitudinal studies. Furthermore, stricter observance of the participants after the intervention is needed in order to decipher whether or not participants continue with the intervention, which will influence the follow-up results.

Do the same interventions work the same on everyone?

In a word, no! This is a very important point to get across. As we are all individuals, with our own idiosyncratic tendencies, each intervention will not suit everyone. This discovery was made by Lyubomirsky and her team as they sought to understand why some interventions worked for some people but not for others (Lyubomirsky et al., 2005; Lyubomirsky, 2006). They concluded that there has to be a good 'fit' with the interventions and three main criteria:

- fit with the source of your unhappiness,
- fit with your strengths,
- fit with your lifestyle.

The Person–Activity Fit Diagnostic (Lyubomirsky, 2008) asks you to consider 12 activities and judge whether they would feel natural or forced. Lyubomirsky's team have found a significant correlation between a person's fit scores and their adherence to interventions as well as wellbeing scores following the intervention. Another contribution from Lyubomirsky concerns the importance of variety. Following several research studies, the team concluded that people who included variety into their interventions had greater increases in wellbeing. The researchers explain these findings as a result of hedonic adaptation theory. Thus, if you are going to take up any of these, it is best to shake things up.

We would like to ask you to flip to the Person–Activity Fit Diagnostic section located at the end of this chapter. Please fill it in and keep it in mind as we go through the interventions.

Validated interventions

So what interventions have been properly validated and are accepted in the positive psychology profession? The following is a list of those interventions/theories that have underpinned the positive psychology research discipline and shown promising results. The section is divided into the main mechanisms that seem to channel the positive outcomes of the intervention.

Gratitude

The first and most robust research falls under the mechanism of expressing gratitude. Gratitude is the underlying concept for many positive psychology interventions as it promotes the savouring of positive events and may counteract hedonic adaptation. Several conceptually related studies have taken a different perspective on how gratitude can increase wellbeing.[1] For example, it appears that when people count their blessings once a week there is an increase in wellbeing. This does not hold true for people who count their blessings more than three times a week. It is postulated that the exercise could become more like a chore and lose meaningfulness and effectiveness. Thus, with gratitude, the method of implementation is key to success!

In another prominent study, people who engaged in counting their blessings (versus burdens) tended to experience more joy, energy, attentiveness and pro-social behaviour. As gratitude and blessings bring up different associations (religious connotations), this intervention has been renamed as 'three good things' (Emmons and McCullough, 2003). Seligman puts another twist on this intervention, asking people to write down three good things that happened to them that day, and their role in bringing about the events. This taps into positive internal explanatory styles, highlighting how we can control our daily positive experiences (Seligman et al., 2005).

Finally, one of the most powerful (albeit fleeting) positive impacts on wellbeing is the Gratitude Visit (Seligman et al., 2005). The Gratitude Visit or Gratitude Letter requires you to write a letter to someone you never properly thanked. You can either read the letter out loud in person or send the letter through the mail (although the first format is ideal). Even more interesting is that this exercise works even when you don't send the letter (Lyubomirsky et al., 2006).

Ultimately, gratitude is an imperative component for wellbeing, which forces people to step back and reflect upon what and whom they have in their life, as well as counteract complacency and 'taken-for-grantedness'. Furthermore, recent findings propose that adolescents and children that are low in positive affect will benefit most from this type of intervention (Froh, Kashdan, Ozimkowski, and Miller, 2009).

Savouring and positive reminiscence

Another underpinning mechanism by which PPIs are believed to work is through the process of *savouring*. You may have already heard of savouring or its other synonyms (basking, rejoicing, enjoying, relishing, luxuriating, cherishing, etc.); however, leading experts in the area, Bryant and Veroff (2007) argue that the latter concepts are much narrower, and that savouring actually encompasses these synonyms.

So what do we mean by savouring? Savouring is defined as 'The capacity to attend to, appreciate and enhance the positive experiences in one's life.' It is important to distinguish savouring as a process and not as an outcome – thus it is something we do, and not something that happens – and it requires active engagement on the person's behalf. Therefore, savouring requires us to slow down and attend intently to our surroundings, feelings, experiences. Stretch out the experience.

So how do we savour?

Bryant and Veroff (2007) propose that savouring can be done in terms of three time orientations, four processes and 10 strategies. How people decide to savour is entirely up to them. In terms of time orientation, people can engage in savouring through (1) the past (reminiscing), (2) the present (savouring the moment) or (3) the future (anticipating). Bryant and Veroff propose four savouring processes including:

(1) thanksgiving (gratitude); (2) basking (pride); (3) marvelling (awe); and (4) luxuriating (physical pleasure).

Finally, there are 10 identified strategies that can be employed in order to enhance savouring across time orientation and process. This section will review these strategies and how you can employ them in your daily life.

1 *Sharing with others.* Sharing positive experiences with others is the single strongest predictor of level of enjoyment. This, of course, is more so with extraverts than introverts. Sharing with others may foster bonding and reinforce healthy relationships for several reasons. First of all, it is pleasant to be with and watch loved ones enjoy themselves. Also, others may point out pleasurable aspects that one may have not noticed and we may become more playful in the presence of others. A desire to share the pleasure makes us more attentive to all the pleasurable details of the experience.

2 *Memory building.* When we experience a positive event we can engage in memory building, which is simply actively taking vivid mental photographs for future recall. This strategy is correlated with a desire to share with others.

3 *Comparing.* Comparing is a difficulty strategy to employ. Research shows us that people who engage in downward social comparison can indeed enhance their own wellbeing; however, when people engage in upward social comparison they may dampen their enjoyment if comparing to someone better off than them.

4 *Sensory-perceptual sharpening.* This strategy asks you to intensify pleasure by focusing on certain stimuli and blocking out others.

5 *Self-congratulation.* Sometimes we just don't have someone beside us or in our life to help us celebrate our accomplishments. This strategy can sometimes be inappropriate but it has its place. It is not to be confused with pride or boasting – it is simple self-congratulation that requires telling yourself how proud you are or how impressed others may be.

6 *Absorption.* This can be described as allowing yourself to get totally immersed in the moment, or akin to self-induced flow.

7 *Behavioural expression.* When we smile, can we actually induce positive emotions/feelings? Can laughing, giggling, jumping up and down and dancing around change our mood? There is a lot of evidence that outwardly expressing positive feelings can intensify them.

8 *Temporal awareness.* This strategy asks you to acknowledge the fleeting moments of time and to engage in *carpe diem.*

9 *Counting blessings.* Of course, we now know the importance of reminding ourselves of our good fortune and thinking about how lucky we are. Take some time to count your blessings at the end of the day or the week.

10 *Killjoy thinking.* The tenth strategy is actually a 'how not to' strategy in the 10 ways of savouring. Basically, it highlights the fact that if you engage in worry, ruminative thought or killjoy thinking, there will be no room for savouring experiences.

What inhibits savouring?

One of the biggest obstacles to savouring is focusing too much on the evaluation of the positive feelings, and not allowing the experiences/feelings to just happen. You have to be careful not to 'push savouring' upon yourself (Lyubomirsky et al., 2006; Bryant and Veroff, 2007).

Studies have been done that reviewed the methods that people use to savour experiences. For example, researchers asked people to either: (1) write about their happiest day or (2) think about it by either (1) systematically analysing or (2) replaying it in their mind.

Replaying of the experience was the most beneficial condition. Researchers concluded that writing and talking require more planning than thinking and infer that overanalysis makes savouring difficult.

However, recent research has tried to separate the difference between systematically analysing happy moments (thereby increasing interest) versus replaying them (thereby increasing positive affect). Researchers have found that while systematically analysing can increase interest it does not induce further pleasantness, whereas simple mental replay can induce both interest and pleasantness (Vittersø, Overwien, and Martinsen, 2009).

Think about it...

OK – it's now practice time! Find a friend, classmate or family member to practise savouring with. Get one person to be the coach and one to be the 'savourer'. Take them through one of the nine savouring processes.
  Activity debrief:

  - Anything surprise you about this exercise?
  - What was challenging for the coach or savourer?
  - What did you learn?

Expressive writing paradigms: optimism and insight

The expressive writing interventions stem from the results of trauma research where scientists found that trauma survivors were able to find meaning through expressive writing (Pennebaker, 1997, 2004). Many studies have replicated and extended the expressive writing design where survivors are asked to write about a painful, distressing experience in detail for 15–30 minutes, for three consecutive days.[2] Individuals who write expressively about past traumatic events make fewer visits to doctors, have enhanced immune functioning, and report less distress and depression than individuals who do not. Pennebaker admits that, although we know that the intervention works, we don't understand why and for whom. One reason proposed is the *catharsis hypothesis,* which dictates that the exercise allows people to write freely without judgement or restraint on paper, and can help organize thoughts and emotions.

So where's the positive side to this? Burton and King (2004) decided to see if the same positive outcomes of writing would work when participants were asked to recall *intensely positive experiences* (IPEs) as opposed to traumatic ones. Intensely positive experiences were operationalized as 'intensely positive emotional experiences (E.g. wonder, happiness, ecstasy, love from graduation, family, children, vacations, etc.).' Following several randomized controlled trials in the same format as Pennebaker's studies, results have concluded that writing about IPEs can enhance mood, health (fewer illnesses and visits to doctor), insight and self-examination.

King (2001) took this concept of writing about positive experiences and created a second, well validated intervention titled 'best possible self'. The best possible self is a narrative description of you as your best possible self, when everything you wish to have come true has. Again, after 15–30 minutes, for three to four consecutive days, results showed that the intervention group had increased subjective wellbeing, decreased illness for five months, enhanced insight into motives and emotions, optimism, self-regulation and confidence. This exercise has been repeatedly shown to enhance positive emotions (Sheldon and Lyubomirsky, 2006). More importantly, this exercise can highlight and restructure priorities by listing main goals and subgoals. Lyubomirsky (2008) recommends taking this further to break down how exactly the person is to achieve these larger goals, using a BPS (best possible selves) diary.

Watkins et al. (2008) married the writing paradigm with the concept of gratefulness. In their experiment, they asked participants to recall an unpleasant open memory. Those that were asked to recall consequences for the event that they felt they could now be grateful for experienced more memory closure, less unpleasant emotional impact and less intrusiveness than those that were asked to only write about the event itself or neutral topics (Watkins et al., 2008).

Random acts of kindness

One of the biggest criticisms of positive psychology is its fixation on hedonic individual happiness (Van Deurzen, 2009). This couldn't be more wrong or disputed as shown by the next intervention. The intervention, *random acts of*

Do it all same day ↓

kindness asks participants to engage in kind acts towards others (for example, holding the door open for a stranger, doing room-mates' dishes). These interventions are thought to bolster self-regard, positive social interactions and charitable feelings towards others. The importance of this exercise is to vary the types of acts that you do and also to do them all on the same day. Reasons for this are that when you repeatedly do the same thing for others, the novelty will wear off and the altruistic act becomes a chore. Likewise, if we are asked to commit five acts of kindness on the same day, we will see and feel a reaction to our kindness.
✗ Researchers have discovered that pro-social behaviour can lose its impact if spread out over the week. Overall, these kindness interventions and many others (for example, Otake et al., 2006) suggest that happiness can be boosted by behavioural intentional activities and that the timing and variety of performing such intentional activities significantly impacts the intervention's effectiveness. As the researchers say, 'Variety is the spice of life', and in PPIs, there is no exception (Lyubomirsky and Sheldon, 2005).

Think about it…

When was the last time you bought something nice for someone else? New research has shown that individuals benefit more from spending money on others then they do spending it on themselves (Dunn et al., 2008). So when you get that birthday money or bonus you were waiting for, think about how and on whom you might spend it!

Active constructive responding

Being truly excited for someone's good news

From Fordyce to Fredrickson, researchers have consistently documented the importance of social relationships to our wellbeing. It goes without saying that when tragedy strikes we need people around us. But what about when things are going well? Gable et al. (2004) decided to look not at how people react to others when they receive bad news but at how they react when someone comes to them with good news. Active constructive responding requires a person to respond with genuine excitement, outwardly displaying their excitement and capitalizing on the other person's success (prolonging discussion of the good news, telling people about it, suggesting celebratory activities). Interestingly Gable found that relationships in which each member engages in active constructive responding tend to flourish as opposed to the other relationships where individuals employ passive constructive, active destructive and passive destructive methods of response (see the 'Think about it . . .' section on the following page).

Think about it…

When someone approaches you with good news, how do you respond?

Are you:

1 Happy for them, but you tend not to make a big deal about it (passive constructive)?
2 Sceptical, and point out why the good news isn't so good at all (active destructive)?
3 Or more of an indifferent reactor (passive destructive)?

The next time a friend comes to you with good news, try and engage in active constructive responding and note the subsequent interactions.

Mindfulness meditation

Mindfulness creates conditions for contentment to develop. Individuals are instructed to practise focusing their attention on the present moment, observing the world and their own thoughts and feelings in a patient, non-judgemental way, without getting caught up in the past or future, or any single line of thinking or preconceived notion (Langer, 2009).

Mindfulness-based stress reduction (Kabat-Zinn) focuses on the management of alterations in body functionality, image, and so forth, while accepting physical changes and attempting to reach mastery over the body. It has been found to enhance management and reduction of pain, psychological distress and control and acceptance of body. It has even been found to reduce stress and depression similar to the effects of cognitive behavioural stress reduction, in addition to enhanced mindfulness, energy and reduced pain beyond 'treatment as usual'.

A new version of meditation currently being tested within positive psychology is *loving-kindness meditation* (Fredrickson et al., 2008). Preliminary results have shown a significant increase in positive emotions and subsequent building of personal resources through the participation in loving-kindness meditation.

Think about it…

Try out a little mindfulness right now by following the personal intervention at the end of the chapter; but remember:

■ Mindfulness means paying attention in a particular way: On purpose, in the present moment, and non-judgmentally . . .

> ■ It does not involve trying to change your thinking. It involves watching thought itself . . .
> ■ It is not to be confused with positive thinking . . .

In conclusion, we believe that positive psychology needs to continue its work on replicating and advancing the PPIs in existence as well as think outside the box when it comes to actual exercises for implementation. For example, and as discussed in the next chapter, PPIs can begin to encompass a more holistic approach, including the body, as well as more active rather than passive leisure activities.

Summary

Reflecting on the learning objectives, you should now understand the concept of positive psychological interventions. More specifically, you should know that:

■ People can choose to adopt either a fixed or growth mindset, with the growth mindset creating more chance for success.
■ Prochaska's transtheoretical model of change demonstrates an interesting perspective on human behaviour change.
■ Grit and perseverance are imperative for success at attaining goals.
■ Self-regulation is important to keep the change going and can be strengthened via self-regulation exercises.
■ There are several ways to evaluate PPIs, with qualitative inquiry enabling a more in-depth understanding.
■ There are not many validated PPIs, however a recent meta-analysis shows that they are helpful in making people happier.
■ Gratitude is a fundamental mechanism in enhancing and maintaining wellbeing.
■ Mindfulness meditation is a fast-growing area, with current scientific evidence to show its positive effects on wellbeing.

Suggested Resources

http://www.carol-dweck.co.uk/
To access information regarding Carol Dweck and a schedule of her upcoming talks, follow the link above. She is one lecturer you don't want to miss!

http://www.faculty.ucr.edu/~sonja/song.html

This will enable you to log onto the leading positive psychology researcher, Sonja Lyubomirsky, to access details on her happiness laboratory as well as publications and updates on wellbeing.

http://www.signalpatterns.com/iphone/livehappy_std.html

Happiness has now entered the twenty-first century, with interventions and tools at your fingertips. Log onto the website, or use ITunes, to download Sonja Lyubomirsky's 'LIVE HAPPY' App for the iphone.

Further questions for you

1 Can you think of an example when you changed your mindset?

2 Of these interventions, how many do you already use?

3 What are your reactions to your Fit scores?

4 Will you engage in any that are not in your top four? Why or why not?

Personal Development Interventions

The exercises presented below ask you to engage in several interventions that have been scientifically shown to enhance your wellbeing. The first relates to strengths, whereas the second is an activity we do with our undergraduate and MSc students.

1 Signature strengths

After Identifying your top five signature strengths, try and use them in a new way, every day, for one week. Alternatively, you could choose your bottom five and try and cultivate them throughout the seven days. Monitor the positive emotions, such as vitality, excitement, authenticity, etc., that you experience but using these strengths in a new and creative way.

2 Portfolio

For the next month, try to incorporate as many PPIs into your daily routine as you can to assess their feasibility and effectiveness. Keep a 'scientific diary' so that you can record your thoughts and experiences and reflect once you have finished the four weeks. How do the results compare to the original research? Did they work? Why or why not?

You can take this further and collate the exercises you completed throughout the textbook (for example, answers to your *Think about it . . .* sections), as well as the questionnaires, and put them into the portfolio for a scrapbook of your personal experiences and journey over the course of the semester.

Measurement Tools

Person–Activity Fit Diagnostic

(Lyubomirsky, 2008)

Directions

Consider each of the following 12 happiness activities. Reflect on what it would be like to do it every week for an extended period of time. Then rate each activity by writing the appropriate number (1–7) in the blank space next to the terms *Natural, Enjoy, Value, Guilty and Situation*.

People do things for many different reasons. Please rate why you might keep doing this activity in terms of each of the following reasons. Use the scale provided:

1	2	3	4	5	6	7
not at all			somewhat			very much

NATURAL: I'll keep doing this activity because it will feel 'natural' to me and I'll be able to stick with it.

ENJOY: I'll keep doing this activity because I will enjoy doing it; I'll find it to be interesting and challenging.

VALUE: I'll keep doing this activity because I will value and identify with doing it; I'll do it freely even when it's not enjoyable.

GUILTY: I'll keep doing this activity because I would feel ashamed, guilty, or anxious if I didn't do it; I'll force myself.

SITUATION: I'll keep doing this activity because somebody else will want me to or because my situation will force me to.

1 Expressing gratitude. Counting your blessings for what you have (either to a close one or privately, through contemplation or a journal) or conveying your gratitude and appreciation to one or more individuals whom you've never properly thanked.

     ✓ NATURAL ___ ENJOY___ VALUE ___ GUILTY ___ SITUATION

2 Cultivating optimism. Keeping a journal in which you imagine and write about the best possible future for yourself or practising to look at the bright side of every situation.

     ✓ NATURAL ___ ENJOY ___ VALUE ___ GUILTY ___ SITUATION

3 Avoiding overthinking and social comparison. Using strategies (such as distraction) to cut down on how often you dwell on your problems and compare yourself with others.

___ NATURAL ___ ENJOY ✔ VALUE ___ GUILTY ___ SITUATION

4 Practising random acts of kindness. Doing good things for others, whether friends or strangers, either directly or anonymously, either spontaneously or planned.

___ NATURAL ✔ ENJOY ___ VALUE ___ GUILTY ___ SITUATION

5 Nurturing relationships. Picking a relationship in need of strengthening, and investing time and energy in healing, cultivating, affirming, and enjoying it.

✔ NATURAL ___ ENJOY ___ VALUE ___ GUILTY ___ SITUATION

6 Developing strategies for coping. Practising ways to endure or surmount a recent stress, hardship, or trauma.

___ NATURAL ___ ENJOY ✔ VALUE ___ GUILTY ___ SITUATION

7 Learning to forgive. Keeping a journal or writing a letter in which you work on letting go of anger and resentment toward one or more individuals who have hurt or wronged you.

___ NATURAL ___ ENJOY ___ VALUE ✔ GUILTY ___ SITUATION

8 Doing more activities that truly engage you. Increasing the number of experiences at home and work in which you 'lose' yourself and are challenging and absorbing (i.e. flow experiences).

___ NATURAL ✔ ENJOY ___ VALUE ___ GUILTY ___ SITUATION

9 Savouring life's joys. Paying close attention, taking delight, and replaying life's momentary pleasures and wonders, through thinking, writing, drawing, or sharing with one another.

___ NATURAL ✔ ENJOY ___ VALUE ___ GUILTY ___ SITUATION

10 Committing to your goals. Picking one, two, or three significant goals that are meaningful to you and devoting time and effort to pursuing them.

___ NATURAL ___ ENJOY ✔ VALUE ___ GUILTY ___ SITUATION

11 Practising religion and spirituality. Becoming more involved in your church, temple, or mosque or reading and pondering spiritually themed books.

___ NATURAL ✔ ENJOY ___ VALUE ___ GUILTY ___ SITUATION

12. Taking care of your body. Engaging in physical activity, meditating, and smiling and laughing.

      ___ NATURAL ___ ENJOY ✓ VALUE ___ GUILTY ___ SITUATION

Scoring

For each of the 12 activities, subtract the average of the GUILTY and SITUATION ratings from the average of the NATURAL, ENJOY and VALUE ratings. In other words, for each of the 12 activities: Fit score = (Natural + Enjoy +Value)/3 – (Guilty + Situation)/2.

Interpretation

The four activities with the highest Fit scores are those that will work best for you. Write down the four activities. Put them to one side for now and keep in mind as we go through the interventions in detail.

Review

This tool was created in order to determine your best fitting activities/interventions. Our classes report mixed, even polarized, reactions to the results of this test. Either the test tells them what they already know, or else it highlights an activity that they would never have thought of doing themselves. Overall, it is an interesting awareness exercise to get you thinking about what interventions you could incorporate easily into your life.

Notes

1 Froh et al. (2009) summarize nine published studies testing the effects of gratitude interventions.
2 Recent research has even shown that two minutes of writing can enhance individuals' health and wellbeing (Burton and King, 2008).

CHAPTER 9

The Body in Positive Psychology

❖ LEARNING OBJECTIVES

This chapter will review the importance of the body within optimal physical and psychological functioning. More specifically we will focus on how the body can produce both hedonic and eudaimonic pleasure via interpersonal touch, sexual behaviours, nutrition, physical activity and physical pain.

List of topics

- Embodiment.
- The importance of interpersonal touch.
- Positive sexual behaviours and wellbeing.
- Nutrition and its role in optimal functioning.
- Physical activity and wellbeing.
- Physical pain and eudaimonic wellbeing.

MOCK ESSAY QUESTIONS

1 Why has psychology ignored the role of the body for so long? Discuss with reference to the five components of a positive body.

2 Critically discuss the role of interpersonal touch in wellbeing (as broadly defined).

3 How can physical activity interventions be employed to enhance societal wellbeing?

As positive psychology continues to make leaps and bounds in terms of scientific advancement and understanding, the focus on the importance of the body within optimal physical and psychological functioning is still lagging. Combining the elements of both hedonic and eudaimonic wellbeing, we propose that we can create a 'positive body' via five core mechanisms: human touch, positive sexual behaviour, physical activity, nutrition and even physical pain. These five components assist either momentary experiences of pleasure or longer lasting feelings of meaning and self-development.

Chapter 9 will commence with a brief review of the history of the body in psychology and the two main 'types of happiness' (hedonic and eudaimonic) (Kashdan et al., 2008: 219) before delving into what Hefferon (in press b) described as the five components of a 'positive body'. Although this is not exhaustive, it is the one of the first of its kind to put these theoretical links together within positive psychology (see Hefferon, in press b). Indeed, it seems unfeasible for positive psychology to continue as a 'neck up focused discipline' (Seligman, 2008) without recognizing the important role of the body in a healthy and happy mind (Resnick et al., 2001; Hefferon et al., 2010; Hefferon and Mutrie, in press).

The body in psychology

For millennia, humans have been grappling with the intricate complexities of mind–body interactions. Commonplace throughout contemporary medicine and psychology (Passer and Smith, 2006), Monism (the foundation of empiricism) maintains that the mind and body are one, holding no separate spiritual properties; what we think and feel is a direct result of physical reactions in the brain. This chapter, however, argues that ultimately, our body affects our emotions, feelings and experiences. The humanistic movement has dedicated much of its time to extending this concept of embodiment (how people experience having and using their body), whilst criticizing positive psychology for its lack of engagement with the body in wellbeing.

Types of happiness

Positive psychology has traditionally conceptualized authentic happiness as a mix of hedonic and eudaimonic wellbeing (Lent, 2007; Seligman and Csikszentmihalyi, 2000). Within the two types of happiness stem three distinct lifestyles: the pleasurable life, the engaged life and the meaningful life. The pleasurable life encompasses feelings of positive emotions, which are integral components to our success and wellbeing. The pleasurable life is further broken down into two further categories: pleasures and gratifications. Pleasures include nice smells, tastes, sexual feelings and so forth whereas gratifications include activities (such as reading, or cooking) that require some forward planning (Rashid, 2009a). Thankfully, our bodies have the ability to induce these feelings of pleasure, desire and positive emotions.

The body can also assist in creating the engaged life. Flow, via participation in physical activity, can induce a sense of engagement, absorption and wellbeing after the fact. Furthermore, engaging in tactical behaviours with your loved ones can develop a deeper and more meaningful relationship.

Finally, the body has a tremendous power to induce the meaningful life, evident in reports of spiritual and embodied transcendence. Individuals, whose bodies have undergone extreme physical pain consistently report a sense of meaning and spiritual connection via the wounded self (Frank, 1995).

Nevertheless, many in our society have forgotten how important it is to have physical bodily pleasures, which can also eventually lead to more eudaimonic achievements. The next section will outline the five proposed components of a positive body in relation to both hedonic and eudaimonic wellbeing.

Five components of a positive body

Interpersonal touch

Over the past few decades, psychologists have become increasingly aware of the importance of human touch for physical and psychological wellbeing (Gallace and Spence, 2010). The first evidence demonstrating the importance of interpersonal touch came from Harry Harlow's studies where baby chimps chose a warm and cuddly, or rather a 'touchable' surrogate mother, with no food, over a steel, unforgiving mother, with an abundance of food (Harlow and Zimmermann, 1959). Today, the Miami based Touch Research Institute has conducted hundreds of clinical studies on the importance of interpersonal touch (massage therapy, clinical reflexology, hugging and so forth) on physical and psychological wellbeing in both clinical and normal populations (Field et al., 2004; Gallace and Spence, 2010). These studies have provided a base for the development of 'touch science'.

The intervention technique with the most considerable amount of research is massage therapy (MT).[2] The evidence suggests that MT has the ability to enhance both physical and psychological functioning. Physically, when employed with infants who are at risk (premature), MT can help their ability to gain weight, increase temperature and gain more sleep (Dieter et al., 2003; Diego et al., 2008). As children grow older, MT has been found to help with attention deficit hyperactivity disorder (ADHD), arthritis, asthma and aggression (Field et al., 1997, 1998; Diego et al., 2002). In adults, MT can reduce migraines (Hernandez-Reif et al., 1998), premenstrual symptoms (Hernandez-Reif et al., 2000), blood pressure (Moyer et al., 2004) and cortisol levels (Field et al., 2005), as well as increase immune and neuro-endocrine functioning in breast cancer and HIV patients (Diego et al., 2001; Hernandez-Reif et al., 2004, 2005) and serotonin and dopamine neurotransmitters (Field et al., 2005).

Psychologically, MT interventions have reported significant reductions in depression (Field et al., 2004), similar to the efficiency of traditional psychotherapy (Moyer et al., 2004). Massage therapy appears to be beneficial even when administered in single doses.

Why does MT seem to have such a positive effect on our physical and psychological wellbeing? Moyer et al. (2004) propose several theories. The first is the 'gate control' theory of pain reduction. More specifically, this proposes that by causing pressure in other areas, apart from the areas of pain, MT will block pain (close the gate) to the original site of trauma. Secondly, it is believed that MT may promote the 'activation of the parasympathetic nervous system', which would reduce anxiety states and may induce wellbeing (Sarafino, 2002). More recently, the theory of 'changes in body chemistry' has been suggested due to evidence of increased serotonin levels and other endorphins in the blood after a session of MT. This change in body chemistry is linked to a further theory, that MT can aid in the 'production of restorative sleep'. Within sports research, MT is believed to work via 'mechanical means', so that 'MT may break down subcutaneous adhesions and prevent fibrosis as well as promote circulation of blood and lymph' (Moyer et al., 2004: 5). Finally, it is thought that the promising effects of MT on pain may be due to the 'interpersonal attention' that one receives from the massage therapist. Like the effects of psychotherapy, it may be the influence of the relationship that changes the wellbeing of the patients and not necessarily the choice of intervention itself (Messer and Wampold, 2002). Although criticisms have been made about the selection criteria for participants, blind controls and randomization techniques, the research shows that for both clinical and normal populations, interpersonal touch via MT can have a significant effect on self-report and objective measurements of physical and psychological wellbeing.

Think about it...

What do you think is causing the beneficial effects of MT? If you have had a massage, what did you like about it? What did you dislike?

Clinical reflexology also has several research bodies attempting to establish proper scientific evidence for the use of reflexology in promoting wellbeing. Following from several randomized controlled trials (RCT), the evidence suggests that reflexology can be used to aid in the reduction of anxiety, depression, headaches and pain symptoms among cancer (Stephenson et al., 2003; Sharp et al., 2010) and multiple sclerosis patients (Siev-Ner et al., 2003) as well as menopausal women (Williamson et al., 2002), in addition to enhancing mental health (Oleson and Flocco, 1993). Again, an explanation for the benefits of reflexology has been the interpersonal connection/influence of the practitioner; however, researchers have started to include control groups that undergo generic foot massages, thus equalizing the effects of simple human contact (Williamson et al., 2002). Issues within this field surround the disagreement among practitioners regarding reflexology mapping and a lack of standardized training centres.

Research into the physiological effects of embracing (hugging) has offered exciting insight into the positive effects of this intimate behaviour. For example, engaging in hugging behaviours, as well as kissing, with your partner can significantly reduce psychological distress and influence proteins that may promote health and wellbeing (Grewen et al., 2005; Matsunaga et al., 2009). Hugs between partners can also reduce cortisol levels, blood pressure and induce higher levels of oxytocin (the bonding hormone) (Grewen et al., 2003; Light et al., 2005).

Thus, interpersonal touch (presented here in the form of MT, clinical reflexology and hugging) has shown mounting evidence of its importance for physical and psychological wellbeing. Hedonically, touch can produce feelings of joy, contentment and serenity (Rolls et al., 2003; Kringelbach, 2004, 2009), while also allowing us to fulfil more eudaimonic achievements, such as connections and bonding with those we love.

Human sexual behaviour

There are very few species that engage in sexual behaviours outwith the purpose of reproduction.[3] Beyond procreation, sexual psychologists have identified several theories (237 in fact) as to why humans have sex (Meston and Buss, 2007). Fundamentally, engaging in sexual activity feels good physically, emotionally and psychologically. Despite this, sexual behaviour is usually associated with risk, shame, guilt and disease. These negative perceptions of human sexual behaviour can be attributed to the rapid increase in the prevalence of sexually transmitted diseases (STDs); rising 63 per cent from 2000 to 2010 in Britain. These diseases (for example, hepatitis C, gonorrhoea, chlamydia, herpes and AIDS) can have detrimental and even fatal consequences, which add to the negative stigma of sexual engagement (NHS Sexual Health, 2010).

Think about it...

W hy do you think STDs are on the rise, around the globe, despite the increase in sexual health education and government campaigns?

Although several scientists were interested in the area of sexuality (for example, Krafft-Ebbing, Freud, Ellis) the discipline of sexual psychology was established by scientist Alfred Kinsey (1894–1956). Kinsey and his research team conducted one of the most fascinating and pioneering studies that remains today one of the leading data sets on sexual practices in the US.[4] After conducting over 18,500 interviews with both males and females on several sexual behaviour practices, they found that, despite a very prudish society 'on the outside', sexual behaviours were quite varied and rampant across society (Kinsey et al., 1953).[5] For example, results demonstrated that most people were not always clearly defined as either heterosexual or homosexual, with nearly 46 per cent of males and 6–14 per cent of females revealing bisexual tendencies. Also, 50 per cent of males and 26 per cent of females admitted to having an extramarital affair. Since the Kinsey reports, sexual behavioural science has improved tremendously in understanding the complexity of human sexuality and how it relates to wellbeing. With sophisticated sexual psychophysiology labs,[6] researchers can study the physiology and anatomy of sexual intercourse.

237

Cindy Meston and David Buss, researchers from the University of Texas at Austin, have spent the past decades researching sexual psychology. In 2007, they conducted a media stirring study that identified 237 reasons why humans have sex, including physical, psychological and emotional rationales. Meston and Buss found that people have sex because they are bored; for spiritual connections; felt sorry for the person; needed to feel power; needed to degrade themselves; to punish themselves; hurt others; express love and many more (Meston and Buss, 2007). Since this study, Meston and Buss have conducted further research into why women specifically have sex. They interviewed 3000 women to discover why they have sex using the 237 reasons as a guideline. They found supportive evidence for their original study's results, as well as in-depth, provocative data from the women interviewed. Overall, sex was often regarded as 'a pleasurable experience, giving the women a sense of excitement, love, connection and self-exploration' (Meston and Buss, 2009:20).

See Meston and Buss (2007, 2009) for the original articles.

Engaging in sexual practices can have physical and psychological benefits for both genders. Physically, scientists have found that engaging in sexual intercourse can have a surprisingly beneficial impact, resulting in better physical shape, reduced blood pressure, increased immune system functioning, reduced cancer risk (prostate) and even a longer life (Janssen and Everaerd, 1993; Davey Smith et al., 1997; Brody et al.,

2000; Bancroft et al., 2003; Brody, 2006, 2010). Neurologically speaking, it appears there is a multitude of connections at work during sexual peak. As in the physiological response to drug taking, the brain's nucleus accumbens activates the 'pleasure centre' (Kringelbach, 2009), releasing neurotransmitters such as dopamine, serotonin, epinephrine and norepinephrine at climax, signalling to the body that what it is experiencing is good.

Immediately following orgasm, the endocrine system (androgens, estrogens, progesterone) kicks in, secreting the hormone prolactin, which can cause the feeling of sleepiness. The body's 'bonding' hormone, oxytocin, is also released at this time inducing feelings of relaxation, sedation, decreased anxiety and connectedness.

Psychologically, sexual intercourse can enhance exposure to moments of intense joy, relaxation and ecstasy; increased self-esteem and confidence (Meston and Buss, 2007); feelings of love and connection to another (Meston and Buss, 2009); reduced anxiety and depression and enhanced overall quality of life (Janssen and Everaerd, 1993; Bancroft et al., 2003). It appears that all of these benefits can come from engaging in sexual practices, as long as the behaviours are engaged in with someone you have a trusting relationship with. People who have sex with someone they care about report much higher levels of wellbeing, confidence and self-esteem than those who engage in sexual practices with strangers. Furthermore, research has shown that engagement in sexual practices can lead to self-development and growth (Meston and Buss, 2009).

Consequently, human sexual behaviours, when practised safely and with a trusted partner, can have positive physiological and psychological effects for those involved. Sexual behaviours can lead to enhanced physical wellbeing, aside from the obvious gratification and ecstasy associated with orgasm (hedonic happiness). Furthermore, people report sexual intercourse as enabling the development of the self, enhancing self-esteem and confidence as well as helping them to become more complete (eudaimonic happiness).

Physical activity and wellbeing

Physical activity (PA) and positive psychology are a match made in heaven – one focuses on the building of happy, fully functioning people (positive psychology) and the other is a tried and tested avenue for creating such positive people (physical activity). Without a doubt, engaging in physical activity is one of the most important things, if not the most important thing, that a person can do to enhance optimal functioning. Not only does physical activity enhance physical functioning, thereby reducing the risks of disease but it can also make us happier, more energized, confident, self-regulated individuals and even make us smarter (Ratey, 2008).[7]

Despite knowing that exercise is good for us, the human species is not functioning as it was originally designed to. Our bodies were and are designed to be hunters and gatherers (Astrand, 1994). However, reports suggest that we are now physically functioning at nearly a third of what we used to 100 years ago (Tudor-Locke and

Bassett, 2004); and considerably less than 10,000 years ago. One of the major barriers to exercise implementation is the misconception that activity needs to be painful and extensive and is only for 'athletic types'. Luckily, we don't need to train like elite athletes to reap the benefits of activity. Physical activity refers to any type of movement that results in energy expenditure (for example, walking, climbing stairs, gardening or yoga). The daily recommendation in the UK is currently 30 minutes of moderate to high intensity physical activity at least five times per week. The good news is that PA can be broken down into short bursts throughout the day (3 × 10 minute sessions), which still gives us a boost in mood and vitality (Backhouse, 2009). The important thing is to get the heart beating above resting level (you would need to operate at between 60 and 75 per cent of your maximum heart rate).[8] Physical activity must not be confused with *exercise*, which is more deliberate and structured with a clear focus on fitness progression. Thus, an aerobic class, training for a run, or anything along the traditional line of activity falls under this category (Biddle and Mutrie, 2007). For the purpose of this chapter, we refer to PA and exercise interchangeably.

Think about it...

Do you exercise? Why or why not? What happens when you start? What happens when you stop?

So what can exercise do for us in terms of promoting optimal functioning? On a physical level, individuals who participate in activity can reduce their risk of developing several illnesses such as obesity, cardiovascular disease, coronary heart disease, stroke, diabetes (type 2), osteoporosis, some sleep disorders, high blood pressure, certain cancers (colon, breast, rectal, lung, prostate, endometrial) and even premature death (Salonen et al., 1983; Paffenbarger et al., 1986). Fortuitously, it is never too late to start. Epidemiological studies show that people who were previously sedentary but start exercising later on in life still live longer than those who never initiated exercise at all (Camacho et al., 1991).

Psychological benefits include enhanced general wellbeing, body image, self-esteem and self-perceptions (Moses et al., 1989; Fox, 2000; Mutrie and Faulkner, 2004); improved general cognitive functioning among older adults (Boutcher, 2000; Rejeski and Mihalko, 2001; Rejeski et al., 2001); reduced emotional distress (Steptoe et al., 1996); reduced anxiety (McDonald and Hodgdon, 1991) and reduced depression (Babyak et al., 2000; Hassmen et al., 2000; Kritz-Silverstein et al., 2001). It is important to note that physical activity does not simply take away or minimize disease but enhances positive health within individuals. For example, many individuals experience an increase in positive affect and wellbeing after participating in activity. The 'feel good factor' or the 'runner's high' is a common response as to why people exercise and these intense positive emotions can be experienced in acute and chronic forms. Linking to the broaden-and-build theory of positive emotions (Fredrickson, 2001), PA enhances levels of positive affectivity, thereby enabling individuals to build psychological, social, intellectual and physical resources (Kobasa et al., 1985).

AEROBICS

Scientific evidence for the benefits of exercise on mental health came from well-designed research studies by Blumenthal et al. (1999) and Babyak et al. (2000). Participants were randomly assigned into one of three groups:

- exercise (30 minutes aerobic classes three times per week);
- medicine (Zoloft, SSRI antidepressant); and
- exercise plus medicine.

After the 16-week intervention, results showed that all three groups improved. Furthermore, there were no significant differences among groups, except that the medication group recovered faster. However, it is the results at 10 months post intervention that really surprise us. In terms of relapse, 38 per cent of participants in the medication group had relapsed, as did 31 per cent of the participants in the combined medication and exercise group. However, only 9 per cent of the participants in the exercise group relapsed, making this an incredible finding for exercise research.

See the Blumenthal et al. (1999) and Babyak et al. (2000) studies for the original articles.

Within clinical populations, we now know that actually, 'rest is not best'! Research on cancer populations demonstrates that activity participation can induce a higher physical and psychological quality of life (Biddleet al., 2000; Courneya et al., 2000, 2002; Courneya, 2003; Campbell et al., 2005; Weert et al., 2005; Mutrie et al., 2007). For HIV patients, PA participation can reduce HIV progression as well as enhance CD4 T-cell counts (Mustafa et al., 1999; Arey and Beal, 2002). Due to the horrible side effects of chemotherapy and HIV antiretroviral treatment, PA can help combat the alterations in body composition. Even participating in yoga, as opposed to moderate activity, can hold some advantages such as restoring somatic control and increasing efficacy and hope in people with physical illness.

And it's not just the individual who benefits from activity engagement. Engaging in community-run PA groups can build a strong identity and sense of cohesiveness (Fox, 2000). Community PA programmes can also access individuals who are socially excluded such as the elderly or people with mental illness and enable them to engage with other people in similar situations, during a productive activity. Thus, activity participation, and the environment it creates, can facilitate the components of Ryff's model of psychological wellbeing (autonomy, environmental mastery, personal growth, positive relationships, purpose in life, self-acceptance) (Ryff and Singer, 2006).[9] Communities have also extreme economic interests in getting people off the couch and out of sedentary lifestyles. It is estimated that in 2002, physical inactivity cost the UK approximately £8.2bn. Today, that figure is much larger and is predicted to keep on rising (Weiler et al., 2010). Community-based interventions currently in place in the UK include access to parks, trails, and centres and cycling schemes such as cycle lanes and free bikes, promoting greener, healthier travel.

Arguably the most astonishing research in the past decade surrounds the discovery of PA's positive influence on cognitive performance in both students and older adults (Boutcher, 2000). Research done in schools with structured daily physical education (PE) programmes has consistently reported reduced absenteeism, aggressive behaviour, disciplinary actions as well as increased academic achievement and improved in-class behaviour and attention (Ratey, 2008). Unfortunately, the demise of physical education has spread rapidly across the globe, with less than 3.8 per cent of students in the US receiving regular PE (Lee, 1995). The demise has been blamed on the increase in standardized testing, lack of budget for experienced teachers and the potential impact on academic performance. Ironically, education systems are ignoring the new neuroscientific research that shows that participation in activity stimulates learning abilities. Exercise itself doesn't make you smarter, but it does better prepare your mind to attend to and absorb more of the information given. Neuroplasticity is the brain's ability to morph and change with experiences. Cells can and do change and activity participation can help us 'rewire' our brains. Exercise elevates concentrations of serotonin, norepinephrine and dopamine (Ratey, 2008). Furthermore, scientists believe that there is a certain protein, brain-derived neurotrophic factor (BDNF) that causes the brain to develop (Ratey, 2008: 40). Exercise increases the amount of BDNF in the brain, thereby escalating the efficiency of learning and memory.

In sum, participation in physical activity can facilitate wellbeing within individuals and societies. Not only does it keep our bodies healthy but it keeps our mind fit and happy as well.

Think about it...

Activity is great for getting the brain going and growing. So at this point, put your book down, and go for a 10 minute light to moderate walk*, either outside or inside your house. There is no time like the present, and when you get back you will hopefully see an improvement in your ability to attend to new information (Ratey, 2008).

*Please consult with your GP whenever you are about to engage in a new exercise routine.

Nutrition

Since positive psychology focuses on wellbeing it is surprising that there has been little reflection on the potential role of nutrition within the discipline. Again, it is important for us to look at wellbeing in a holistic sense, acknowledging the links between what we do and what we put into the body that can potentially affect our wellbeing. In particular, the following section reviews how maintaining a healthy weight and diet, in addition to the consumption of selected food groups, can positively affect our mental health and wellbeing (Benton and Donohoe, 1999).

Think about it...

How do you feel after eating a high-fat, calorie-laden dinner? Like you want to take on the world? Chances are that this isn't the case. Research has shown that when we gorge on unhealthy food high in saturated fats, we might experience what is called a *high-fat hangover* (Weissmann, 2009; as cited in Rath and Harter, 2010: 205), which can cause our cognitive functioning to decline – although this research was conducted on rats (Murray et al., 2009; Wincour and Greenwood, 2005; as cited in Rath and Harter, 2010). Next time, try to reflect upon how the food choices you make affect your thinking patterns.

Epidemiological evidence has provided researchers and policy makers with convincing evidence as to the importance of maintaining a healthy weight via proper nutrition and physical activity. Having a healthy BMI range (body weight (kg)/height (m^2)) of 18–25 can significantly reduce the risk of several illnesses including certain cancers (for example, of the kidney, oesophagus, colon, gallbladder, and pancreas) (Uhley and Jen, 2007). Nutrition is one of the best ways to fight and prevent obesity, including diets with high levels of fruit, vegetables, fibre and reduced fat intake (Pierce et al., 2004). The United States Department of Agriculture (USDA)[10] recommended daily diet for promotion of physical wellbeing includes:

- grains and grain products (6–11 servings)
- fruits (2–4)
- vegetables (3–5)
- dairy (2)
- lean meats, fish, poultry (2–3)

Why is it that certain foods are better for us than others? Foods that contain the amino acid tryptophan (for example, turkey and bananas) can be absorbed by the body to produce the metabolite 5-Hydroxytryptophan (5HTP), which finally transforms into serotonin (5HT). Serotonin, of course, is the neurotransmitter associated with improved mental health, sleep patterns, energy and lowered levels of depression, stress and premenstrual symptoms (Isaac and Isaac, 2004).

Dopamine is another neurotransmitter frequently linked to the experience of pleasure or hedonic wellbeing. It can be manufactured by breaking down foods that are rich with the amino acid tyrosine. Eating tyrosine-rich foods, such as cheese and chocolate can help fight stress and anxiety and may induce momentary experiences of gratification (Isaac and Isaac, 2004).

With regards to physical illness, the use of food to prevent cancer and cognitive decline has gained rapid popularity. Wolk et al. (2006) found a 74 per cent reduction in developing kidney cancer when women ate one or more servings of fatty fish per week. In addition, other promising connections have been made between omega-3 fatty acids and other physical and mental disorders, such as Alzheimer's, mood, depression and heart disease (El-Mesry et al., 2009, as cited in Rath and Harter, 2010).

The nutritional properties of two other food products in particular are of interest in clinical research on nutrition and wellbeing: chocolate and wine. Ancient civilizations such as Maya and Aztec made use of cacao (chocolate) for pleasure and medicinal purposes. In Britain, during the sixteenth to twentieth centuries, chocolate had many medicinal uses, ranging from the alleviation of emaciation, apathy, fatigue, digestion, fever, gout, kidney stones to poor sexual functioning (Dillinger et al., 2000; Cooper et al., 2008).

Modern-day researchers believe that it is the existence of polyphenols – more specifically, flavanols (flavan-3-ols or catechins) – that account for the physical health benefits of pure chocolate. The theories claim that these catechins increase the number of antioxidants within the blood and aid in the elimination of free radicals. Antioxidants have recently been hailed as *the* anticancer substances and have gained some notoriety. In all, there have been approximately 230 human trials (28 clinical trials) on the effects of chocolate on physical and mental health. These studies have mainly administered and studied only single doses, however researchers argue that the beneficial effects may accumulate. Overall, there is some evidence, both cross-sectional and epidemiological, to show positive links between dark chocolate consumption (100 g/day) and cognition, cancer, diabetes, cardiovascular disease and even all-cause mortality (Mink et al., 2007).[11] A catch, of course, is that the chocolate that has the most impact is dark chocolate (at least 70 per cent). When mixed with milk, it appears that any benefits of the chocolate are dissipated into the bloodstream (Serafini et al., 2003).

Another substance proposed to have positive effects on physical and mental wellbeing is wine. Although the research is not conclusive, it appears that drinking red wine (150 ml/day), particularly older wines from Sardinia and the south-east Mediterranean, can help decrease cardiovascular disease and can increase longevity

(Di Castelnuovo et al., 2003). The research again points to polyphenols (Reservatol) contained in the grape skins, which increase antioxidants and work in much the same way that dark chocolate is thought to work. White wine and beer do not contain these antioxidants to the same extent as red wines, and therefore do not enhance physical wellbeing to the same degree (Di Castelnuovo et al., 2002).

Taken as a whole, the importance of maintaining a healthy weight via a nutritionally balanced diet (with the occasional treat of chocolate and wine) must not be underestimated. Further clinical and independent research is needed to create a solid evidence base, although at present, researchers within clinical illness settings support the use of nutrition as an aid to physical wellbeing (Lent, 2007).

Physical pain

Although controversial and counterintuitive, research suggests that it is possible to experience a sense of eudaimonic wellbeing via the experience of physical pain, such as that experienced during physical illness and body modification (BM).[12]

Although cancer survivorship can be wrought with negative physical and psychological side-effects of diagnosis and treatment, there are also reports of co-existing perceptions of development of the self via the endurance of physical pain. Increased self-efficacy and confidence as well as hope and meaning are common reports after cancer treatment (Low et al., 2007). Some patients even believe that their pain is a form of sanctification, to be redeemed in the after life (Cuevas-Renaud et al., 2000).

A metasynthesis conducted by Hefferon et al. (2009) found that illness survivors perceived that the physical stripping of the body via illness side-effects was imperative for their eventual attainment of psychological growth. Hefferon et al. (2010) also reported that people could gain a sense of inner strength as well as an appreciation for their body when they experience physical deterioration. Furthermore, people can develop a healthier and more appreciative relationship with their body after the experience of physical pain (Hefferon et al., 2008).

Engaging in body modification has traditionally been regarded as a practice of marginalized populations (Fisher, 2002). Within psychology, research has mainly focused on the psychopathology associated with such painful, self-initiated behaviour (Jeffreys, 2000; Cardasis et al., 2008). This has not, however, always been the case. Greek and Roman societies used body art as a symbol of leadership and status, including courage in battle. Other societies have used the practices to solidify individual and group identity, such as Canadian and American First Nations. Lately, researchers have acknowledged the positive experiences and psychological wellbeing (for example, enhanced confidence, authenticity, completeness) that may stem from certain forms of BM.

Current rationales for engaging in BM include reasons of a decorative nature (fashion accessory) (Sweetman, 1999) to more eudaimonic (self-development) pursuits. Tattooing, specifically, can be a form of self-expression and authenticity, allowing tattooed individuals to show their personality as well as their value and belief system. The pain and permanence of tattooing are also major motivators for engaging in BM. Tattooees can derive a sense of achievement and pride via the painful procedure and aftercare process. Reports of increased self-confidence and feelings of 'completeness' (Sweetman, 1999: 19) stem from the fact that not everyone can endure such pain; a person must earn their body modification.

Think about it…

Do you have a tattoo? Think back to when you got it. What were your motivations? Are you still happy with it? If you do not have a tattoo, what are your reasons for not getting one? Is it the permanence or the pain? Or something else? Why do you think others choose to get a tattoo?

By adding such artistic permanence to the self, people derive a sense of pleasure in creating something meaningful, which becomes part of their body (corporeal artefact). They derive authenticity by having the final say in how they look and how they portray themselves to the world. Body modification not only enhances individual identity, but also connects and solidifies certain social groups. From the pleasurable to the more meaningful consequences, the body can derive a sense of wellbeing from pain by way of illness and BM.

Throughout this brief chapter on some of the wonderful, positive effects that the body can bring, there is enough argument to support a shift in the focus of positive psychology to understand how to create positive bodies in addition to positive psychological flourishing. The subject matters of interpersonal touch, sexual behaviours, physical activity, nutrition and even physical pain are just the start of understanding the body and its effects on wellbeing. As with most of the subject matters in positive psychology, there is a need for more rigorous research in all areas and it is exciting to think about the future in this respect.

Ultimately, positive psychology is the science of wellbeing and this should therefore include research on the body and the role it plays in this. Overall, the information presented in this chapter highlights interesting and exciting developments for the discipline of positive psychology. Combining and extending research on positive bodies is what we believe to be part of the future of positive psychology.

Summary

Reflecting on the learning objectives you should now understand the concept of a 'positive body'. More specifically, you should know:

- The body is under-recognized both in positive psychology and psychology in general.
- Interpersonal touch, such as massage therapy and personal contact with others, is important for development and wellbeing.
- Positive sexual behaviours, with a trusted partner, can influence both hedonic and eudaimonic wellbeing.
- Nutrition can play an interesting role in our creation of a 'positive body'.
- Physical activity is one of the most important things we can do for our physical and mental wellbeing.
- The experience of physical pain can cause a transformative experience, thereby enhancing eudaimonic wellbeing.

Suggested Resources

www6.miami.edu/touch-research/
This is Tiffany Field's Touch Research Institute website, which outlines all of the research findings from her work with touch and wellbeing.

www.mestonlab.com/
You can access all of Dr Cindy Meston's work on sexual psychology and also take part in online studies.

http://homepage.psy.utexas.edu/homepage/Group/BussLAB/index.htm
This is the 'Buss Lab' of David Buss, famous evolutionary psychologist, where you can learn more about psychology and evolution.

www.nhs.uk/livewell/fitness/Pages/Fitnesshome.aspx
This NHS website has links for you to learn more about health and fitness, as well as take health check tests and plan your fitness for the New Year.

Further questions for you

1 How often do you give or receive hugs?
2 Why do you think most of the world population does not engage in physical activity?

Personal Development Interventions

We created the following personal development tools to help you reflect on your relationship with your body and how it affects your overall wellbeing.

1 Human touch

For the next seven days, and only when appropriate, try and hug significant others as much as possible. Aim for at least eight hugs a day increasing to 12 if possible, for at least 5 seconds each. Record your reactions and their reactions in a diary at the end of the day. If this is not possible, or appropriate, book into a massage and record your feelings of this interaction. Many universities offer free or discounted sport massages so their students can practise, and you can get a free treatment!

2 Exercise

After consulting with your GP, try and start your own light to moderate physical activity programme. You will be asked, upon clearance from your general practitioner, to engage in 30 minutes of physical activity, at 65 per cent maximum heart rate, three days a week. This can include: aerobics, cleaning, walking, biking and so forth. You can split this into 3 × 10 minute sessions. Please record your thoughts before and after as well as what exercise was achieved (see the table below for an example of a record of activity). Remember to build upon where you are starting from. Take the activity questionnaire to see where you fall in terms of activity levels.

Record of activity

Date	Type of Activity	Duration	Feelings before	Feelings after

Measurement Tools

International Physical Activity Questionnaire (IPAQ)

Directions

We are interested in finding out about the kinds of physical activities that people do as part of their everyday lives. The questions will ask you about the time you spent being physically active in the last seven days. Please answer each question even if you do not consider yourself to be an active person. Please think about the activities you do at work, as part of your house and yard work, to get from place to place and in your spare time for recreation, exercise or sport.

Section 1

Think about all the *vigorous* activities that you did in the *last seven days*. Vigorous physical activities refer to activities that take hard physical effort and make you breathe much harder than normal. Think *only* about those physical activities that you did for at least 10 minutes at a time.

1. During the *last 7 days,* on how many days did you do **vigorous** physical activities like heavy lifting, digging, aerobics, or fast bicycling?

   _____   **days per week**

   ☐ No vigorous physical activities ⟶ *Skip to question 3*

2. How much time did you usually spend doing **vigorous** physical activities on one of those days?

   _____   **hours per day**

   _____   **minutes per day**

   ☐ Don't know/Not sure

Section 2

Think about all the *moderate* activities that you did in the *last 7 days. Moderate* activities refer to activities that take moderate physical effort and make you breathe somewhat harder than normal. Think only about those physical activities that you did for at least 10 minutes at a time.

3. During the *last 7 days,* on how many days did you do **moderate** physical activities like carrying light loads, bicycling at a regular pace, or doubles tennis? Do not include walking.

_____ **days per week**

☐ No moderate physical activities ⟶ ***Skip to question 5***

4. How much time did you usually spend doing *moderate* physical activities on one of those days?

_____ **hours per day**

_____ **minutes per day**

☐ Don't know/Not sure

Section 3

Think about the time you spent *walking* in the *last 7 days.* This includes at work and at home, walking to travel from place to place, and any other walking that you might do solely for recreation, sport, exercise, or leisure.

5. During the *last 7 days,* on how many days did you *walk* for at least 10 minutes at a time?

_____ **days per week**

☐ No walking ⟶ ***Skip to question 7***

6. How much time did you usually spend *walking* on one of those days?

_____ **hours per day**

_____ **minutes per day**

☐ Don't know/Not sure

Section 4

The last question is about the time you spent *sitting* on weekdays during the *last 7 days.* Include time spent at work, at home, while doing course work and during leisure time. This may include time spent sitting at a desk, visiting friends, reading, or sitting or lying down to watch television.

7. During the *last 7 days,* how much time did you spend *sitting* on a *week day?*

_____ **hours per day**

_____ **minutes per day**

☐ Don't know/Not sure

Scoring and interpretation

This tool is based on categorical scores, with three proposed levels of physical activity:

1 Low (category 1)
This is the lowest level of physical activity. Those individuals who do not meet the criteria for categories 2 or 3 are considered inactive.

2 Moderate (category 2)
Any one of the following three criteria:
- 3 or more days of vigorous activity of at least 20 minutes per day OR
- 5 or more days of moderate-intensity activity or walking of at least 30 minutes per day OR
- 5 or more days of any combination of walking, moderate-intensity or vigorous-intensity activities achieving a minimum of at least 600 MET-minutes/week.

3 High (category 3)
Any one of the following two criteria:
- Vigorous-intensity activity on at least three days and accumulating at least 1500 MET-minutes/week OR
- 7 or more days of any combination of walking, moderate-intensity or vigorous-intensity activities achieving a minimum of at least 3000 MET-minutes/week.

Review

This questionnaire has been used internationally and exists in several forms. The one presented here is the short form, self-administered questionnaire, although there is the long form version as well as telephone and self-administered versions. The scales are also offered in several languages. The long version is quite detailed and asks a lot of the participant, therefore we would suggest this version if dealing with research projects.

Notes

1 This chapter is an adapted version of Hefferon (in press a).
2 Massage therapy is defined as 'involving rubbing and stroking different parts of the body with some pressure and usually with oil' (Field, 1998: 779).
3 The bonobos, a cousin of the chimpanzee, and dolphins are the only other known communities that engage in sex 'for fun' (Martin, 2009).
4 Today, only the National Health and Social Life Survey, conducted in 1992, has rivalled the Kinsey reports.

5 Contrary to popular belief, the average experience of coitus during late teens was 2.8 times a week, followed by 2.2 times a week by age 30 and 1.0 times a week by age 50.

6 These labs also study preferential mate selection, sexual desires, sexual responses, sexual dysfunction due to psychological issues and much more.

7 The top thriving countries around the world have citizens who report participating in activity one or two times per week (Gallup, as cited in Buetner, 2010).

8 To calculate your target heart rate range, minus your age from 220 and calculate 60 and 75 per cent of this.

9 See Hefferon and Mutrie (in press) for a detailed review of physical activity and Ryff's model of psychological wellbeing.

10 See www.usda.gov/ (USDA website) for serving sizes.

11 Another caveat is to look out for who has funded the research in question. With chocolate there appears to be an increased proportion of funding from interested parties, which readers must take into consideration.

12 Body modification is defined as scarification, brandings, body manipulation, tattooing and piercing.

CHAPTER 10

Applying Positive Psychology

How can psychotherapists and other clinicians facilitate optimal functioning and psychological wellbeing? Since the strengths-based approach is used in most areas when applying positive psychology, this chapter commences by reviewing different approaches to conceptualizing and classifying human strengths, focusing specifically on the Values in Action (VIA) inventory. The rest of the chapter discusses some of the recent advances on the interface between psychotherapy, coaching and positive psychology. Finally, the chapter considers the applications of positive psychology to educational and organizational settings.

List of topics

- The concept and application of strengths.
- How positive psychology and coaching connect.
- 'Positive therapy' and its cousins.
- Positive psychology in organizations.
- Positive education curriculums.
- Enabling institutions and their place in society.

MOCK ESSAY QUESTIONS

1 From what is wrong to what is strong. To what extent could the focus on strengths (as opposed to weaknesses) contribute to good functioning?
2 Discuss how positive psychology's empirical research can be used in one-to-one environments.
3 Discuss how research findings from positive psychology can inform other areas of applied psychology, such as educational and organizational psychology.

Character strengths and virtues

So what exactly are strengths and how can they be used to enhance and maintain 'the good life'? Studying strengths of character is a difficult notion at the best of times. Science is supposedly predicated on the basis of 'fact and objective truths', whereas values and characters are fluffy, philosophical notions, seemingly impossible to pin down. Some researchers argue that psychology should maintain its focus on the study of character, whereas other researchers believe that character is a philosophical matter rather than a psychological one.

Christopher Peterson and Martin Seligman, however, believe otherwise (Peterson and Seligman, 2004). Following an extensive review of thousands of pieces of literature, science, and text, from across the world and across the centuries, they identified 24 character strengths that are organized into six virtues[1] (see Table 10.1). Thus, the Values in Action (VIA) Classification of Strengths and Virtues has become known within the positive psychology world as the 'un-DSM', or rather a book/reference guide to which psychologists can refer in recognition of strengths and positive functioning, rather than classifications of disorder and dysfunction.

As positive psychology advocates, good character is more than bad character negated or minimized. Furthermore, human strengths are not secondary to weaknesses. Through the hard work of Peterson and Seligman human strengths are now amenable to scientific assessment and understanding.

Strengths versus talents

Within psychology, terminology is never straightforward. Thus, some researchers study *strengths* whereas others study *talents*. So how are these two different when they are used interchangeably in common speech? Strengths are argued to be distinguishable from talents because talents can be considered to be more innate and non-moral and can be wasted. On closer inspection, someone may have a talent for football or singing but decide not to develop or use that talent. However, strengths appear naturally in our daily life and we very rarely waste our strengths.

Think about it…

What do you think of this distinction? Are we ever really born with talent, or do we develop talent with hard work and effort?

Definition of a strength

In order to be classified as a character strength, Peterson and Seligman set out several inclusion criteria, some but not all of which are listed below:

- It must be present in a range of the individual's behaviours, thoughts, feelings, and actions, generalizable across situations and times.
- It must contribute to fulfilment of the good life for self and others.
- It must be morally valued in its own right, irrespective of the beneficial outcomes it can lead to.

Wisdom and Knowledge	• Curiosity and interest • Love of learning • Judgement, critical thinking, open-mindedness • Practical intelligence, creativity, originality, ingenuity • Perspective
Courage	• Valour • Industry, perseverance • Integrity, honesty, authenticity • Zest, enthusiasm
Love	• Intimacy, reciprocal attachment • Kindness, generosity, nurturance • Social intelligence, personal intelligence, emotional intelligence
Justice	• Citizenship, duty, loyalty, teamwork • Equity, fairness • Leadership
Temperance	• Forgiveness, mercy • Modesty, humility • Prudence, caution • Self-control, self-regulation
Transcendence	• Awe, wonder, appreciation of beauty and excellence • Gratitude • Hope, optimism, future-mindedness • Playfulness, humour • Spirituality, sense of purpose, faith, religiousness

TABLE 10.1 VIA strengths

- Furthermore, displaying the strength does not diminish others, but may rather benefit them.
- The larger society provides institutions and associated rituals for cultivating strengths and virtues.
- It can be measured.
- It can be distinguished from other character strengths (adapted from Boniwell, 2008).

> ## Think about it...
>
> Have a go at completing the VIA Questionnaire at www.authentic happiness.org. You will receive a readout of your Top 5 signature strengths and information on what to do with the results.

The alternative or rival to the VIA is the Clifton Strengths Finder, which is organized into 34 talent themes (Lopez and Ackerman, 2009). Its authors propose that talents are the basis of strengths, which are produced when talents are refined with knowledge and skills. This tool was created by Donald Clifton, who interviewed thousands of top performers within several organizational contexts (mainly business and academia) and analysed the data accordingly to determine success. These data were then used to develop a semi-structured interview schedule, which was delivered to millions of participants across skill, job, and culture contexts. Statistical analysis reduced the data to 34 themes. The tool is said to have high validity and internal reliability, although most data collection with the Strengths Finder is conducted internally, with outside unbiased researchers having limited access to its properties. At present, millions of people from across the world have taken this tool and research suggests that organizations that focus on their employees' strengths, rather than weaknesses, can reduce turnover, increase productivity and, in turn, profitability (Delichte and Evers-Cacciapaglia, 2010).

> ## Think about it...
>
> You can access the Strengths Finder via http://www.strengthsfinder.com or by purchasing one of the several Clifton Strengths Finder books.

Realise2

The Realise2 strengths assessment was developed at the Centre for Applied Positive Psychology (CAPP) in Warwickshire, England. The creator of the tool,

Alex Linley, is a well renowned positive psychologist who mainly works within the area of business and positive psychology. You can access the Realise2 online, and take the test that asks you to assess 60 attributes (ranging from Spotlight to Courage to Relationship deepener) and determine three major factors: whether or not these attributes have the ability to re-energize you, whether you are good at them and how often you get to use them in your daily life.

According to this model, Realise2 divides an individual's attributes into four dimensions:

- *Realized strengths* are the strengths of which you are aware already and use, which in turn enable you to perform at your best.
- *Unrealized strengths* are strengths that you may not be able to express on a daily basis due to your environment and work situation. However, when you do display them you derive energy and satisfaction from exhibiting these attributes.
- *Learned behaviours* encompass the behaviours that you have, over time, learned to do well; however, you do not derive pleasure or energy from completing them. These are not considered strengths in the Realise2 but attributes that you have learned to do well, but drain you, therefore inhibiting your ability to perform and live at your best.
- *Weaknesses* encompass the behaviours that you have not managed to do well over time and they drain you. These attributes can create issues and need to be managed so that they do not hinder your success in life (Adapted from CAPP website: www.cappeu.com/realise2.htm for more information.)

The first two dimensions can hold up to seven attributes, whereas learned behaviours can hold up to four and weaknesses can hold up to three. In your report, the order in which the attributes are numbered demonstrates the potency of the attribute.

Once you have completed the online assessment tool at www.realise2.com, and reviewed the detailed report, the Realise2 creates a development and prioritization plan for you to enhance your unrealized strengths, moderate your learned behaviours and minimize your weaknesses. By doing this, Realise2 intends to maximize your daily performance.

One caveat is that due to the fact that this tool is so new, little research has been completed on the usefulness of it. Scientific data on the impact of the Realise2 are expected in the near future.

Think about it...

Check out CAPP's *Strength2020* website at http://www.strengths2020.com for daily tips, links to Realise2 and books relating to this specific tool.

The value of strengths

Now that we have taken the tests and know our strengths, what is their value and how can they be applied to help us live life to its fullest? Research has demonstrated that by simply following our strengths we can gain insight and perspective into our lives, generate optimism, confidence and even enhanced sense of vitality (Clifton and Anderson, 2001). More importantly, strengths appear to have a preventative mechanism in terms of buffering against certain types of physical dysfunction such as allergies, diabetes, chronic pain and even some mental disorders. Strengths help build psychological resilience with the use of signature strengths in work, love, play and parenting generating positive emotions. Finally, the strengths approach is argued to be at the heart of successful psychological therapies (Peterson and Seligman, 2004).

Distribution and demographics

One of the most common questions we are asked is whether or not certain strengths are more amenable to certain demographics, countries and even age groups. The answer seems to be 'yes' to all three. Based on the data from 117,676 respondents, within the US and other Western nations, the most commonly endorsed strengths are kindness, fairness, honesty, gratitude, and judgement, and the lesser strengths include prudence, modesty and self-regulation (Park et al., 2004). Hope, teamwork and zest are more common among adolescents than adults whereas appreciation of beauty, authenticity, leadership and open-mindedness are more common among adults (Park et al., unpublished).

Biswas-Diener (2006) conducted an in-depth empirical examination of strengths and virtues from a cross-cultural perspective. Among 123 members of the Kenyan Maasai, 71 seal hunters in Northern Greenland, and 519 University of Illinois students, there was a high rate of agreement about the existence, desirability and development of virtues. Despite strong similarities, there were differences between cultures based on gender, the perceived importance of specific virtues (such as modesty) and the existence of cultural institutions that promote each strength. In the UK, both genders tend to score similarly among four of their top five strengths (open-mindedness, fairness, curiosity and love of learning). In addition, as British citizens get older, they tend to have higher strengths relating to curiosity and love of learning, fairness, forgiveness and self-regulation (Linley et al., 2007).

In relation to wellbeing, it appears that it is better to have some strengths rather than others. Research suggests that the strengths of curiosity, gratitude, hope, love and zest are most robustly associated with life satisfaction (Park et al., 2004). So, should we be worried that we are doomed to never be happy if we don't have these correlated strengths? We would argue, on the basis of other well documented research, that there is a lot you can do, regardless of what strengths you have, to enhance your wellbeing. For example, simply by taking the VIA online and identifying your Top 5 signature strengths can significantly enhance your wellbeing levels (Seligman et al., 2005). From there, you can do many things with this information to create a strength-based approach to life. First of all, when you are deciding on what career to follow or what job to take, try to match your Top 5 strengths with your job, as the most valued job, relationship and hobbies are the ones congruent with people's strengths. Thus, if your top strength is kindness, then try and source a job with some form of mentoring element. Or if you score high on curiosity, try to inject some adventure into your romantic relationships.

Finally, you can try using your signature strengths in a new way every day, for at least one week. Infusing your daily life with variety in how you express your strengths has a lasting effect on increased happiness and decreased depressive symptoms for up to 6 months (Seligman et al., 2005).

Can my strengths change over time?

Your strengths have the ability to morph over time and circumstances. Although the test is considered reliable, it is subject to changes in environment. One of the biggest influences is tragedy. For example, after 9/11, researchers compared pre- and post-9/11 VIA surveys and found a significant increase in faith, hope and love (Peterson and Seligman, 2003). Furthermore, Peterson and his colleagues have started to look into the connections between illness (both physical and mental) and strengths. More specifically, they have found, from a large sample of US citizens, that individuals who recover from a serious physical illness (such as cancer or heart disease) score higher on greater appreciation of beauty, bravery, curiosity, fairness, forgiveness, gratitude, humour, kindness, love of learning and spirituality. Those who have recovered from a psychological disorder score higher on appreciation of beauty, creativity, curiosity, gratitude and love of learning (Peterson et al., 2006).

Think about it...

If you don't like online tests, we would suggest reviewing the strengths lists (either the VIA or Clifton Strengths Finder) and pick the top five you feel are most authentic to you. When you are doing this, think about:

- Whether or not the strength identifies who you really are.
- When you are demonstrating this strength, do you truly enjoy yourself?
- Are you energized during and after its use?

How else can we use the strengths within our daily lives?

A very cheesy way to break the ice with new members of a group is to say your name, where you are from and maybe why you are there. Whenever we ask people to do this, we inevitably get the eyes rolling and disengagement immediately. This is why a *positive introduction* can cage the cynicism and enhance the enjoyment of a classroom and indeed a group. The next time you are chairing a group, or meeting new people, try out a positive introduction, like the following, and see how things become a little more interesting.

Think about it...

Try out an example of a positive introduction:

Please turn to the person on your left and ask them to describe a situation when they were at their best last week. What did it feel like? Describe the beginning, middle and the end. Once they have finished, please switch roles and complete the introduction yourself.

Make a beautiful day using your strengths

Seligman offers several ideas for incorporating strengths into our daily lives, for example, creating 'a beautiful day' or going on a 'strengths date'. To create a 'beautiful day', use your talents and attributes to create the perfect day (or even half day). Thus, if your top strengths are love of learning and curiosity, your day might include a trip to a favourite museum or a few hours with a book that you've been meaning to read. If the capacity to love crowns your list you might spend an evening with old friends or summon family for a dinner. You can also take your 'strengths day' further and design a date with your significant other together so that both of you can express your talents.

Developing strengths

But how do we develop strengths? In order to do this, we must first identify our non-signature strengths. If you are 'low' on curiosity and interest, you may try expanding your knowledge in an area of interest through books, journals, magazines, TV, radio or Internet, for half an hour, three times a week.

Furthermore you could attend a function/lecture/colloquium of a culture that differs from yours. In order to develop curiosity of others, find a person in an area of your interest and learn how he/she increased his/her expertise in that area. Go and eat food of a different culture, explore its cultural context and become aware of your thoughts.

If you feel that you need to enhance your appreciation of beauty, try and note at least one expression of natural beauty around you every day (sunrise, clouds, sunset, sunshine, snowfall, rainbow, trees, moving leaves, birds, flowers, fruits, vegetables, and so forth). You can listen to a piece of music or a watch a film and evaluate how it touches you. Visit a museum and pick a piece of art and evaluate how it aesthetically touches you.

Interventions for zest and enthusiasm include pushing yourself to do something that you already do, but with more energy and in creative and different ways. To enhance zest, try to exercise at least three times a week and notice how it affects your energy level. Try a physically rigorous activity (bike riding, running, sports, singing, playing) you always wanted to do but have not done yet.

Interventions targeting emotional intelligence can ask you to listen to your friends and siblings empathically, without preparing rebuttals and just try to reflect on your feelings. Notice and compliment the positive gestures of others. Finally, in order to examine your emotional vocabulary (a key component to emotional intelligence), write five personal feelings daily for four weeks and monitor patterns.

Finally, a moving exercise involves asking yourself and identifying a time when you felt at your personal best. You need to reflect on the personal strengths displayed throughout the event and then review the story every day for one week. By engaging in the suggested exercises you can help develop areas or strengths that may need some additional focus (Kauffman, 2006).

The next section will move away from strengths to focus more on positive therapy, coaching and associated techniques.

Positive therapy

When we hear the word 'therapy', many of us automatically equate it to something negative, defunct, broken. Positive psychology therapy is, at present, a non-governed field (Joseph and Linley, 2006, 2009). Many psychologists who affiliate themselves with the positive psychology movement offer ideas on how to conduct 'positive psychology therapy'. The underlying principles are that therapy shouldn't focus just on diagnosing and treating disorder, maladjustment, suffering, etc. (Joseph and Linley, 2009; Rashid, 2009b). In addition, therapy should recognize, use and build a patient's existing strengths and resources rather than view the client as flawed and disordered.

time out

Types of therapy

What is therapy and what type of therapies are currently in practice? In modern day psychology, you can choose a variety of schools of thought when considering therapy, such as:

1 *Behavioural* (aims to change behaviour and thus thought processes).

2 *Cognitive behavioural* (aims to change thought processes and thus your action).

3 *Psychoanalytic* (aims to uncover and deal with unconscious emotional issues developed from the past).

4 *Psychodynamic* (similar to the above methods, however less intense and shorter in duration).

5 *Gestalt* (part of the existential branch, this therapy aims to uncover personal responsibility).

6 *Client-centred* (aims to be non-directive and assumes that the client is better equipped to figure out their own answers to their own problems).

7 *Transactional analysis* (a mixture of several therapies, it assumes that all people are ok, we can all think for ourselves, and that we have the power to change our situation).

8 *Integrative therapy* (aims to adopt a pragmatic approach to therapy, thereby using the positive elements of several types of therapy and combining them into one new cohesive framework).

(Adapted from Boniwell, 2008: 110–11)

Positive therapy is not just concerned with enhancing strengths and qualities within the individual but also with the prevention of mental illness and ill-being (Seligman, 2002). There are issues with trying to decipher the effects of psychotherapy. As Seligman points out, field studies versus controlled lab settings consistently show better results; furthermore, when researchers try to isolate the specific elements that appear to be working, there appears to be no large difference between techniques. Finally, as in all psychology, we have to negotiate the placebo effect (Goldacre, 2009), with on average 50 per cent of clients demonstrating positive effects when being administered placebo drugs/therapies (Seligman, 2002).

THERAPIES

Do all therapies work the same? And if not, which ones have shown better results than others? In 2002, Lambert and Barley wrote and published a controversial chapter on the effects of the therapeutic relationship and positive outcomes of psychotherapy. After reviewing the psychotherapy literature, they concluded that only 15 per cent of therapy success could be attributed to the therapeutic technique (method used).

The remainder was attributed to expectancy (15 per cent), common factors (such as empathy, warmth confidentiality) (30 per cent) and extratherapeutic change (40 per cent). Wampold (2005) conducted a similar review of laboratory controlled psychotherapy interventions, and found evidence supporting Lambert and Barley's findings. His results showed that it was the therapists themselves who were the largest predictor of therapy success whereas the treatment technique had only a minute effect on the final outcome.

See Lambert and Barley (2001; 2002) and Wampold (2005) for the original articles.

Seligman argues that generic therapy works because it can be broken down in tactics and deep strategies, and that the utilization of these can be accounted for the beneficial outcomes of psychotherapy. Tactics that all good therapy must include are: attention, authority figure, rapport, paying for services, trust, opening up, naming the problem and utilizing tricks of the trade (for example, 'Let's pause here', rather than 'Let's stop here') (Seligman 2002: 6). Deep strategies are arguably theoretical and scientifically based techniques within positive psychology. These strategies include: instilling hope and building strengths (such as courage, rationality and capacity for pleasure). By using these strategies, therapists will engage with enhancing and nurturing what is already strong, rather than trying to fix or remedy what is wrong.

Indeed, even in late 1960s, therapists were aware that therapy existed in two formats: helping with psychological disorders and enabling psychological growth (Mahrer, as cited in Bernard et al., 2010). A positive therapy stands in sharp contrast to attempts that seek to classify every problem of living as a psychological disorder. The next section will review the main therapies that have existed, and continue to assist individuals to thrive, including rational emotional behavioural therapy (REBT), wellbeing therapy (WBT) and quality-of-life therapy (QoLT). Of course, this is not an exhaustive review of all the types of 'positive therapies' available, however they are the ones with the most evidence behind them to date.

Positive clinical psychology[2]

Rational emotional behavioural therapy (REBT)

Contrary to popular belief (even within positive psychology), Ellis's rational emotional behavioural therapy (REBT) was aimed at both helping individuals, with and without emotional problems, to deal with emotional distress as well as lead a fulfilling and happy life (Bernard et al., 2010). Based on the concept of rationality, this scientific model aimed at restructuring cognition, which enables individuals to harness their own inner strengths and abilities to live rational lives: 'rationality is characterized by positive emotions (pleasure, joy, excitement), an absence of dysfunctional negative emotions, a determination to solve life's problems and goal directed behaviour' (Bernard et al., 2010: 303). By doing so, individuals can experience short-term positive affect as well as long-term goal attainments and psychological wellbeing.

Ellis proposes that there are 11 rational principles of living including:

- Self-interest – individuals need to pursue their own interests before others; not to give over themselves to others (be kind to yourself).
- Social interest – while you are pursing your happiness makes sure it is not at the expense of others and be kind to others.
- Self-direction: do not wait for others to 'serve' you happiness or remove dissatisfaction; you need to do this yourself.
- Self-acceptance: remove the belief in a 'rating scale' when comparing yourself to others. There is no 'global standard'.
- Tolerance of others: people who understand that all humans are fallible will be better equipped to deal with flaws and diversity.
- Short-term/long-term hedonism: it's about the short-term and the long-term happiness of individuals. Don't take the easy route.
- Commitment to creative, absorbing activities and pursuits: similar to the concept of flow, try and engage in activities of 'vital absorption'.
- Risk taking and experimenting: continue to explore and take on new projects – this will expand your mind and help development of the self. Also take risks: failure is a part of life so take a chance!
- High frustration tolerance and willpower.
- Problem solving.
- Scientific thinking (as cited in Bernard et al., 2010: 303).

Even Ellis was a balanced scientist, highlighting the importance of negative emotions. He argued that people who exhibit sadness are rational and therefore able to deal with their situation. The next section will move away from REBT and focus on Rogers' concept of unconditional positive regard.

Organismic valuing process

Therapists are also directed to encourage clients to use the *organismic valuing process* (Rogers) and provide unconditional positive regard to strip away external and internal conditions of worth. Therapists should form an authentic relationship with clients (Rogers) as this satisfies the need for relatedness and has been shown to be the strongest predictor of therapy outcome (Orlinsky et al., 1994; Wampold, 2001). Thus, it is not so important what therapists do (the techniques that they use) but the extent to which they use 'deep strategies', such as instilling hope, building strengths, facilitating coherence in mental functioning (Joseph and Linley, 2006).

Positive psychologists also acknowledge that some psychopathologies (for example, schizophrenia, bipolar disorders, temporal lobe epilepsy and organic brain diseases) are best considered disorders and treated within the medical field by psychiatrists and clinical psychologists.

Wellbeing therapy

Wellbeing therapy consists of eight sessions, 30–50 minutes in length, with an emphasis on self-observation with a structured diary. This type of therapy is conceptually based on Ryff's Psychological Wellbeing (PWB) model, targeting environmental mastery, personal growth, purpose in life, autonomy, self-acceptance and positive relations with others. Essentially, clients simply monitor whether or not episodes of PWB occur. Episodes (or the lack thereof) are then discussed in therapy, and obstacles are targeted with traditional CBT techniques (for example, refuting negative automatic thoughts). Preliminary evidence suggests the potential of this therapy for relapse prevention in mood and anxiety disorders (Ruini and Fava, 2004; Fava and Ruini, 2009).

Quality of life (QOL) therapy

Quality of life therapy is a comprehensive approach that has been evaluated as a package, thus it is the sum of its parts (Frisch, 1998, 2006; Frisch et al., 2005). In the next section we will review a selection of QOL therapy interventions such as the *most feared obituary* and *playlist* (to view the entire QOLT programme, please see Frisch, 2006).

My most feared obituary

This exercise is considered a 'dark version' of the best possible self exercise, which asks people to think of their life, and pretend that they never changed all those bad habits they promised to do when they were alive. Although it is implied that such a reflection may provide additional fuel for change, we are not big of fans of this intervention; indeed, we feel that its darkness overshadows the good it is apparently trying to do. Furthermore, students find it quite morbid and counterproductive, flying in the face of focusing on and developing strengths.

Playlist

Adults aren't really good 'players'. We tend to leave imagination and the fun stuff to children. However, recreational activities are essential ways to relax, have fun, forget worries, be creative and learn something new. These activities can renew and refresh us so that we perform better in our work and relationships. We spend too little time 'playing' when we are adults. So this exercise asks you to list the activities that you think you might enjoy as a recreational outlet. Do not think about what is best, most practical, or easy to do. If possible, try to choose active rather than passive leisure activities as these are proved to enhance, rather than hinder wellbeing (Holder et al., 2009). Ideas on the playlist can include visiting your favourite (or new) sections of a book, video, or music store; playing cards or board games, singing, dancing, going to the museum or the botanical garden, visiting a neighbour, sightseeing in the city, going to an antique sale, doing woodwork, hiking, bird watching, people watching, bowling, reading do-it-yourself materials, baking, scrap booking, looking at pictures, cuddling and many others! Try to follow a leisure plan in which you regularly – preferably daily even for just 5 minutes – engage in some of these activities.

In conclusion, there is no specific 'positive psychology therapy', however, as demonstrated, some therapy approaches are developing genuine positive psychology therapies based on positive psychology-related models (for example, Fava and Ruini, 2009). Strangely, no SDT therapy exists yet (Deci and Ryan, 2008) although this is hailed as one of the most promising future directions. Seligman et al. are busy developing specific positive psychology interventions to target VIA strengths and virtues.

Critiques of 'positive therapy' stem from the perception that many conventional therapies already use positive psychology principles to reduce suffering and increase happiness and wellbeing (but usually without making this explicit). For example, some therapies facilitate positive emotions; meaning and purpose (self-determination/autonomy); self-efficacy, perceived competence/mastery; relatedness and interpersonal functioning (Weinberger, 1995). Thus, a clearer distinction in the separation of the two is needed.

Positive psychology and coaching

Since the year 2000 the integration of positive psychology (theory and practice) into the coaching world has increased exponentially (Kauffman and Scouler, 2004; Grant, in press; Grant and Spence, in press; Hefferon, in press). Although an obvious pairing, it is only recently that the publication of accessible, scientifically supported positive psychology manuals (for example, *Authentic Happiness; The HOW of Happiness; Positivity; Positive Psychology and Coaching*) has enabled coaches to access the existing validated positive psychology interventions (PPIs), which offer innovative and invigorating exercises for coaches to use in their client sessions. Positive psychology provides an excellent theoretical framework for coaching and, likewise, coaching can serve as a good soundboard to their scholarly ideas (such as positive emotions, resilience and strengths) (Hefferon, in press).

Coaching is defined as 'a process that enables learning and development to occur and thus performance to improve' (Parsloe, 1999: 8). Coaching typically involves identification and development of strengths and competencies, goal setting and a focus on achieving results within a specified timescale. Coaching psychology is for enhancing performance in work and personal life domains with normal, non-clinical populations, underpinned by models of coaching grounded in established therapeutic approaches (Grant and Palmer, 2002). Executive coaching takes place in a business context and is commonly aimed at 'key' employees at times of change and transition. Furthermore, when coaching is undertaken by professional versus peer coaches, research shows a greater commitment and progression, as well as higher levels of wellbeing (environmental mastery) (Spence and Grant, 2007).

Positive psychology research found that the combination of several coaching interventions (360-degree feedback, one-half day leadership workshop and four one-to-one coaching sessions)[3] over 12 weeks significantly increased employees' goal attainment, resilience, workplace wellbeing and reduced depression and stress when compared to controls (Grant et al., 2009).

Positive psychology and coaching both claim that attention should be redirected away from 'fixing' the client, from looking for signs of pathology or viewing the client as 'broken', flawed, disordered, etc. Both coaching and positive psychology are natural allies in sharing an explicit concern with the enhancement of optimal functioning and wellbeing, arguing for performance improvement, finding what is right with the person and working on enhancing it. Good coaching helps clients to discover their skills and resources and fits with the premise of positive psychology: helping clients identify their strengths and find ways to use them more often in all aspects of their lives.

Applying positive psychology to education

One of the fastest growing directions in applied positive psychology is within the domain of positive educational curricula. At the present time, several curriculums worldwide incorporate the principles of positive psychology to varying degrees.

The reasons for the focus on the development of wellbeing in children are twofold. On the one hand, Western countries are facing an unprecedented increase in childhood and adolescent depression. At any point in time, approximately 2 per cent of children aged 11–15 and 11 per cent of youth aged 16–24 in the UK suffer a major depressive disorder (Green et al., 2005). In the US, approximately one in five adolescents has a major depressive episode by the end of high school (Lewinsohn et al., 1993). A similar picture is observed in Australia (Noble and McGrath, 2005).

Children and adolescents who suffer from high levels of depressive symptoms or depressive disorders are more likely to have academic and interpersonal difficulties. They are more likely to smoke, use drugs and alcohol and attempt suicide (Covey et al., 1998; Garrison et al., 1989).

Positive education aims to develop the skills of wellbeing, flourishing and optimal functioning in children, teenagers and students, as well as parents and educational institutions. In doing that it adopts both the preventative and enabling developmental functions. Importantly, positive education is underpinned by the principles and methods of empirical validation, which is what differentiates positive psychology from self-help initiatives.

Schools in the US, UK, Australia and across the world have, for some time, included work on social and emotional issues in the curriculum (for example, personal, social and health education, service learning, citizenship) and helped pupils reflect on the importance of good social and emotional skills. Although much has been done to promote such learning through stand-alone programmes and/or the whole-school environment, relatively few such programmes have been evaluated empirically through randomized controlled studies.

Primary and secondary schools

Globally, empirically tested programmes such as the Penn Resilience Program in the US (Gillham et al., 1995) and the Bounce Back! programme in Australia (McGrath and Noble, 2003) have provided evidence that the teaching of social competence, resilience and optimism can offer benefits to children through reducing psychological disorders.

The Penn Resilience Program (PRP) has been developed and researched for over 16 years and consequently has acquired a solid base of evidence (Reivich and Shatté, 2002; Seligman, 2002, 2007; Reivich et al., 2007). This evidence suggests that it prevents both depression and anxiety and has long-lasting effects. More specifically, in the 13 randomized, placebo-controlled trials carried out with over 2000 participants, 11 of the studies demonstrate reductions in depressive symptoms, with three studies also showing positive effects on anxiety and behavioural problems. At its best, the PRP has been shown to reduce the incidence of depression and anxiety by 50 per cent at three-year follow-up (Gillham et al., 2007).

The PRP is a schools-based intervention curriculum designed to increase resilience and promote optimism, adaptive coping skills and effective problem solving through the application of the principles of cognitive behaviour therapy to normal populations. Based on the seven 'learnable' skills of resilience, the programme teaches children how to identify their feelings; tolerance of ambiguity; the optimistic explanatory style; how to analyse causes of problems; empathy; self-efficacy and how to reach out or try new things. The PRP, therefore, educates adolescents to challenge a habitual pessimistic explanatory style by looking at the evidence and considering what is realistic whilst avoiding unrealistic optimism.

The PRP is delivered to US school grades 5–8 (ages 10–14) in 12 sessions of 90–120 minutes. It has also been pioneered in three local authorities in the UK with children in Year 7 (ages 11–12). Although no UK data are available at the moment, informal evaluations indicate that the programme is being well received by teachers and young people.

A further applied classroom resilience programme is Bounce Back! Devised by two Australian psychologists, Dr Helen McGrath and Dr Toni Noble (2003), it is a highly practical, teacher-friendly programme. It is based on the conclusions, reached by a meta-review of school-based programmes, that the benefits of the vast majority of short-term programmes are, in fact, not sustainable. Bounce Back! is delivered in both primary and secondary schools, revisiting fundamental concepts in developmentally appropriate ways over time. Emerging research evidence indicates beneficial effects of the programme on depression (McGrath and Noble, 2003).

Although being able to decrease depression and anxiety in children and adolescents permanently is a striking achievement that cannot be understated, the above programmes do not go far enough in enhancing wellbeing, rather than simply alleviating possible psychological problems. Wellbeing is not a mere absence of depression, just as the person who is not ill is not necessarily in good physical shape. Development of wellbeing needs to include skills over and above successful coping, including the enhancement of positive emotions, flow, positive relations and meaningfulness.

With the expansion of the positive psychology field, the last decade has seen a surprising wealth of curricula being developed around the world to address different aspects of positive functioning. For example, the Wisdom Curriculum encourages the intellectual and moral development of children through the medium of mainstream subjects (Reznitskaya and Sternberg, 2004). Students can formulate their own ideas about wise thinking – thus it is not about what to think but how to think. This education programme incorporates 16 pedagogical principles and six procedures such as reflective thinking, dialogical thinking and dialectical thinking.

A number of projects accentuating hope in schoolchildren include Making Hope Happen and Making Hope Happen for Kids (Lopez et al., 2004), a five-session programme based on the Hope model intertwined with psychodrama (goals, obstacles, pathways and willpower). Basically, children create a story about navigating obstacles in addition to engaging in the Hope Game of multiple goal pursuits, designing hope cartoons, emphasizing hopeful language, writing hope stories about own goals, and so forth. The results of this programme are promising, with significant gains in hope scores (CHS).

A strengths-based development programme, developed by the Gallup Foundation, has been found to significantly improve academic performance (Hodges and Clifton, 2004). In the UK, the Celebrating Strengths approach, targeting the development of strengths through storytelling, has been widely implemented in primary schools in the north of England (Eades, 2008). Emotional intelligence has been widely used as an umbrella concept for various programmes around social and emotional learning, the most successful of which are Self Science and The South Africa Emotional Intelligence

Curriculum (Salovey et al., 2004). Some of the programmes, such as Going for the Goal, which teaches adolescents the skills of positive goal setting and facilitation of goal attainment, have been carried out on a very large scale (Danish, 1996). Key School, in Indianapolis, aims to cultivate pupils' experience of flow (full engagement in an activity). Their programme provides opportunities for pupils to challenge their abilities, and the school has a Flow Activities Center, where pupils have the time and space to engage in activities related to their own interests. The Culver Academies, a group of boarding high schools in Indiana, have integrated character strengths and positive emotions throughout the school. Teaching staff have been trained in strengths and positive emotions, and staff performance reviews are based on the strengths approach (Yeager, 2007). The Hawn Foundation, a US charity, has developed a mindfulness education curriculum that is being piloted in schools in Canada and the US.

In September 2006, Wellington College – a private, co-educational school in the UK – embarked on a two-year Skills of Wellbeing programme for its pupils. The course was designed by Ian Morris and Dr Nick Baylis and is delivered fortnightly to years 10 and 11 (ages 14–16) with the specific aim of 'redressing the imbalance in modern education caused by an emphasis on exam results and measured outcomes' (Baylis and Morris, 2006: 3). The ultimate outcome of the course is to give Wellington College pupils practical skills for living well that are useful, easily understood and can be applied on a daily basis. Although the course is still in its infancy, the passionate desire to deliver these skills is driving an ongoing review of the course. This is coupled with an intention to avoid a 'myopic' approach and broaden the breadth and depth of the course to include knowledge from positive psychology, drawing on the latest evidence-based research and practical interventions. In common with other programmes aimed at the development of positive functioning, Skills of Wellbeing has, at present, very limited scientific validation. Despite this fact, it has attracted unprecedented media coverage, placing the wellbeing debate firmly in the heart of the British political agenda.

In the US, a comprehensive programme of 17 lessons, each two hours in length, was developed to introduce positive psychology to high-school students. Developed around Martin Seligman's Authentic Happiness (Seligman, 2002a) ideas and including a substantial resilience component, the programme incorporates several tested and innovative positive psychology interventions, such as savouring (Bryant and Veroff, 2007), gratitude letters and counting blessings (Seligman et al., 2005) and forgiveness and letting go of grudges (McCullough and Witvliet, 2002).

Whole-school approach to wellbeing

Looking beyond programmes targeting the development of specific skills, evidence suggests that school-wide programmes (involving all staff and pupils) to promote psychological wellbeing are more likely to be effective than class-based interventions (Wells et al., 2003), probably owing to the impact of all staff modelling positive behaviours outside of class time. A positive climate in the school as a whole is associated with teacher and student satisfaction, lower stress levels and better academic results (Sangsue and Vorpe, 2004).

Although it is difficult to define what makes a good school, researchers agree that it is a type of school that encourages students to be engaged with and enthusiastic about learning. Common features of such schools include a safe environment, an articulated and shared vision of the school's purpose, explicit goals for students, emphasis on the individual student and rewarding their efforts or improvements (Peterson, 2006). Student satisfaction with the school, feelings of security and belonging play a crucial role in their engagement in learning and achievement (Brand et al., 2003).

Currently, a project aiming to create a 'positive school' is being implemented in Geelong Grammar, a fee-charging Australian boarding school. Under the leadership of Professor Martin Seligman, a team of 35 positive psychologists from the University of Pennsylvania are spending several months redesigning the school on the basis of positive psychology principles. All staff are being trained in positive psychology and resilience using the Penn Resilience Program and elements of the Positive Psychology Programme for High School Students. However, in addition to introducing the above programmes as stand-alone elements, the positive psychology team is collaborating with subject teachers to discover and highlight elements of optimal functioning in mainstream subjects, such as English, history and maths.

Caveat: positive parenting

Of course, schools are not enough. Wellbeing of young people depends to a large extent on what is going on at home, so tackling the issue of parenting is unavoidable. Parenting is one of those activities that people take for granted: most parents learn their skills from their parents and 'on-the-spot' in the process of bringing up their own children. Although there are different views on what constitutes 'good' parenting, child psychologists generally agree that it is essential to support healthy development, social adjustment, academic achievement and self-esteem. Authoritative parenting – a high level of parental control combined with high sensitivity to and interest in the child – is generally recognized as the most conducive way to raise psychologically healthy children (Baumrind, 1991, 1993). Recent research in positive psychology took the question of positive parenting even further and identified seven Pillars of

Parenting that focus on the psychological needs of children (Cameron and Maginn, 2008):

- Care and protection – sensitivity to a child's basic needs shows the child that we care and that the child is important.

- Secure attachment – appears to act as a buffer against anxiety and to operate as a protective mechanism.

- Positive self-perception – essential to allow the development of a positive self-image.

- Emotional competence – this ability underpins the successful development of relationships outside the family and may moderate susceptibility to and propensity for later mental health problems.

- Self-management – prevents inappropriate behaviour when enticing or compelling outside factors try to intrude.

- Resilience – resilient individuals seem to be able to understand what has happened to them in life (insight), develop understanding of others (empathy) and gain control over their life experiences (achievement).

- A sense of belonging – research on relationships has established human beings as fundamentally social and highlighted the need to belong.

Higher education

Research and implementation of the findings related to wellbeing do not, of course, stop with young children. Positive psychology courses are becoming increasingly popular in higher education too. At present, there are hundreds of undergraduate courses taught in the US, UK and Australia. At Harvard University, the positive psychology class led by Tal Ben-Shahar attracts 1400 students per semester – approximately 20 per cent of all undergraduates – making it the largest class in Harvard's history.

As we have already discussed, the establishment of two Master's programmes in Applied Positive Psychology (MAPP), one at the University of Pennsylvania in the US and one at the University of East London in the UK,[4] offer students an opportunity to develop a depth of knowledge and critical understanding of the theory and research within positive psychology, as well as to study and use a range of positive psychology interventions and assessment methods, applying findings of this science to the areas that need it most.

A comparison between the two programmes on the two different continents revealed an unexpected similarity in the student experience, described by some as 'a life-changing experience' or 'the combustion of the being' and characterized by very high levels of intrinsic motivation, engagement and sustained commitment. Despite being taught by different faculty members, with the programmes operating across somewhat distinct cultural contexts and adopting different modes of study, students' descriptions of their experience have converged. A study by Boniwell and Seligman (in preparation) revealed six major factors of this 'Magic of MAPP', including being 'called' towards this profession, openness to personal transformation, experience of fun or positive emotions, intense intellectual stimulation and rigour, connectedness with others and being a part of something larger (or larger meaning). With the projected rapid growth of postgraduate programmes in Argentina, Australia, Italy and other countries, further research will be needed to establish if a similar phenomenon would occur.

With governments around the world taking an active interest in children's wellbeing, availability of research and science in positive psychology and a multitude of initiatives, positive education is set for a positive future. Nevertheless, it is important to recognize that we are still at the very beginning of the journey. For these programmes and interventions to succeed, active research needs to continue.

Positive psychology and business organizations

Positive organizing is the term used to describe the links between positive psychology and organizational theory, 'in general terms, it refers to the generative dynamics in and of the organizations that enable individuals, groups and organizations as a whole to flourish (Fredrickson and Dutton, 2008: 1). *Positive organization scholarship* regards organizations as macro contexts that shape positive states and positive outcomes for individuals, groups and whole organizations (Cameron et al., as cited in Fredrickson and Dutton, 2008: 1). *Positive organizational behaviours* is a vein of this work that focuses more narrowly on developed positive psychological states that enhance human performance.

In 2004, Jane Henry proposed several practices of positive organizations including:

- *Job variety:* employers can offer the opportunity to try out another area/skill of the job in order to engage their workers.
- *Intrinsic motivation:* as employers move away from setting external rewards, organizations can enhance intrinsic motivation by increasing their employees' autonomy (flexible working time), relatedness (social groups, networking) and competence (allowing employees to shadow, attend development courses).
- *Confidence:* organizations recognize the importance of confidence and therefore help target confidence levels within their employees.
- *Creativity:* positive organizations have an open ethos and encourage creative thinking.
- *Strengths work:* the organization can use a strengths-based approach to their staff development plans, rather than fixating on weaknesses.
- *Team building:* the organization invests in new teams and develops old teams through team-building weekends or exercises.
- *Metaperspective:* the organization maintains a balanced perspective with regards to strengths and competencies; they can be either positive or negative.

- *Flow:* the organization provides clear goals, feedback and appropriate challenges for the employee.

- *Participatory working practices:* the organization allows their employees to determine how they work, e.g. from home, over the telephone, etc.

- *Open climate, empowerment and self-organization:* the organization allows the employee to govern his/her own teams, invest into the company.

Although the tide is turning, many organizations still adopt a weakness, troubleshooting approach, which has been found to be inefficient in enhancing productivity and flourishing within the organization and the employees themselves. Furthermore, the manager role holds one of the keys for engagement and flourishing within business organizations. For example, employees who feel ignored by their manager have a 40 per cent likelihood of disengaging from their job. Conversely, managers who listen to their employees, and encourage them to utilize their strengths reduced the likelihood of disengagement to only 1 per cent.

Think about it...

To what extent do you think your boss influences your overall wellbeing? Interestingly, new research shows that when asked to rank the people we **DON'T** like to be around, both genders ranked their boss as number one! (Krueger et al., 2008)

Positive psychology interventions within business organizations

In business, the application of a 'reflected best selves exercise' (RBSE) intervention has gained increasing popularity. New research has shown that when RBSE uses both professional and personal sources, individuals experience enhanced positive emotions, agency and relation resources than when it is just delivered by the professional source. Furthermore, the exercise can be strengthened by adding improvement suggestions as well as strengths-based RBSE (Spreitzer et al., 2009).

Flow interventions are argued to be very important for a 'good business' (Csikszentmihalyi, 2003). The main reasons why flow doesn't happen on the job stem from the idea of not bringing out the *best* in people but getting the *most* out of them. Few jobs have clear goals and feedback is seldom provided. Furthermore, when the skills and the opportunities for action are not well matched, the employee will experience a sense of lack of control.

At present, a strengths approach as a framework for career development, performance appraisal and team building has been adopted by several companies. A strengths-based approach includes incorporating a strengths language into the environment in which to communicate or discuss issues with colleagues. Recent research has found that people who are thriving in career wellbeing are able to use their strengths on a regular basis within their work environment. By using their strengths, workers have been found to be up to six times more engaged than those who do not. Furthermore, people who use their strengths report enjoying up to 40-hour work weeks whereas those that do not report experiencing burn out at the 20-hour mark (Rath and Harter, 2010).

Some companies use strengths assessment tools such as the VIA for recruitment and selection purposes, however this should not be the sole determinant in the final decision. In terms of appropriateness of job allocation, businesses have started to match people with their strengths with promising results. Furthermore, constructing teams on the basis of complementary strengths profiles and managing weaknesses through complementary partnering or strengths-matched teams has also delivered successful outcomes. Ultimately, businesses that create further opportunities for the use of strengths report enhanced productivity and wellbeing among employees (Buckingham and Clifton, 2005).

Positive psychology interventions within health organizations

Unfortunately, there are several issues when attempting to apply positive psychology within healthcare settings (Harris and Thoresen, 2006), especially since strengths-based approaches are not commonplace. However, when applied to hospitals, community mental health centres and disorder-focused psychotherapy centres, the use of positive psychology based interventions (for example, forgiveness; self-efficacy training) can have a tremendous effect on healthcare settings that have traditionally been focused on reducing suffering rather than building strengths.

Research has also shown that within healthcare work settings, such as nursing, organizational respect (defined as 'esteem, dignity, care for others' positive self-regard and the collective nature of organizational life', Ramarajan et al., 2008: 5) can have a significant effect on the reduction of burnout and emotional exhaustion of its employees (Ramarajan et al., 2008). Additionally, organizations can implement interventions to enhance organizational respect, which have been found to significantly reduce emotional tiredness (Ramarajan et al., 2008).

Positive psychology and public policy

Countries around the world have traditionally measured the wealth of their nation by gross domestic product (GDP). Robert Kennedy famously criticized this method of analysis, claiming that governments measure everything but what makes life worth living. Positive psychologists have made progress within the area of public policy, recommending the implementation of subjective wellbeing measures into a government's assessment of individuals and societal quality of life and subjective wellbeing (Diener et al., 2009). Not only can these tools give governments an idea of how 'happy' their people are, it can help distinguish between what projects and schemes actually increase/decrease their citizens' wellbeing. Governments around the world have heeded this information (for example, Britain) and are currently employing wellbeing measurements in their general citizen polls (Stiglitz et al., 2009).

Overall, the application of positive psychology to therapy, coaching, education, the organizational setting and public policy is rapidly growing. The increase in funding for evaluating larger scale and longitudinal programmes will further validate positive psychology within the psychological sciences.

Summary

Reflecting on the learning objectives, you should now understand the concept of strengths and several applications of positive psychology. More specifically, you should know:

- There are three main models of strengths, including the VIA, Clifton Strengths Finder and Realise2.
- Most research in positive psychology is on the VIA and its 24 strengths, classified into six virtues (wisdom, courage, humanity, justice, temperance and transcendence).
- Coaching is an excellent medium for testing out theories within positive psychology, helping to bridge the gap between the ivory tower and the real world.
- Positive therapy uses 'deep strategies' approaches.
- Rational emotional behavioural therapy, wellbeing therapy and quality of life therapy attempt to work on building strengths.
- Organizations that adopt a positive psychology approach can increase productivity, reduce turnover and enhance the wellbeing of their staff.
- The use of positive psychology within schools is growing, ranging from one-off workshops to three-month interventions, or even the reorganization of entire curricula to embed the theoretical concepts of positive psychology.
- Positive psychology measurement tools are currently being adopted by governments to assess their citizens' subjective wellbeing scores.

Suggested Resources

http://www.ppc.sas.upenn.edu/prpsum.htm
Log on to this website to access information regarding the Penn Resilience Program, as well as training opportunities.

http://www.flourishingschools.org/
If you want to see how schools are implanting positive psychology into their school ethos, check out the above website.

http://www.businessweek.com/magazine/content/09_62/s0902044518985.htm
BusinessWeek magazine wrote an article on how to use positive psychology in business. A very interesting read for students with a business drive.

http://www.bus.umich.edu/Positive/
This is a positive organization lab at the University of Michigan.

Further questions for you

1 What would the good university be like?

2 How would you create a truly positive psychology department?

3 What do you think children should be learning in school? Are academic skills enough?

4 What three things could your workplace do to create a flourishing environment?

Personal Development Interventions

Mindfulness

- Make sure you have a relaxed position, closed eyes;
- Become aware of your position, your body, your breathing;
- Become aware of sensations and feelings . . . watch them come and go;
- Become aware of how your mind wanders, notice it, and gently bring yourself back to just observing this;
- Even if you're having thoughts or feelings that you don't like, try to not push them away . . . adopt an attitude of acceptance toward all parts of your experience (Davidson et al., 2003).

Notes

1 Whereby building these strengths, a person can achieve the associated virtue.
2 For more information, please see Seligman and Peterson's (2003) chapter on positive clinical psychology.
3 Using a cognitive behavioural solution focused approach, with trained, external coaches.
4 Our students include: psychologists, business, health and education professionals, executive and life coaches, and charity and NGO workers.

CHAPTER 11

Summing Up Positive Psychology

❖ *LEARNING OBJECTIVES*

Does positive psychology overemphasize the positive and neglect the useful functions of negative psychological processes, such as pessimism, complaining and doubt? Does this emerging field overemphasize psychological factors, such as positive affect and cognition, at the expense of social and environmental predictors of adjustment? This chapter discusses some of the limitations of positive psychology and recent criticisms aimed at it.

List of topics

- Top ten critiques of positive psychology.
- The many futures of positive psychology.

- A summary of the textbook.

MOCK ESSAY QUESTIONS

1 Does the positive psychology movement have legs?
2 Discuss the criticism of imbalance.
3 Is positive psychology all about the positive? Critically argue for or against.

Top ten critiques of positive psychology

So is positive psychology all it's cracked up to be? There are a number of critics who would vehemently oppose this, arguing that, in fact, positive psychology is the curse of the twenty-first century. With chronic natural disasters, a crippling global recession and widespread diseases, isn't it criminal to want to enhance the good life when others around suffer greatly? Is positive psychology just another by-product of capitalist America's selfish, individualistic fixation on the pursuit of happiness? We have collated the top ten criticisms of positive psychology that encompass critics from all areas of science and the humanities.

1 Why study positive when negative is more important and immediate?

One of the biggest critiques comes from the well renowned emotion/coping researcher Richard Lazarus. In 2003, his critique mainly stemmed from the belief that positive psychology is indeed just another fad that promises too much and won't deliver. He deemed the focus of positive psychology was to 'accentuate the positive, eliminate the negative, and don't mess with Mr. In-between' (p. 93). Fundamentally, the *positive* in positive psychology implies that positive can be separated from negative, which is dangerous in itself, as we shouldn't emphasize one *at the expense* of the other (Lazarus, 2003).

2 Methodology

Furthermore, Lazarus argues that positive psychology relies on problematic methods, with too much emphasis on the abundance of cross-sectional correlation research. These types of methods are able to show us relationships but not causal directions. However, this limitation in research design is one that plagues psychology in general and not positive psychology alone. Most positive psychologists agree with this psychology-wide limitation and, as the discipline grows, the issues of methodology (cross sectional, self-report) are becoming less prominent, with longitudinal research and world surveys becoming more commonplace.

3 The concept of positive and negative

Another oft-used criticism of positive psychology is its simplistic viewpoint on the dimensionality of emotions; emotions are regarded as either positive or negative but in reality they are often mixed (Larsen et al., 2001, 2004). For example, hope (positive), which is a wish for a desired outcome, can cause incredible amounts of uncertainty and anxiety (negative). Joy may be pleasant but is usually short lived. Pride is one of seven deadly sins. Love is pleasant but only when reciprocated. Anger can be positive when one needs to assert oneself. Thus, positive psychology would do well to heed this critique and continually identify the complexity of emotions and the blends that can occur within human life.

Held (2002) supports this argument, claiming that positive psychologists convey polarizing messages without nuances (positive is good, negativity is bad). Some positive psychologists (such as Seligman) seem to suggest that 'we must think positive thoughts, we must cultivate positive emotions and attitudes, and we must play to our strengths to be happy, healthy, and wise.'

4 Unbalanced perspective on topics and research findings

Lazarus also criticizes positive psychology's advocacy of optimism, which is incredibly one-sided and unbalanced. In reality, pessimists ('realists') mobilize valuable outrage against cruelty, murder, slavery, genocide, prejudice and discrimination.

Lazarus also argues that 'psychology as usual' was not as unbalanced as previously claimed. This is actually a difficult critique to unravel. Research within the areas of self-esteem, confidence, positive reappraisal and so forth has been going on for decades. This is again where new positive psychologists need to be aware of what research and topic areas have come before them in order to understand what is 'new' and what is now simply extensions of previous theory.

Held proposes that Seligman's message was sometimes too one-sided and messianic: 'Pessimists are losers on many fronts' (authentic happiness). There is an implicit message that 'accentuating the positive' (and ignoring the negative) is maximally beneficial (Held, 2004). However, research suggests that co-activation of negative emotions and memories is also necessary for integration and growth (Larsen et al., 2003). However, on a side note, researchers propose that there is no evidence to suggest that a healthy balance of positive and negative experiences is needed (King, 2003). Furthermore, people who experience positive illusions are better off than those who are realistic.

Not only do critics criticize the unbalanced perspective in topic coverage; they also believe that critical reporting on the subjects and the research findings is unbalanced as well. Positive psychologists often claim that positive emotions/cognitions uniformly lead to better health and longevity. Some research suggests that mildly depressed older women live longer (Hybels et al., 2002) and that cheerfulness (optimism and sense of humour) is associated with younger age of death in a longitudinal study (Friedman et al., 1993).

5 Negative as necessary

Van Deurzen's (2009) critique of positive psychology focuses on the notion of positive psychology filling a void in this century's lost people, who find their lives devoid of meaning. Most notably, Van Deurzen states that struggle and hardship are necessary in human existence and that positive psychology fixates on a happy ending. In response to the latter criticism, the areas of resilience and post-traumatic growth (PTG) focus specifically on these concepts and on how, through suffering, we can learn something and change something valuable about ourselves. This argument shows a lack of understanding for the areas outwith authentic happiness and subjective wellbeing, which, as you will know by now, are not the sole focus of positive psychology.

Ultimately, Van Deurzen and several other notable researchers miss the area of PTG when critiquing what positive psychology suggests makes life worth living. Critics even use Frankl as a perfect example of something we should aspire to; we would agree with this and remind critics that Frankl is a figurehead for the area of meaning and PTG, which falls within the realm of positive psychology.

6 Positive psychology as a cult

Is positive psychology little more than an ideological movement? A dogma for the increasingly secular societies in which we live? Some researchers argue that positive psychology gives people a bandwagon to hop onto, however this comparison clearly oversimplifies the issue. Yes, positive psychology might have overemphasized novelty, but this was understandable to identify, from the start, its perspective shift. Researchers and students in positive psychology work hard to put scientific evidence behind important topics and phenomena, and not to advocate self-help techniques that have not been properly validated through psychological experimentation.

7 Ethics of positive psychologists

Van Deurzen argues that positive psychologists offer quick fixes, taking complex issues and turning them into easy to access sellable commodities. But aren't we always trying to bridge the gap between research and the ivory tower and practice–application? What good are ideas if not put into practice?

Van Deurzen argues that positive psychology's aim is to change unhelpful and negative thoughts/emotions into more productive/positive entities, likening it to a sort of mind control. However, traditional clinical psychology has for decades 'interfered' with patients' negative thinking and attempted to remove detrimental patterns. The difference we see is that positive psychology offers not just the removal but also the addition of adaptive thought processes. Positive psychology is not asking for the exclusivity of positive thoughts; rather it understands and highlights the importance of a healthy balance to negative thinking. The positive psychology movement does not endorse unconscious satisfaction.

8 Tyranny of positive thinking

Held (2002) argues that there is a major 'dark downside' to the positive psychology movement, a side effect being that victims of unfortunate circumstances, and other sufferers, are blamed for their own misery. When victims fail to exhibit the necessary optimism, strength, virtue and willpower, it is their own fault. The tyranny of the positive attitude may paradoxically reduce subjective wellbeing, the very condition it is designed to enhance. The implicit cultural mandate that unhappiness is intolerable and should be abolished may be harmful (Held, 2002):

> ❝ The single most remarkable fact of human existence is how hard it is for human beings to be happy. If we add up all those humans who are or have been depressed, addicted, anxious, angry, self-destructive, alienated, worried, compulsive, workaholic, insecure, painfully shy, divorced, avoidant of intimacy, stressed, and so on, we are compelled to reach this startling conclusion: Suffering is a basic characteristic of human life.
>
> *– (Hayes, Strosahl, and Wilson, 1999 – see also the ACT website at http://contextualpsychology.org/act)* ❞

9 The separatist stance of (some) positive psychologists

Seligman dismisses humanistic psychology as unscientific (Taylor, 2001; Held, 2004) and simultaneously defines quantitative, empirical research as the only legitimate scientific basis for positive psychology. 'This dismissal can be understood in the context of positive psychology's dominant, separatist Message: If one claims that one's movement constitutes a "discrete approach within the social sciences," then one must eliminate competing approaches that can challenge that distinction' (Held, 2004).

9½ Lack of cohesive guiding theory

Critics argue that neither logical nor empirical relationships between variables are clearly established within the area of positive psychology. We put this as 9½ because we feel that there is a guiding theory that binds the areas of research. Yes, there are several areas that seem not to link well; however, each area is trying to understand how humans flourish. Furthermore, if you were to look within cognitive psychology, many of the topic areas bear little resemblance or connection to the others, with the main thread being to look at the brain and how it influences human behaviour.

10 Positive psychology neglects positive aspects of 'negative thinking'

Critics would argue that there is a definite case for the positive effects of negative thinking. For example, defensive pessimism, as discussed in Chapter 5, can be a good thing, depending on the individual. Furthermore, there is some evidence to support the 'case for complaining' (Kowalski, 2002). Although chronic complainers tend to be disliked and ostracized, and chronic complaining facilitates negative moods in oneself and others, there are benefits to the initiation of complaints. For example, complaining in novel, unpleasant situations can be an effective form of social bonding (for instance, when in a waiting room, at a new college, or any other unfamiliar situation – expression of complaints about unpleasant circumstances is effective ice breaking). In conclusion, Kowalski argues that 'positive psychology has neglected to focus on the positive features of negative interpersonal behaviours.'

The future of positive psychology

Interestingly, the major figures within the discipline (for example, Diener, Linley, Joseph) believe that the integration of positive psychology (and therefore its disappearance) is the ideal future of the field. Ultimately the purpose of Seligman's APA terms as president was to readdress the imbalance within 'psychology as usual'. Now that this has been addressed, perhaps there is no 'need' for a separate discipline. The timeline over which this could potentially take place is debatable. Integration and a shift in perspective may continue for another decade or longer, depending on funding, researchers and a need for developed theories and applications (Linley et al., 2006).

As researchers, consultants and lecturers within the field of positive psychology we have a unique insight and have made an educated prediction for the future of positive psychology. We feel that if positive psychology continues with what Joseph and Linley once described as marginalization (the segregation of positive psychology from the other fields within psychology), it would damage the integrity and growth of the subject. Within our own departments and fields, we as academics can feel the destructive consequences of such a narrow-minded focus and strongly deter our students from thinking in this way. The more a discipline isolates itself, the more it loses in terms of depth, richness and understanding of its counterparts.

Indeed, we feel that as positive psychology progresses and grows, its strength will double with integration into other areas of the science, with continued specialization. This proposed future has elements of pragmatism in it in terms of the funding and structural issues guaranteed to exist within psychological bureaucracy. Positive psychology must recognize, however, that while studying the positive there needs to be an acknowledgement of the negative, because imbalance was what originally drove us to the field in the first place.

Summary

Reflecting on the learning objectives, you should now understand the current critiques of positive psychology. More specifically, you should know:

- We have identified ten major critiques of the positive psychology movement, most of which are the result of a misunderstanding of the discipline.
- As the discipline grows and ages, the issues of methodology (cross-sectional studies, self-reports) are becoming less prominent, with longitudinal research and world surveys becoming more prominent.
- As you can see from Chapter 6, positive psychology recognizes that negative experiences are part of life and via research on resilience and growth it attempts to understand a more holistic sense of being than critics assume.

- There are still several questions left to answer, such as why interventions work for some people and not others. Is it genetics?
- There are several perceived futures for the area of positive psychology: separation, integration and complete dissolution.

Suggested Resources

http://www.uel.ac.uk/psychology/programmes/postgraduate/positive-msc.htm
For access to information regarding our MAPP course at the University of East London, UK, please log on and view the details.

http://www.sas.upenn.edu/lps/graduate/mapp/
If you fancy an American perspective, check out the following MAPP USA website for information on their programme.

http://www.intentionalhappiness.com/workbooks.html
For workbooks in the area of positive psychology, log onto Robert Biswas-Diener's selection of workbooks for you to use in your own time.

http://www.uel.ac.uk/psychology/lp4/index.htm

http://positivepsychologynews.com
This website will keep you updated on all the recent developments, book reviews and debates within the field of positive psychology.

http://www.centreforconfidence.co.uk

http://www.bowdoin.edu/faculty/b/bheld/

Textbook summary

So as the textbook, and your course, comes to the end of its journey, let's review what we set out to achieve with this textbook, as well as with the course in general.

We set out to give undergraduates an up-to-date, critical textbook that could lead them on a clear journey through positive psychology. We wanted to present readings that are relevant beyond the traditional, narrow positive psychological perspective, on topics such as the positive influence of the body and existential positive death. During the next stages of your education in positive psychology, you can push the boundaries of what you have learned here. Try out the suggested resources, look into the MAPP MSc programmes or contact your local or national positive psychology centre.

Over the past 12 weeks, we hope you have engaged with the textbook, taking the time to stop and reflect on the 'think about it' sections. Furthermore, we hope you have enjoyed reading the interesting and sometimes obscure experiments that we feel each positive psychology student should know.

Finally, we hope that you have taken the time, each week, to attempt the personal development interventions that we have chosen according to the topics within the relevant chapters. These are based on scientific evidence and, if initiated with intrinsic engagement, can have a significant impact on your wellbeing.

Overall, we hope you have gained a balanced perspective of positive psychology through critical thinking and we wholeheartedly encourage you to undertake further independent study.

Further questions for you

1 What do you intend to do with your knowledge of positive psychology?

2 Do you think the discipline is biased and exclusive?

3 How would you describe the discipline in one sentence?

4 What would your ideal future be for positive psychology?

Personal Development Interventions

1 Creating your own mind map
We would like you to now set aside some time, review the mind map you created within the first chapter, and create a new, more intricate version. How does it compare to the mind map you created 11 weeks ago? What do your main branches look like? What now stems off of them? If you need reminding of how to do the mind map, use the example in the first chapter to guide you.

2 Creating an 'emotion' scrapbook
This last intervention is aimed at giving you a personal development intervention that you can keep doing long after the course has finished. It is similar in concept to the portfolio from Chapter 8. We would like you to create a portfolio based on one of the ten positive emotions (for example, a gratitude or serenity portfolio) (Fredrickson, 2009). For this intervention, you need to collect photographs, memorabilia and so forth that help you feel the emotion you are trying to encapsulate. You can be as creative as you like – just make sure you are choosing meaningful and relevant entries. Once you have completed one, try to create, in your own time, a portfolio for all ten emotions (Fredrickson, 2009). Remember, this is an ongoing task that you can return to many weeks, months from now and reflect upon or add to.

References

Abramson, L. Y., Seligman, M. E. P. and Teasdale, J. D. (1978) Learned helplessness in humans – critique and reformulation. *Journal of Abnormal Psychology,* 87(1): 49–74.

Ackerman, C. (2009) Dopamine. In S. Lopez (ed.) *The Encyclopedia of Positive Psychology* (pp. 288–90). Chichester: Blackwell Publishing Ltd.

Adelmann, K. (1987) Occupational complicity, control and personal income – their relationship to well being in men and women. *Journal of Applied Psychology,* 72(4): 529–37.

Affleck, G., Tennen, H., Croog, S. and Levine, S. (1987) Causal attribution, perceived benefits, and morbidity after a heart attack: an 8-year study. *Journal of Consulting and Clinical Psychology,* 55: 29–35.

Ai, A. L., Tice, T. N., Whitsett, D. D., Ishisaka, T. and Chim, M. (2007) Posttraumatic symptoms and growth of Kosovar war refugees: the influence of hope and cognitive coping. *Journal of Positive Psychology,* 2(1): 55–65.

Ajzen, I. (1988) *Attitudes, Personality, and Behavior.* Milton Keynes: Open University Press.

Ajzen, I. (1991) The theory of planned behaviour. *Organisational Behaviour and Human Decision Processes,* 50: 179–211.

Ajzen, I. and Fishbein, M. (1980) *Understanding Attitudes and Predicting Social Behaviour.* Englewood Cliffs, NJ: Prentice-Hall.

Aked, J., Marks, N., Cordon, C. and Thompson, C. (2008) *Five Ways to Wellbeing.* London: New Economics Foundation.

Amabile, T. M. (1983a) *The Social Psychology of Creativity.* New York: Springer-Verlag.

Amabile, T. M. (1983b) The social psychology of creativity: a componential conceptualization. *Journal of Personality and Social Psychology,* 45: 357–76.

Antoni, M. H., Lehman, J. M., Kilbourn, K. M. et al. (2001) Cognitive-behavioral stress management intervention decreases the prevalence of depression and enhances benefit finding among women under treatment for early-stage breast cancer. *Health Psychology,* 20(1): 20–32.

Antonovsky, A. (1979) *Health, Stress and Coping.* San Francisco, CA: Jossey-Bass.

Antonovsky, A. (1987) *Unraveling the Mystery of Health – How People Manage Stress and Stay Well.* San Francisco, CA: Jossey-Bass Publishers.

Antonovsky, A. (1993) The structure and properties of the Sense of Coherence Scale. *Social Science and Medicine,* 36: 725–33.

Antonovsky, H. and Sagy, S. (2001) The development of a sense of coherence and its impact on response to stress situations. *Journal of Social Psychology,* 126(2): 213–25.

Arey, B. D. and Beal, M. W. (2002) The role of exercise in the prevention and treatment of wasting in acquired immune deficiency syndrome. *Journal of the Association of Nurses in AIDS Care,* 13: 29–49.

Åstrand, P. O. (1994) Physical activity and fitness: evolutionary perspective and trends for the future. In C. Bouchard, R.J. Shephard, and T. Stephens (eds) *Physical Activity, Fitness, and Health: International Proceedings and Consensus Statement* (pp. 98–105). Champaign, IL: Human Kinetics.

Babyak, M., Blumenthal, J. A., Herman, S. et al. (2000) Exercise treatment for major depression: maintenance of therapeutic benefit at 10 months. *Psychosomatic Medicine,* 62(5): 633–8.

Backhouse, S. (2009) Aerobic activity. In S. Lopez (ed.) *The Encyclopedia of Positive Psychology* (pp. 18–21). Chichester: Blackwell Publishing Ltd.

Baltes, P., Staudinger, U., Maercker, A. and Smith, J. (1995) People nominated as wise: a comparative study of wisdom-related knowledge. *Psychology and Aging,* 10: 155–66.

Bancroft, J., Janssen, E., Strong, D. et al. (2003) The relation between mood and sexuality in heterosexual men. *Archives of Sexual Behavior,* 32(3): 217–30.

Bandura, A. (1977) *Social Learning Theory.* Englewood Cliffs, NJ: Prentice-Hall.

Bandura, A. (1986) *Social Foundations of Thought and Action: A Social Cognitive Theory.* Englewood Cliffs, NJ: Prentice-Hall.

Bandura, A. (1997) *Self-Efficacy: The Exercise of Control.* New York: Freeman Press.

Bandura, A., Ross, D. and Ross, S. A. (1961) Transmission of aggression through imitation of aggressive models. *Journal of Abnormal and Social Psychology,* 63: 575–82.

Baumeister, R. F. (2003) Ego depletion and self-regulation failure: a resource model of self-control. *Alcoholism: Clinical and Experimental Research,* 27(2): 281–4.

Baumeister, R. F., Bratslavsky, E., Muraven, M. and Tice, D. M. (1998) Ego depletion: is the active self a limited resource? *Journal of Personality and Social Psychology,* 74(5): 1252–65.

Baumeister, R. F., Gailliot, M., DeWall, C. N. and Oaten, M. (2006) Self-regulation and personality: how interventions increase regulatory success, and how depletion moderates the effects of traits on behavior. *Journal of Personality,* 74(6): 1773–801.

Baumeister, R. F., Muraven, M. and Tice, D. M. (2000) Ego depletion: a resource model of volition, self-regulation, and controlled processing. *Social Cognition,* 18(2): 130–50.

Baumrind, D. (1991) The influence of parenting style on adolescent competence and substance use. *Journal of Early Adolescence,* 11: 56–95.

Baumrind, D. (1993) The average expectable environment is not good enough. *Child Development,* 64: 1299–1317.

Baylis, N. and Morris, I. (2006) *The Skills of Wellbeing: Course Overview.* Tonbridge Wells: Wellington College.

Beck, A. T. (1976) *Cognitive Therapy and the Emotional Disorders.* New York: International Universities Press.

Benton, D. and Donohoe, R. T. (1999) The effects of nutrients on mood. *Public Health Nutrition,* 2(3A): 403–9.

Bernard, M. E., Froh, J. J., DiGiuseppe, R., Joyce, M. R. and Dryden, W. (2010) Albert Ellis: unsung hero of positive psychology. *Journal of Positive Psychology,* 5: 302–10.

Biddle, S. J. H., Fox, K. R., Boutcher, S. H. and Faulkner, G. (2000) The way forward for physical activity and the promotion of psychological wellbeing. In S. J. H. Biddle, K. Fox and S. H. Boutcher (eds) *Physical Activity and Psychological Wellbeing* (pp. 154–68). London: Routledge.

Biddle, S. J. H. and Mutrie, N. (2007) *Psychology of Physical Activity: Determinants, Wellbeing and Interventions* (2nd edn). London: Routledge.

Biswas-Diener, R. (2006) From the equator to the north pole: a study of character strengths. *Journal of Happiness Studies,* 7: 293–310.

Biswas-Diener, R. and Diener, E. (2006) The subjective wellbeing of the homeless, and lessons for happiness. *Social Indicators Research,* 76: 185–205.

Black, A. E. and Deci, E. L. (2000) The effects of instructors' autonomy support and students' autonomous motivation on learning organic chemistry: a self-determination theory perspective. *Science Education,* 84: 740–56.

Blanchflower, D. G. (2001) Unemployment, wellbeing, and wage curves in eastern and central Europe. *Journal of the Japanese and International Economies,* 15(4): 364–402.

Blanchflower, D. G., Oswald, A. J. and Stutzer, A. (2001) Latent entrepreneurship across nations. *European Economic Review,* 45(4–6): 680–91.

Blumenthal, J. A., Babyak, M. A., Moore, K. A. et al. (1999) Effects of exercise training on older patients with major depression. *Archives of Internal Medicine,* 159: 2349–56.

Bohart, A. (1993) Emphasizing the future in empathy responses. *Journal of Humanistic Psychology,* 33(2): 12–29.

Boniwell, I. (2008) *Positive Psychology in a Nutshell.* London: Personal Wellbeing Centre.

Boniwell, I. (2009) European Network for Positive Psychology. In S. Lopez (ed.) *The Encyclopedia of Positive Psychology* (pp. 357–9). Chichester: Blackwell Publishing Ltd.

Boniwell, I. and Seligman, M. (in preparation) The 'magic' of MAPP: factors behind optimal engagement of students studying for a Master's in Applied Positive Psychology.

Boutcher, S. H. (2000) Cognitive performance, fitness and aging. In S. J. H. Biddle, K. R. Fox and S. H. Boutcher (eds) *Physical Activity and Psychological Wellbeing* (pp. 118–129). London: Routledge.

Bower, J. E., Kemeny, M. E., Taylor, S. E. and Fahey, J. L. (1998) Cognitive processing, discovery of meaning, CD4 decline, and AIDS-related mortality among bereaved HIV-seropositive men. *Journal of Consulting and Clinical Psychology,* 66(6): 979–86.

Brackett, M., Crum, A. and Salovey, P. (2009) Emotional intelligence. In S. Lopez (ed.) *The Encyclopedia of Positive Psychology* (pp. 310–15). Chichester: Blackwell Publishing Ltd.

Brand, S., Felner, R., Shim, M., Seitsinger, A. and Dumas T. (2003) Middle school improvement and reform: development and validation of a school-level assessment of climate, cultural pluralism, and school safety. *Journal of Educational Psychology,* 95: 570–88.

Branden, N. (1994) *The Six Pillars of Self-esteem.* New York: Bantam Books.

Braun, V. and Clarke, V. (2006) Using thematic analysis in psychology. *Qualitative Research in Psychology,* 3: 77–101.

Brickman, P., Coates, D. and Janoff-Bulman, R. (1978) Lottery winners and accident victims – is happiness relative? *Journal of Personality and Social Psychology,* 36(8): 917–27.

Bridges, S. and Wertz, F. (2009) Abraham Maslow. In S. Lopez (ed.) *The Encyclopedia of Positive Psychology* (pp. 599–600) Chichester: Blackwell Publishing Ltd.

Brody, S. (2006) Blood pressure reactivity to stress is better for people who recently had penile-vaginal intercourse than for people who had other or no sexual activity. *Biological Psychology,* 71(2): 214–22.

Brody, S. (2010) The relative health benefits of different sexual activities. *Journal of Sexual Medicine,* 7(4): 1336–61.

Brody, S., Veit, R. and Rau, H. (2000) A preliminary report relating frequency of vaginal intercourse to heart rate variability, Valsalva ratio, blood pressure, and cohabitation status. *Biological Psychology,* 52(3): 251–7.

Brunstein, J. (1993) Personal goals and subjective wellbeing: a longitudinal study. *Journal of Personality and Social Psychology,* 65: 1061–70.

Brunstein, J., Schultheiss, O. C. and Grassman, R. (1998) Personal goals and emotional wellbeing: The moderating role of motive dispositions. *Journal of Personality and Social Psychology,* 75: 494–508.

Bryant, F. B. and Veroff, J. (2007) *Savoring: A New Model of Positive Experience.* Mahwah, NJ: Lawrence Erlbaum Associates.

Buckingham, M. and Clifton, D. (2005) *Now Discover Your Strengths: How to Develop Your Talents and Those of the People You Manage.* New York: Pocket Books.

Buettner, D. (2010) *Thrive: Finding Happiness the Blue Zones Way.* Washington, DC: National Geographic Society.

Burton, C. M. and King, L. A. (2004) The health benefits of writing about intensely positive experiences. *Journal of Research in Personality,* 38(2): 150–63.

Burton, C. M. and King, L. A. (2008) Effects of (very) brief writing on health: the two-minute miracle. *British Journal of Health Psychology,* 13: 9–14.

Cadell, S., Regehr, C. and Hemsworth, D. (2003) Factors contributing to post-traumatic growth: a beginning structural equation model. *American Journal of Orthopsychiatry,* 73(3): 279–87.

Calhoun, L. G. and Tedeschi, R. G. (2004) The foundations of posttraumatic growth: new considerations. *Psychological Inquiry,* 15(1): 93–102.

Calhoun, L. G. and Tedeschi, R. G. (2008) The paradox of struggling with trauma: guidelines for practice and directions for research. In S. Joseph and A. Linley (eds) *Trauma, Recovery, and Growth: Positive Psychological Perspectives on Posttraumatic Stress* (pp. 325–37). Hoboken, NJ: John Wiley & Sons, Inc.

Camacho, T. C., Roberts, R. E., Lazarus, N. B., Kaplan, G. A. and Cohen, R. D. (1991) Physical activity and depression: evidence from the Almeda county study. *American Journal of Epidemiology,* 134(2): 220–31.

Cameron, R. and Maginn, C. (2008) The authentic warmth dimension of professional childcare. *British Journal of Social Work,* 38: 1151–72.

Cameron, R. J. and Maginn, C. (manuscript submitted for publication) The authentic warmth dimension of professional childcare.

Campbell, A., Mutrie, N., White, F., McGuire, F. and Kearney, N. (2005) A pilot study of a supervised group exercise programme as a rehabilitation treatment for women with breast cancer receiving adjuvant treatment. *European Journal of Oncological Nursing,* 9: 56–63.

Cantor, N. and Sanderson, C. (1999) Life task participation and wellbeing: the importance in taking part in daily life. In D. Kahneman, E. Diener and N. Schwarz (eds) *Wellbeing: The Foundations of Hedonic Psychology* (pp. 230–243). New York: Russell Sage Foundation.

Cantril, H. (1965) *The Pattern of Human Concerns.* New Brunswick, NJ: Rutgers University Press.

Cardasis, W., Huth-Bocks, A. and Silk, K. (2008) Tattoos and anti-personality disorder. *Personality and Mental Health,* 2: 171–82.

Carr, A. (2004) *Positive Psychology: The Science of Happiness and Human Strengths.* Hove: Brunner-Routledge.

Carstensen, L. L. and Charles, S. T. (2002) Human aging: Why is even good news taken as bad? In L. Aspinwall and U. Staudinger (eds) *A Psychology of Human Strengths: Perspectives on an Emerging Field.* Washington, DC: American Psychological Association.

Carver, C. S. and Scheier, M. F. (1982) Control theory – a useful conceptual-framework for personality, social, clinical and health psychology. *Psychological Bulletin,* 92(1): 111–35.

Carver, C. S. and Scheier, M. F. (1990) Origins and functions of positive and negative affect – a control process view. *Psychological Review,* 97(1): 19–35.

Carver, C. S. and Scheier, M. F. (1998) *On the Self-regulation of Behavior.* New York: Cambridge University Press.

Carver, C.S and Scheier, M. F. (2009) Optimism. In S. Lopez (ed.) *The Encyclopedia of Positive Psychology* (pp. 656–63). Chichester: Blackwell Publishing Ltd.

Cassel, L. and Suedfelda, P. (2006) Salutogenesis and autobiographical disclosure among Holocaust survivors. *Journal of Positive Psychology,* 1(4): 212–25.

Charney, D. (2004) Psychobiological mechanisms of resilience and vulnerability: implications for successful adaptation to extreme stress. *American Journal of Psychiatry,* 161: 195–216.

Cheavens, J. and Dreer, L. (2009) Coping. In S. Lopez (ed.) *The Encyclopedia of Positive Psychology* (pp. 232–9). Chichester: Blackwell Publishing Ltd.

Christakis, N. and Fowler, J. (2009) *Connected: The Surprising Power of Our Social Networks and How They Shape Our Lives.* New York: Little, Brown & Company.

Ciarrocchi, J. W., Dy-Liacco, G. S. and Deneke, E. (2008) Gods or rituals? Relational faith, spiritual discontent, and religious practices as predictors of hope and optimism. *Journal of Positive Psychology,* 3(2): 120–36.

Claessens, B., Van Eerde, W., Rutte, C. and Roe, R. (2007) A review of the time management literature. *Personnel Review,* 36: 255–76.

Clark, A. E., Diener, E., Heorgellis, Y. and Lucas, R. (2008) Lags and leads in life satisfaction: a test of the baseline hypothesis. *The Economic Journal,* 118: 222–43.

Clifton, D. O. and Anderson, E. C. (2001) *StrengthsQuest.* Washington: The Gallup Organization.

Cohen, S., Doyle, W. J., Turner, R. B., Alper, C. M. and Skoner, D. P. (2003) Emotional style and susceptibility to the common cold. *Psychosomatic Medicine,* 65(4): 652–7.

Cohn, M. and Fredrickson, B. (2009) Broaden-and-build theory of positive emotions. In S. Lopez (ed.) *The Encyclopedia of Positive Psychology* (pp. 105–10). Chichester: Blackwell Publishing Ltd.

Collins, R. L., Taylor, S. E. and Skokan, L. A. (1990) A better world or a shattered vision? Changes in perspectives following victimization. *Social Cognition,* 8: 263–85.

Compton, W. C., Smith, M. L., Cornish, K. A. and Qualls, D. L. (1996) Factor structure of mental health measures. *Journal of Personality and Social Psychology,* 71(2): 406–13.

Cook, T. D. and Campbell, D.T. (1979) *Quasi Experimentation: Design and Analysis Issues for Field Settings.* Chicago: Rand-McNally.

Cooper, K. A., Donovan, J. L., Waterhouse, A. L. and Williamson, G. (2008) Cocoa and health: a decade of research. *British Journal of Nutrition,* 99(1): 1–11.

Cordova, M. (2008) Facilitating posttraumatic growth following cancer. In S. Joseph and A. Linley (eds) *Trauma, Recovery and Growth: Positive Psychological Perspectives on Posttraumatic Stress* (pp. 185–206) Hoboken, NJ: John Wiley & Sons, Inc.

Cordova, M., Cunningham, L., Carlson, C. and Andrykowski, M. (2001) Posttraumatic growth following breast cancer: a controlled comparison study. *Health Psychology,* 20: 176–85.

Costa, P. T. and McCrae, R. R. (1992) *Revised NEO Personality Inventory (NEO-PI-R) and NEO Five-Factor Inventory (NEO-FFI) Manual.* Odessa, FL: Psychological Assessment Resources.

Costa, T. and McCrae, R. R. (1980) Influence of extraversion and neuroticism on subjcetive wellbeing: Happy and unhappy people. *Journal of Personality and Social Psychology,* 38(4): 668–78.

Courneya, K. S. (2003) Exercise in cancer survivors: an overview of research. *Medicine and Science in Sports and Exercise,* 35(11): 1846–52.

Courneya, K. S., Mackey, J. and Jones, L. (2000) Coping with cancer: can exercise help? *The Physician and Sportsmedicine,* 28: 49–73.

Courneya, K. S., Mackey, J. R. and McKenzie, D. C. (2002) Exercise for breast cancer survivors – research evidence and clinical guidelines. *Physician and Sportsmedicine,* 30(8): 33–42.

Covey, L. S., Glassman, A. H. and Stetner, F. (1998) Cigarette smoking and major depression. *Journal of Addictive Diseases,* 17: 35–46.

Craig, C. (2007) *Creating Confidence: A Handbook for Professionals Working with Young People.* Glasgow, UK: Centre for Confidence and Wellbeing.

Crawford, S., Diener, E., Wirtz, D., Lucas, R. and Oishi, S. (2002) Wanting, having and satisfaction: Examining the role of desire discrepancies in satisfaction with income. *Journal of Personality and Social Psychology*, 83: 725–34.

Crocker, J. and Wolfe, C. T. (2001) Contingencies of self-worth. *Psychological Review*, 108: 593–623.

Csikszentmihalyi, M. (1975) *Beyond Boredom and Anxiety*. San Franscisco: Jossey-Bass.

Csikszentmihalyi, M. (1990) *Flow: The Psychology of Optimal Experience*. New York: Harper & Row.

Csikszentmihalyi, M. (1992) *Flow: The Psychology of Happiness*. New York: Rider & Co.

Csikszentmihalyi, M. (1993) *The Evolving Self: A Psychology for the Third Millenium*. New York: Harper Collins.

Csikszentmihalyi, M. (1997) *Finding Flow: The Psychology of Engagement with Everyday Life*. New York: Basic Books.

Csikszentmihalyi, M. (2002) *Flow: The Classic Work on How to Achieve Happiness*. New York: Harper & Row.

Csikszentmihalyi, M. (2003) *Good Business: Flow, Leadership and The Making of Meaning*. New York: Viking.

Csikszentmihalyi, M. (2009) Flow. In S. Lopez (ed.) *The Encyclopedia of Positive Psychology* (pp. 394–400). Chichester: Blackwell Publishing Ltd.

Csikszentmihalyi, M. and Csikszentmihalyi, I. (1988) *Optimal Experience: Psychological Studies of Flow In Consciousness*. New York: Cambridge University Press.

Csikszentmihalyi, M. and Larson, R. (1984) *Being Adolescent: Conflict and Growth in the Teenage Years*. New York: Basic Books.

Cuevas-Renaud, C., Sobrevilla-Calvo, P. and Almanza, J. (2000) Development of a scale to measure psychosocial concerns of Mexican women with advanced cancer. *Psycho-Oncology*, 9: 73–83.

Curley, J. and Keverne, E. (2009) Epigenetics. In S. Lopez (ed.) *The Encyclopedia of Positive Psychology* (pp. 345–7). Chichester: Blackwell Publishing Ltd.

Danish, S. J. (1996) Going for the goal: a life-skills program for adolescents. In G. W. Abele and T. P. Gullotta (eds) *Primary Prevention Works*. Newbury Park, CA: Sage.

Davey Smith, G., Frankel, S. and Yarnell, J. (1997) Sex and death: are they related? Findings from the Caerphilly Cohort Study. *British Medical Journal*, 315(7123): 1641–4.

Davidson, R. J. (2001) Toward a biology of personality and emotion. *Unity of Knowledge: the Convergence of Natural and Human Science*, 935: 191–207.

Davidson, R. J. (2003) Affective neuroscience and psychophysiology: toward a synthesis. *Psychophysiology*, 40(5): 655–65.

Davidson, R. J. and Irwin, W. (1999) The functional neuroanatomy of emotion and affective style. *Trends in Cognitive Sciences*, 3(1): 11–21.

Davidson, R. J., Jackson, D. C. and Kalin, N. H. (2000) Emotion, plasticity, context, and regulation: Perspectives from affective neuroscience. *Psychological Bulletin*, 126(6): 890–909.

Davidson, R. J., Kabat-Zinn, J., Schumacher, J. et al. (2003) Alterations in brain and immune function produced by mindfulness meditation. *Psychosomatic Medicine*, 65(4): 564–70.

Davidson, R. J., Marshall, J. R., Tomarken, A. J. and Henriques, J. B. (2000) While a phobic waits: Regional brain electrical and autonomic activity in social phobics during anticipation of public speaking. *Biological Psychiatry*, 47(2): 85–95.

Davies, M., Stankov, L. and Roberts, R. D. (1998) Emotional intelligence: in search of an elusive construct. *Journal of Personality and Social Psychology*, 75: 989–1015.

Day, A. and Carroll, S. (2008) Faking emotional intelligence (EI): comparing response distortion on ability and trait-based EI measures. *Journal of Organizational Behavior,* 29: 761–84.

De Volder, M. (1979) Time orientation: a review. *Psychologica Belgica,* 19: 61–79.

De Volder, M. and Lens, W. (1982) Academic achievement and future time perspective as a cognitive-motivational concept. *Journal of Personality and Social Psychology,* 42: 566–71.

Deaton, A. (2008) Income, health and wellbeing around the world: Evidence from the Gallup World Poll. *Journal of Economic Perspectives,* 22: 2.

Deci, E., Connell, J. and Ryan, R. (1989) Self-determination in a work organisation. *Journal of Applied Psychology,* 74: 580–90.

Deci, E. L. and Ryan, R. M. (1995) Human agency: The basis for true self-esteem. In M. H. Kernis (ed.) *Efficacy, Agency, and Self-esteem* (pp. 31–50). New York: Plenum.

Deci, E. L. and Ryan, R. M. (2000) The 'what' and 'why' of goal pursuits: human needs and the self-determination of behavior. *Psychological Inquiry,* 11(4): 227–68.

Deci, E. L. and Ryan, R. M. (2008) Self-determination theory: a macrotheory of human motivation, development, and health. *Canadian Psychology-Psychologie Canadienne,* 49(3): 182–5.

Delichte, J. and Evers-Cacciapaglia, R. (2010) The science and application of strengths. Lecture presented 16 April, UEL MAPP.

Delle Fave, A. and Massimini, F. (2004) Bringing subjectivity into focus: optimal experiences, life themes, and person-centred rehabilitation. In P. A. Linley and S. Joseph (eds) *Positive Psychlogy in Practice* (pp. 581–97) Hoboken, NJ: John Wiley & Sons, Inc.

DeNeve, K. M. and Cooper, H. (1998) The happy personality: a meta-analysis of 137 personality traits and subjective wellbeing. *Psychological Bulletin,* 124(2): 197–229.

Di Castelnuovo, A., Rotondo, S. and de Gaetano, G. (2003) Protective effects of alcohol or wine consumption: wishful thinking? In J. Arnout, G. de Gaetano, M. Hoylaerts et al. (eds.) *Thrombosis: Fundamental and Clinical Aspects* (pp. 679–703). Leuven: Leuven University Press.

Di Castelnuovo, A., Rotondo, S., Iacoviello, L., Donati, M. B. and de Gaetano, G. (2002) Meta-analysis of wine and beer consumption in relation to vascular risk. *Circulation,* 105(24): 2836–44.

Diab, D. L., Gillespie, M. A. and Highhouse, S. (2008) Are maximizers really unhappy? The measurement of maximizing tendency. *Judgment and Decision Making,* 3: 364–70.

Diego, M. A., Field, T. and Hernandez-Reif, M. (2008) Temperature increases in preterm infants during massage therapy. *Infant Behavior and Development,* 31(1): 149–52.

Diego, M. A., Field, T., Hernandez-Reif, M. et al. (2001) HIV adolescents show improved immune function following massage therapy. *International Journal of Neuroscience,* 106(1–2): 35–45.

Diego, M. A., Field, T., Hernandez-Reif, M. et al. (2002) Aggressive adolescents benefit from massage therapy. *Adolescence,* 37(147): 597–607.

Diener, E. (1984) Subjective wellbeing. *Psychological Bulletin,* 95: 542–75.

Diener, E. (2000) Subjective wellbeing – the science of happiness and a proposal for a national index. *American Psychologist,* 55(1): 34–43.

Diener, E. (2003) What is positive about positive psychology: the curmudgeon and Pollyanna. *Psychological Inquiry,* 14: 115–20.

Diener, E. (2009) *The Science of Wellbeing: The Collected Works of Ed Diener.* New York: Springer.

Diener, E. and Biswas-Diener, R. (2008) *Happiness: Unlocking the Mysteries of Psychological Wealth.* Boston, MA: Blackwell Publishing.

Diener, E. and Diener, M. (1995) Cross-cultural correlates of life satisfaction and self-esteem. *Journal of Personality and Social Psychology,* 68: 653–63.

Diener, E., Emmons, R. A., Larsen, R. J. and Griffin, S. (1985) The Satisfaction with Life Scale. *Journal of Personality Assessment,* 49(1): 71–5.

Diener, E., Horowitz, J. and Emmons, R. A. (1985) Happiness of the very wealthy. *Social Indicators Research,* 16: 263–74.

Diener, E., Kahneman, D., Arora, R., Harter, J. and Tov, W. (2009) Income's differential influemce on judgements of life versus affective wellbeing. In A. C. Michalos (ed.) 'Social Indicators Research Series', vol. 39. *Assessing Well-being: The Collected Works of Ed Diener.* London: Springer.

Diener, E. and Larsen, R. (1984) Temporal stability and cross-situational consistency of affective, behavioral, and cognitive responses. *Journal of Personality and Social Psychology,* 47: 871–83.

Diener, E., Lucas, R. E., Oishi, S. and Suh, E. M. (2002) Looking up and looking down: weighting good and bad information in life satisfaction judgments. *Personality and Social Psychology Bulletin,* 28(4): 437–45.

Diener, E., Lucas, R., Schimmack, U. and Helliwell, J. (2009) *Wellbeing for Public Policy.* Oxford: Oxford University Press.

Diener, E. and Oishi, S. (2000) Money and happiness: Income and subjective wellbeing across nations. In E. Diener and E. M. Suh (eds.) *Subjective Wellbeing Across Cultures.* Cambridge, MA: MIT Press.

Diener, E., Sandvik, E., Pavot, W. and Gallagher, D. (1991) Response artifacts in the measurement of subjective wellbeing. *Social Indicators Research,* 24(1): 35–56.

Diener, E., Suh, E. M., Lucas, R. E. and Smith, H. L. (1999) Subjective wellbeing: three decades of progress. *Psychological Bulletin,* 125: 276–302.

Diener, E., Wirtz, D., Tov, W. et al. (2009) New measures of wellbeing: flourishing and positive and negative feelings. *Social Indicators Research,* 39: 247–66.

Dieter, J. N. I., Field, T., Hernandez-Reif, M., Emory, E. K. and Redzepi, M. (2003) Stable preterm infants gain more weight and sleep less after five days of massage therapy. *Journal of Pediatric Psychology,* 28(6): 403–11.

Dillinger, T. L., Barriga, P., Escarcega, S. et al. (2000) Food of the gods: cure for humanity? A cultural history of the medicinal and ritual use of chocolate. *Journal of Nutrition,* 130(8): 2057S–2072S.

Duckworth, A. L. and Seligman, M. E. P. (2005) Self-discipline outdoes IQ in predicting academic performance of adolescents. *Psychological Science,* 16(12): 939–44.

Duckworth, A. L. and Seligman, M. E. P. (2006) Self-discipline gives girls the edge: gender in self-discipline, grades, and achievement test scores. *Journal of Educational Psychology,* 98(1): 198–208.

Dunigan, J. T., Carr, B. I. and Steel, J. L. (2007) Posttraumatic growth, immunity and survival in patients with hepatoma. *Digestive Diseases and Sciences,* 52(9): 2452–9.

Dunn, E. W., Aknin, L. B. and Norton, M. I. (2008) Spending money on others promotes happiness. *Science,* 319: 1687–8.

Dweck, C. S. (2006) *Mindset: The New Psychology of Success.* New York: Random House.

Dweck, C. S. and Bempechat, J. (1983) Children's theories of intelligence: implications for learning. In S. Paris, G. Olson and H. Stevenson (eds) *Learning and Motivation in Children.* Hillsdale, NJ: Erlbaum.

Dweck, C. S., Chiu, C. and Hong, Y. (1995) Implicit theories: elaboration and extension of the model. *Psychological Inquiry,* 6: 322–33.

Eades, J. (2008) *Celebrating Strengths: Building Strengths-based Schools.* Warwick: Capp Press.

Ekman, P. (2003) *Emotions Revealed: Recognizing Faces and Feelings to Improve Communication and Emotional Life.* New York: Henry Holt and Company, LLC.

Emerson, H. (1998) Flow and occupation: A review of the literature. *Canadian Journal of Occupational Therapy,* 65: 37–43.

Emmons, R. A. (1991) Personal strivings, daily life events, and psychological and physical well-being. *Journal of Personality,* 59: 453–72.

Emmons, R. A. and McCullough, M. E. (2003) Counting blessings versus burdens: An experimental investigation of gratitude and subjective wellbeing in daily life. *Journal of Personality and Social Psychology,* 84(2): 377–89.

Epel, E., Bandura, A. and Zimbardo, G. (1999) Escaping homelessness: The influences of self-efficacy and time perspective on coping with homelessness. *Journal of Applied Social Psychology,* 29: 575–96.

Falkenstern, M., Schiffrin, H., Nelson, K., Ford, L. and Keyser, C. (2009) Mood over matter: can happiness be your undoing? *Journal of Positive Psychology,* 4: 365–71.

Fava, G. and Ruini, C. (2009) Well–being therapy. In S. Lopez (ed.) *The Encyclopedia of Positive Psychology* (pp. 1034–6). Chichester: Blackwell Publishing Ltd.

Festinger, L., Riecken, H.W. and Schachter, S. (1956) *When Prophecy Fails.* Minneapolis, MN: University of Minnesota Press.

Festinger, L., Riecken, H. and Schachter, S. (2008) *When Prophecy Fails,* 2nd edn. London: Pinter & Martin.

Field, T. (1988) Stimulation of preterm infants. *Pediatrics in Review,* 10: 149–54.

Field, T., Diego, M. A., Hernandez-Reif, M., Schanberg, S. and Kuhn, C. (2004) Massage therapy effects on depressed pregnant women. *Journal of Psychosomatic Obstetrics and Gynecology,* 25(2): 115–22.

Field, T., Hemandez-Reif, M., Diego, M. et al. (2004) Massage therapy by parents improves early growth and development. *Infant Behavior and Development,* 27(4): 435–42.

Field, T., Henteleff, T., Hernandez-Reif, M. et al. (1998) Children with asthma have improved pulmonary functions after massage therapy. *Journal of Pediatrics,* 132(5): 854–8.

Field, T., Hernandez-Reif, M., Diego, M. et al. (2005) Cortisol decreases and serotonin and dopamine increase following massage therapy. *International Journal of Neuroscience,* 115(10): 1397–413.

Field, T., Hernandez-Reif, M., Seligman, S. et al. (1997) Juvenile rheumatoid arthritis: benefits from massage therapy. *Journal of Pediatric Psychology,* 22(5): 607–17.

Field, T., Quintino, O., Hernandez-Reif, M. and Koslovsky, G. (1998) Adolescents with attention deficit hyperactivity disorder benefit from massage therapy. *Adolescence,* 33(129): 103–8.

Findley, M. J. and Cooper, H. M. (1983) Locus of control and academic achievement: a literature review. *Journal of Personality and Social Psychology,* 44: 419–27.

Fine, M. and Gordon, S. M. (1989) Feminist transformations of/despite psychology. In M. Crawford and M. Gently (eds) *Gender and Thought: Psychological Perspectives* (pp. 146–74). New York: Springer-Verlag.

Fisher, J. (2002) Tattooing the body, marking culture. *Body and Society,* 8(4): 91–107.

Ford, M. E. and Nichols, C. W. (1991) Using goal assessments to identify motivational patterns and facilitate behavioral regulation and achievement. In M. L. Maehr and P. Pintrich (eds) *Advances in Motivation and Achievement* (Vol. 7, pp. 51– 84). Greenwich, CT: JAI.

Ford, J. D., Tennen, H. and Albert, D. (2008) A contrarian view of growth following adversity. In S. Joseph and P. A. Linley (eds) *Trauma, Recovery and Growth: Positive Psychological Perspectives on Posttraumatic Stress* (pp. 297–324). Hoboken, NJ: Wiley.

Fordyce, M. (1977) Development of a program to increase personal happiness. *Journal of Counseling Psychology,* 24(6): 511–21.

Fordyce, M. (1981) *The Psychology of Happiness: A Brief Version of the 14 Fundamentals.* Fort Myers, FL: Cypress Lake Media.

Fordyce, M. (1983) A program to increase happiness – further studies. *Journal of Counseling Psychology,* 30(4): 483–98.

Foret, M. and Steger, M. F. (2004, October) Valence of Temporal Perspective: An Important Dimension in the Relation between Time Perspective and Well-being. Presented at the International Positive Psychology Summit, Washington, DC.

Forrester, M. A. (ed.) (2010) *Doing Qualitative Research in Psychology: A Practical Guide.* London: Sage.

Fowler, J. and Christakis, N. (2008) Dynamic spread of happiness in a large social network: longitudinal analysis over 20 years in the Framingham heart study. *British Medical Journal,* 337: 1–9.

Fox, K. R. (2000) Self-esteem, self-perceptions and exercise. *International Journal of Sport Psychology,* 31(2): 228–40.

Frank, A. W. (1995) *The Wounded Storyteller; Body, Illness and Ethics.* Chicago: University of Chicago Press.

Frankl, V. (1963) *Man's Search for Meaning.* New York: Pocket Books.

Fredrickson, B. (2001) The role of positive emotions in positive psychology – the broaden-and-build theory of positive emotions. *American Psychologist,* 56(3): 218–26.

Fredrickson, B. (2009) *Positivity: Groundbreaking Research Reveals how to Embrace the Hidden Strength of Positive Emotions, Overcome Negativity, and Thrive.* New York: Crown.

Fredrickson, B., Cohn, M. A., Coffey, K. A., Pek, J. and Finkel, S. M. (2008) Open hearts build lives: positive emotions, induced through loving-kindness meditation, build consequential personal resources. *Journal of Personality and Social Psychology,* 95: 1045–62.

Fredrickson B. and Dutton, J. (2008) Unpacking positive organizing: organizations as sites of individual and group flourishing. *Journal of Positive Psychology,* 3: 1–3.

Fredrickson, B. and Levenson, R. W. (1998) Positive emotions speed recovery from the cardiovascular sequelae of negative emotions. *Cognition and Emotion,* 12(2): 191–220.

Fredrickson, B. and Losada, M. F. (2005) Positive affect and the complex dynamics of human flourishing. *American Psychologist,* 60(7): 678–86.

Friedman, H. S., Tucker, J. S., Tomlinson-Keasey, C. et al. (1993) Does childhood personality predict longevity? *Journal of Personality and Social Psychology,* 65: 176–85.

Frisch, M. (2006) *Quality of Life Therapy: A Life Satisfaction Approach to Positive Psychology and Cognitive Therapy.* Hoboken, NJ: John Wiley & Sons, Inc.

Frisch, M. B. (1998) Quality of life therapy and assessment in health care. *Clinical Psychology – Science and Practice,* 5(1): 19–40.

Frisch, M. B., Clark, M. P., Rouse, S. V. et al. (2005) Predictive and treatment validity of life satisfaction and the quality of life inventory. *Assessment,* 12(1): 66–78.

Froh, J. J., Fives, C. J., Fuller, J. R. et al. (2007) Interpersonal relationships and irrationality as predictors of life satisfaction. *Journal of Positive Psychology,* 2(1): 29–39.

Froh, J. J., Kashdan, T. B., Ozimkowski, K. M. and Miller, N. (2009) Who benefits the most from a gratitude intervention in children and adolescents? Examining positive affect as a moderator. *Journal of Positive Psychology,* 4(5): 408–22.

Fromm, E. (1976) *To Have or to Be.* London: Abacus.

Gable, S. L., Reis, H. T., Impett, E. A. and Asher, E. R. (2004) What do you do when things go right? The intrapersonal and interpersonal benefits of sharing positive events. *Journal of Personality and Social Psychology,* 87(2): 228–45.

Gailliot, M. T. and Baumeister, R. F. (2007) The physiology of willpower: linking blood glucose to self-control. *Personality and Social Psychology Review,* 11: 303–27.

Gailliot, M. T., Baumeister, R. F., DeWall, C. N. et al. (2007) Self-control relies on glucose as a limited energy source: Willpower is more than a metaphor. *Journal of Personality and Social Psychology,* 92(2): 325–36.

Gainotti, G. (1972) Emotional behavior and hemispheric side of the lesion. *Cortex,* 8(1): 41–55.

Galati, D., Manzano, M. and Sotgiu, I. (2006) The subjective components of happiness and their attainment: a cross-cultural comparison between Italy and Cuba. *Social Science Information Sur Les Sciences Sociales,* 45(4): 601–30.

Gallace, A. and Spence, C. (2010) The science of interpersonal touch: An overview. *Neuroscience and Biobehavioral Reviews,* 34(2): 246–59.

Garbarino, J. (1975) The impact of anticipated reward upon cross-aged tutoring. *Journal of Personality and Social Psychology,* 32: 421–8.

Gardner, H. (1993) *Frames of Mind: The Theory of Multiple Intelligences.* 2nd edn. New York: Basic Books.

Gardner, J. and Oswald, A. (2006) Money and mental wellbeing: a longitudinal study of medium-sized lottery wins. *Journal of Health Economics,* 26(1): 49–60.

Garrison, C. Z., Addy, C. L., Jackson, K. L., McKeown, R. E. and Waller, J. L. (1992) Major depressive disorder and dysthymia in young adolescents. *American Journal of Epidemiology,* 135: 792–802.

Garrison, C. Z., Schluchter, M. D., Schoenbach, V. J. and Kaplan, B. K. (1989) Epidemiology of depressive symptoms in young adolescents. *Journal of the American Academy of Child and Adolescent Psychiatry,* 28: 343–51.

Gilbert, D. (2007) *Stumbling on Happiness.* London: Harper Perennial.

Gilbert, D., Pinel, E. C., Wilson, T. D., Blumberg, S. J. and Wheatley, T. (1998) Immune neglect: A source of durability bias in affective forecasting. *Journal of Personality and Social Psychology,* 75: 617–38.

Gilbert, P., McEwan, K., Mitra, R. et al. (2008) Feeling safe and content: A specific affect regulation system? Relationship to depression, anxiety, stress, and self-criticism. *Journal of Positive Psychology,* 3(3): 182–91.

Gillham, J. E., Reivich, K. J., Freres, D. R. et al. (2007) School-based prevention of depressive symptoms: a randomized controlled study of the effectiveness and specificity of the Penn Resiliency Program. *Journal of Consulting and Clinical Psychology,* 75(1): 9–19.

Gillham, J. E., Reivich, K. J., Jaycox, L. H. and Seligman, M. E. P. (1995) Prevention of depressive symptoms in schoolchildren: Two-year follow-up. *Psychological Science,* 6(6): 343–51.

Goldacre, B. (2009) *Bad Science.* London: Harper Collins Publishers.

Goldenberg, J. and Shackelford, T. (2005) Is it me or is it mine? Body self-integration as a function of self-esteem, body esteem and mortality salience. *Self and Identity,* 4: 227–41.

Goleman, D. (1996) *Emotional Intelligence: Why It Can Matter More Than IQ.* New York: Bantam Books.

Gomez, M. (2009) Albert Bandura. In S. Lopez (ed.) *Encyclopedia of Positive Psychology* (pp. 98–9). Chichester: Blackwell Publishing Ltd.

Grant, A. (in press) Coaching and positive psychology. In K. M. Sheldon, T. B. Kashdan and M. Steger (eds) *Designing the Future of Positive Psychology.* Oxford: Oxford University Press.

Grant, A., Curtayne, L. and Burton, G. (2009) Executive coaching enhances goal attainment, resilience and workplace wellbeing: a randomised controlled study. *Journal of Positive Psychology,* 4(5): 396–407.

Grant, A. and Palmer, S. (2002) Coaching psychology. Meeting held at the annual conference of the Division of Counselling Psychology, British Psychological Society, Torquay, 18 May.

Grant, A. and Spence, G. B. (in press) Using coaching and positive psychology to promote a flourishing workforce: a model of goal-striving and mental health. In A. Linley, S. Harrington and N. Page (eds) *Oxford Handbook of Positive Psychology and Work.* Oxford: Oxford University Press.

Green, H., McGinnity, A., Meltzer, H., Ford, T. and Goodman, R. (2005) *Mental Health of Children and Young People in Great Britain 2004.* London: Office for National Statistics.

Grewen, K. M., Anderson, B. J., Girdler, S. S. and Light, K. C. (2003) Warm partner contact is related to lower cardiovascular reactivity. *Behavioral Medicine,* 29(3): 123–30.

Grewen, K. M., Girdler, S. S., Amico, J. and Light, K. C. (2005) Effects of partner support on resting oxytocin, cortisol, norepinephrine, and blood pressure before and after warm partner contact. *Psychosomatic Medicine,* 67(4): 531–38.

Grolnick, W. S. and Ryan, R. M. (1987a) Autonomy-support in education: Creating the facilitating environment. In N. Hastings and J. Schwieso (eds) *New Directions in Educational Psychology,* Volume 2: Behavior and motivation. London: Falmer Press.

Grolnick, W. S. and Ryan, R. M. (1987b) Autonomy in children's learning: an experimental and individual difference investigation. *Journal of Personality and Social Psychology,* 52: 890–8.

Grubb, W. and McDaniel, M. (2007) The fakability of Bar-On's Emotional Quotient Inventory Short Form: catch me if you can. *Human Performance,* 20: 43–59.

Hafstrom, J. L. and Paynter, M. A. (1991) Time use satisfaction of wives: home, farm, and labor force workload. *Lifestyles,* 12(2): 131–43.

Haidt, J. (2006) *The Happiness Hypothesis: Finding Modern Truth in Ancient Wisdom.* New York: Basic Books.

Harker, L. A. and Keltner, D. (2001) Expressions of positive emotion in women's college yearbook pictures and their relationship to personality and life outcomes across adulthood. *Journal of Personality and Social Psychology,* 80(1): 112–24.

Harlow, H. F. and Zimmermann, R. R. (1959) Affectional responses in the infant monkey. *Science,* 130(3373): 421–32.

Harmon-Jones, E., Simon, L., Greenberg, J. et al. (1997) Terror management theory and self-esteem: evidence that increased self-esteem reduces mortality salience effects. *Journal of Personality and Social Psychology,* 72: 24–36.

Harris, A. H. S. and Thoresen, C. E. (2006) Extending the influence of positive psychology interventions into health care settings: lessons from self-efficacy and forgiveness. *Journal of Positive Psychology,* 1(1): 27–36.

Harter, J. (2009) Employee engagement. In S. Lopez (ed.) *The Encyclopedia of Positive Psychology* (pp. 330–334). Chichester: Blackwell Publishing Ltd.

Hassmen, P., Koivula, N. and Uutela, A. (2000) Physical exercise and psychological wellbeing: a population study in Finland. *Preventive Medicine,* 30(1): 17–25.

Hayes, S. C., Strosahl, K. and Wilson, K. G. (1999) *Acceptance and Commitment Therapy: An Experiential Approach to Behavior Change.* New York: Guilford Press.

Headey, B. (2008) Life goals matter to happiness: a revision of set-point theory. *Social Indicators Research*, 86: 213–31.

Headey, B., Schupp, J., Tucci, I. and Wagner, G. (2010) Authentic happiness theory supported by impact of religion on life satisfaction: a longitudinal analysis with data for Germany. *Journal of Positive Psychology*, 5: 73–82.

Headey, B., Veenhoven, R. and Wearing, A. (1991) Top-down versus bottom-up theories of subjective wellbeing. *Social Indicators of Research*, 24: 81–100.

Headey, B. and Wearing, A. (1989) Personality, life events, and subjective wellbeing: toward a dynamic equilibrium model. *Journal of Personality and Social Psychology*, 57: 731–9.

Hefferon, K. (in press a) Creating 'positive bodies': corporality in hedonic and eudaimonic wellbeing. In C. Martin-Krumm (ed.) *Handbook of Positive Psychology*.

Hefferon, K. (in press b) Positive psychology and coaching. In L. Wildflower and D. Brennan (eds) *Theories, Concepts and Applications of Evidence Based Coaching: A User's Manual*. San Francisco, CA: Jossey-Bass.

Hefferon, K., Grealy, M. and Mutrie, N. (2008) The perceived influence of an exercise class intervention on the process and outcomes of posttraumatic growth. *Journal of Mental Health and Physical Activity*, 1(2): 47–88.

Hefferon, K., Grealy, M. and Mutrie, N. (2009) Posttraumatic growth and life threatening physical illness: a systematic review of the qualitative literature. *British Journal of Health Psychology*, 14(2): 343–78.

Hefferon, K., Grealy, M. and Mutrie, N. (2010) Transforming from cocoon to butterfly: the potential role of the body in the process of posttraumatic growth. *Journal of Humanistic Psychology*, 50(2): 224–47.

Hefferon, K. and Mutrie, N. (in press) Physical activity as a 'stellar' positive psychology intervention. In E.O. Acevedo (ed.) *Oxford Handbook of Exercise Psychology*. Oxford: Oxford University Press.

Hefferon, K. and Ollis, S. (2006) 'Just clicks': an interpretive phenomenological analysis of professional dancers' experience of flow. *Research in Dance Education*, 7: 141–59.

Held, B. S. (2002) The tyranny of the positive attitude in America: observation and speculation. *Journal of Clinical Psychology*, 58(9): 965–91.

Held, B. S. (2004) The negative side of positive psychology. *Journal of Humanistic Psychology*, 44(1): 9–46.

Hernandez-Reif, M., Dieter, J., Field, T., Swerdlow, B. and Diego, M. (1998) Migraine headaches are reduced by massage therapy. *International Journal of Neuroscience*, 96(1–2): 1–11.

Hernandez-Reif, M., Field, T., Ironson, G. et al. (2005) Natural killer cells and lymphocytes increase in women with breast cancer following massage therapy. *International Journal of Neuroscience*, 115(4): 495–510.

Hernandez-Reif, M., Ironson, G., Field, T. et al. (2004) Breast cancer patients have improved immune and neuroendocrine functions following massage therapy. *Journal of Psychosomatic Research*, 57(1): 45–52.

Hernandez-Reif, M., Martinez, A., Field, T. et al. (2000) Premenstrual symptoms are relieved by massage therapy. *Journal of Psychosomatic Obstetrics and Gynecology*, 21(1): 9–15.

Hewitt, J. (2009) Self-esteem. In S. Lopez (ed.) *The Encyclopedia of Positive Psychology* (pp. 880–6). Chichester: Blackwell Publishing Ltd.

Hodges, T. D. and Clifton, D. O. (2004) Strengths-based development in practice. In P. A. Linley and S. Joseph (eds) *Positive Psychology in Practice* (pp. 256–68). Hoboken, NJ: John Wiley & Sons, Inc.

Hodgins, D. and Engel, A. (2002) Future time perspective in pathological gambling. *Journal of Nervous and Mental Disease,* 190(11): 775–80.

Holder, M. and Klassen, A. (2009) Personality. In S. Lopez (ed.) *The Encyclopedia of Positive Psychology* (pp. 689–91). Chichester: Blackwell Publishing Ltd.

Holder, M. D., Coleman, B. and Sehn, Z. L. (2009) The contribution of active and passive leisure to children's wellbeing. *Journal of Health Psychology,* 14(3): 378–86.

Howell, A. J. (2009) Flourishing: achievement-related correlates of students' wellbeing. *Journal of Positive Psychology,* 4(1): 1–13.

Howitt, D. and Cramer, D. (2008) *Introduction to Research Methods in Psychology,* 2nd edn. Harmondsworth: Pearson Education Limited.

Huta, V., Park, N., Peterson, C. and Seligman, M. E. P. (2003, October) Pursuing pleasure versus eudaimonia: which leads to greater satisfaction? Poster presented at the International Positive Psychology Summit, Washington, DC.

Hybels, C., Pieper, C. and Blazer, D. (2002) Sex differences in the relationship between subthreshold depression and mortality in a community sample of older adults. *American Journal of Geriatric Psychiatry,* 10: 283–91.

Isaac, M. T. and Isaac, M. B. (2004) *Eat Yourself Happy.* London: Carroll & Brown.

Iyengar, S. S. and Lepper, M. R. (2000) When choice is demotivating: can one desire too much of a good thing? *Journal of Personality and Social Psychology,* 79(6): 995–1006.

James, O. (2007) *Affluenza.* London: Vermillion.

James, W. (1890) *The Principles of Psychology* (2 vols.). New York: Henry Holt (reprinted Bristol: Thoemmes Press, 1999).

Janoff-Bulman, R. (1992) *Shattered Assumptions: Towards a New Psychology of Trauma.* New York: Free Press.

Janoff-Bulman, R. (2004) Posttraumatic growth: three explanatory models. *Psychological Inquiry,* 15(1): 30–4.

Janssen, E. and Everaerd, W. (1993) Determinants of male sexual arousal. *Annual Review of Sex Research,* 4: 211–45.

Jeffreys, S. (2000) Body art and social status: cutting, tattooing and piercing from a feminist perspective. *Feminism and Psychology,* 10(4): 409–29.

Jimenez, S. (2009) Suffering. In S. Lopez (ed.) *The Encyclopedia of Positive Psychology* (pp. 979–83). Chichester: Blackwell Publishing Ltd.

Johnson, K. J., Waugh, C. M. and Fredrickson, B. L. (2010) Smile to see the forest: facially expressed positive emotions broaden cognition. *Cognition and Emotion,* 24(2): 299–321.

Joseph, S. and Hefferon, K. (in press) Posttraumatic growth: eudaimonic happiness. In I. Boniwell and S. David (eds) *Oxford Handbook of Happiness.* Oxford: Oxford University Press.

Joseph, S. and Linley, A. (2006) *Positive Therapy: A Meta-theory for Positive Psychological Practice.* Hove: Routledge.

Joseph, S. and Linley, A. (eds) (2008) *Trauma, Recovery, and Growth: Positive Psychological Perspectives on Posttraumatic Stress.* Hoboken, NJ: John Wiley & Sons, Inc.

Joseph, S. and Linley, A. (2009) Positive therapy. In S. Lopez (ed.) *The Encyclopedia of Positive Psychology* (pp. 758–9). Chichester: Blackwell Publishing Ltd.

Joseph, S., Linley, A. and Harris, G. J. (2005) Understanding positive change following trauma and adversity: structural clarification. *Journal of Loss and Trauma,* 10(1): 83–96.

Joseph, S., Williams, R. and Yule, W. (1993) Changes in outlook following disaster: The preliminary development of a measure to assess positive and negative responses. *Journal of Traumatic Stress,* 6: 271–9.

Judge, T., Erez, A., Bono, J. and Thorensen, C. (2002) Are measures of self-esteem, neuroticism, locus of control, and generalized self-efficacy indicators of a common core construct? *Journal of Personality and Social Psychology,* 23: 693–710.

Kahana, E. and Kahana, B. (1983) Environmental continuity, futurity and adaptation of the aged. In G. D. Rowles and R. J. Ohta (eds) *Aging and Milieu* (pp. 205–28). New York: Haworth Press.

Kahneman, D. (1999) Objective happiness. In D. Kahneman, E. Diener and N. Schwarz (eds) *Well-being: Foundations of Hedonic Psychology* (pp. 3–25). New York: Russell Sage Foundation Press.

Kahneman, D., Krueger, A., Schkade, D., Schwarz, N. and Stone, A. (2004) A survey method for characterizing daily life experience: the day reconstruction method. *Science,* 306: 1776–80.

Kangas, M., Henry, J. L. and Bryant, R. A. (2002) Posttraumatic stress disorder following cancer – a conceptual and empirical review. *Clinical Psychology Review,* 22(4): 499–524.

Karpinski, A. and Steinberg, R. (2006).The single category implicit association test as a measure of implicit social cognition. *Journal of Personality and Social Psychology,* 91: 16–31.

Kashdan, T. B., Biswas-Diener, R. and King, L. A. (2008) Reconsidering happiness: the costs of distinguishing between hedonics and eudaimonia. *Journal of Positive Psychology,* 3: 219–33.

Kasser, T. and Ryan, R. M. (2001) Be careful what you wish for: optimal functioning and the relative attainment of intrinsic and extrinsic goals. In P. Schmuck and K. M. Sheldon (eds) *Life Goals and Well-being: Towards a Positive Psychology of Human Striving* (pp. 116–31). Gottingen: Hogrefe & Huber Publishers.

Kasser, T., Ryan, R. M., Zax, M. and Sameroff, A. J. (1995) The relations of maternal and social environments to late adolescents'materialistic and prosocial aspirations. *Developmental Psychology,* 31: 907–14.

Kauffman, C. (2006) Positive psychology: the science at the heart of coaching. In D. R. Stober and A. M. Grant (eds) *Evidence Based Coaching Handbook: Putting Best Practices to Work for your Clients* (pp. 219–53). Hoboken, NJ: John Wiley & Sons, Inc.

Kauffman, C. and Scouler, A. (2004) Towards a positive psychology of executive coaching. In A. Linley and S. Joseph (eds) *Positive Psychology in Practice.* New York: John Wiley & Sons, Inc.

Kazakina, E. (1999) Time perspective of older adults: relationships to attachment style, psychological wellbeing, and psychological distress. *Dissertation Abstracts International: Section B: The Sciences and Engineering,* 60(l-b), 0368.

Keith, M. and Schafer, R. B. (1982) A comparison of depression among employed single-parent and married women. *Journal of Psychology,* 110(2): 239–47.

Keough, K. A., Zimbardo, G. and Boyd, J. N. (1999) Who's smoking, drinking and using drugs? Time perspective as a predictor of substance use. *Basic and Applied Social Psychology,* 21: 149–64.

Kesebir, P. and Diener, E. D. (2008) In pursuit of happiness: empirical answers to philosophical questions. *Perspectives on Psychological Science,* 3(2): 117–25.

Keyes, C. and Annas, J. (2009) Feeling good and functioning well: distinctive concepts in ancient philosophy and contemporary science. *Journal of Positive Psychology,* 4: 197–201.

Keyes, C. and Michalec, B. (2009) Mental health. In S. Lopez (ed.) *The Encyclopedia of Positive Psychology* (pp. 614–17). Chichester: Blackwell Publishing Ltd.

Keyes, C., Shmotkin, D. and Ryff, C. D. (2002) Optimizing wellbeing: the empirical encounter of two traditions. *Journal of Personality and Social Psychology,* 82(6): 1007–22.

King, L. A. (2001) The health benefits of writing about life goals. *Personality and Social Psychology Bulletin,* 27(7): 798–807.

King, L. A. (2003) Some truths behind the trombones? *Psychological Inquiry,* 14(2): 128–31.

King, L. A. and Napa, C. K. (1998) What makes a life good? *Journal of Personality and Social Psychology,* 75(1): 156–65.

Kinsey, A. C., Pomeroy, W. B., Martin, C. E. and Gebhard, H. (1953) *Sexual Behavior in the Human Female.* New York: Pocket Books.

Kirschenbaum, D. S. (1984) Self-regulation and sport psychology: nurturing an emerging symbiosis. *Journal of Sport Psychology,* 6: 159–83.

Kobasa, S., Maddi, S., Puccetti, M. and Zola, M. (1985) Effectiveness of hardiness, exercise and social support as resources against illness. *Journal of Psychosomatic Research,* 29: 525–33.

Kowalski, R. (2002) Whining, griping, and complaining: positivity in the negativity. *Journal of Clinical Psychology,* 58: 1023–35.

Kringelbach, M. (2004) Food for thought: Hedonic experience beyond homeostasis in the human brain. *Neuroscience,* 126(4): 807–19.

Kringelbach, M. (2009) *The Pleasure Centre: Trust Your Animal Instincts.* New York: Oxford University Press.

Kritz-Silverstein, D., Barrett-Connor, E. and Corbeau, C. (2001) Cross-sectional and prospective study of exercise and depressed mood in the elderly – The Rancho Bernardo study. *American Journal of Epidemiology,* 153(6): 596–603.

Krueger, A., Kahneman, D. Schkades, D., Schwartz, N. and Stone, A. (2008) *National Time Accounting: The Currency of Life.* Princeton, NJ: Princeton University, Department of Economics, Industrial Relations Section.

Lambert, M. J. and Barley, D. E. (2001) Research summary on the therapeutic relationship and psychotherapy outcome. *Psychotherapy,* 38(4): 357–61.

Lambert, M. J. and Barley, D. E. (2002) Research summary on the therapeutic relationship and psychotherapy outcome. In J. C. Norcross (ed.) *Psychotherapy Relationships that Work: Therapist Contributions and Responsiveness to Patients.* New York: Oxford University Press.

Lambert, N. M., Fincham, F. D., Stillman, T. F. and Dean, L. R. (2009) More gratitude, less materialism: the mediating role of life satisfaction. *Journal of Positive Psychology,* 4(1): 32–42.

Landis, S. K., Sherman, M. F., Piedmont, R. L. et al. (2009) The relation between elevation and self-reported prosocial behavior: Incremental validity over the Five-Factor Model of Personality. *Journal of Positive Psychology,* 4(1): 71–84.

Langdridge, D. (2004a) Fundamentals of qualitative analysis. In D. Langdridge (ed.) *Introduction to Research Methods and Data Analysis in Psychology* (pp. 249–60). London: Pearson Education.

Langdridge, D. (2004b) Research in the social sciences. In D. Langdridge (ed.) *Introduction to Research Methods and Data Analysis in Psychology.* London: Pearson Education.

Langer, E. (2009) Mindfulness. In S. Lopez (ed.) *The Encyclopedia of Positive Psychology* (pp. 618–22). Chichester: Blackwell Publishing Ltd.

Langer, E. and Rodin, J. (1976) The effects of choice and enhanced personal responsibility for the aged: a field experiment in an institutional setting. *Journal of Personality and Social Psychology,* 134: 191–8.

Larsen, J. T., Hemenover, S. H., Norris, C. J. and Cacioppo, J. T. (2003) Turning adversity to advantage: on the virtues of the coactivation of positive and negative emotions. In L. G. Aspinwall and U. M. Staudinger (eds) *A Psychology of Human Strengths: Perspectives on an Emerging Field* (pp. 211–26). Washington, DC: American Psychological Association.

Larsen, J. T., McGraw, A. P. and Cacioppo, J. T. (2001) Can people feel happy and sad at the same time? *Journal of Personality and Social Psychology,* 81: 684–96.

Larsen, J. T., McGraw, A. P., Mellers, B. A. and Cacioppo, J. T. (2004) The agony of victory and thrill of defeat: mixed emotional reactions to disappointing wins and relieving losses. *Psychological Science,* 15: 325–30.

Larsen, R. and Diener, E. (1992) Promises and problems with the circumplex model of emotion. In M. S. Clark (ed.) *Review of Personality and Social Psychology* Vol. 13 (pp. 25–59). Newbury Park, CA: Sage.

Lazarus, R. S. (2003) Does the positive psychology movement have legs? *Psychological Inquiry,* 14(2): 93–109.

Lazarus, R. S. and Folkman, S. (1984) *Stress, Appraisal, and Coping.* New York: Springer.

Leary, M. R., Tambor, E. S., Terdal, S. K. and Downs, D. L. (1995) Self-esteem as an interpersonal monitor: the sociometer hypothesis. *Journal of Personality and Social Psychology,* 68: 518–30.

Lechner, S. (2009) Benefit finding. In S. Lopez (ed.) *The Encyclopedia of Positive Psychology* (pp. 99–102). Chichester: Blackwell Publishing Ltd.

Lechner, S., Stoelb, B. and Antoni, M. (2008) Group-based therapies for benefit finding in cancer. In S. Joseph and A. Linley (eds) *Trauma, Recovery, and Growth: Positive Psychological Perspectives on Posttraumatic Stress* (pp. 207–31). Hoboken, NJ: Wiley.

Lee, I. M. (1995) Exercise and physical health: cancer and immune function. *Research Quarterly for Exercise and Sport,* 66(4): 286–91.

Lent, R. (2007) Restoring emotional wellbeing: a model. In M. Feuerstein (ed.) *Handbook of Cancer Survivorship.* New York: Springer Science.

Lent, R. and Hackett, G. (2009) Social cognitive theory. In S. Lopez (ed.) *The Encyclopedia of Positive Psychology* (pp. 908–12). Chichester: Blackwell Publishing Ltd.

Lepore, S. and Revenson, T. (2006) Resilience and posttraumatic growth: recovery, resistance and reconfiguration. In R. G. Tedeschi and L. G. Calhoun (eds) *Handbook of Posttraumatic Growth* (pp. 24–46). Mahwah, NJ: Lawrence Erlbaum Associates.

Lev-Wiesel, R. and Amir, M. (2003) Posttraumatic growth among holocaust child survivors. *Journal of Loss and Trauma,* 8(4): 229–37.

Levy, B. (1996) Improving memory in old age by implicit self-stereotyping. *Journal of Personality and Social Psychology,* 71: 1092–1107.

Levy, B. (2009) Stereotype embodiment: a psychological approach to aging. *Current Directions in Psychological Science,* 18: 332–3.

Levy, B., Hausdorff, J., Hencke, R. and Wei, J. Y. (2000) Reducing cardiovascular stress with positive self-stereotypes of aging. *Journal of Gerontology: Psychological Sciences,* 55B: P205–P213.

Levy, B. R., Slade, M., Kunkel, S. and Kasl, S. (2002) Longevity increased by positive self-perceptions of aging. *Journal of Personality and Social Psychology,* 83: 261–70.

Lewinsohn, P. M., Hops, H., Roberts, R. and Seeley, J. (1993) Adolescent psychopathology: I. Prevalence and incidence of depression and other DSM-III-R disorders in high school students. *Journal of Abnormal Psychology,* 102: 110–20.

Light, K. C., Grewen, K. M. and Amico, J. A. (2005) More frequent partner hugs and higher oxytocin levels are linked to lower blood pressure and heart rate in premenopausal women. *Biological Psychology,* 69(1): 5–21.

Linley, A. (2003) Positive adaptation to trauma: wisdom as both process and outcome. *Journal of Traumatic Stress,* 16: 601–10.

Linley, A. (2009) Positive psychology (history). In S. Lopez (ed.) *The Encyclopedia of Positive Psychology* (pp. 742–6). Chichester: Blackwell Publishing Ltd.

Linley, A. and Joseph, S. (2004) Positive change following trauma and adversity: a review. *Journal of Traumatic Stress*, 17(1): 11–21.

Linley, A. and Joseph, S. (2009) Posttraumatic growth. In S. Lopez (ed.), *The Encyclopedia of Positive Psychology* (pp. 769–73). Chichester: Blackwell Publishing Ltd.

Linley, A., Joseph, S., Harrington, S. and Wood, A. (2006) Positive psychology: past, present, and (possible) future. *Journal of Positive Psychology*, 1(1): 3–16.

Linley, A., Maltby, J., Wood, A. M. et al. (2007) Character strengths in the United Kingdom: The VIA Inventory of Strengths. *Personality and Individual Differences*, 43(2): 341–51.

Litovsky, V. G. and Dusek, J. B. (1985) Perceptions of child rearing and self-concept development during the early adolescent years. *Journal of Youth and Adolescence*, 14: 373–88.

Lopes, M. P. and Cunha, M. P. (2008) Who is more proactive, the optimist or the pessimist? Exploring the role of hope as a moderator. *Journal of Positive Psychology*, 3(2): 100–9.

Lopez, S. and Ackerman, C. (2009) Clifton Strengths Finder. In S. Lopez (ed.) *The Encyclopedia of Positive Psychology* (pp. 163–7). Chichester: Blackwell Publishing Ltd.

Lopez, S. J., Snyder, C. R., Magyar-Moe, J. L. et al. (2004) Strategies for accentuating hope. In P. A. Linley and S. Joseph (eds) *Positive Psychology in Practice* (pp. 388–403). Hoboken, NJ: John Wiley & Sons, Inc.

Low, C., Beran, T. and Stanton, A. (2007) Adaptation in the face of advanced cancer. In M. Feuerstein (ed.) *Handbook of Cancer Survivorship*. New York: Springer Science.

Lucas, R. E. (2005) Time does not heal all wounds: a longitudinal study of reaction and adaptation to divorce. *Psychological Science*, 16: 945–50.

Lucas, R. E. (2007) Long-term disability has lasting effects on subjective wellbeing: evidence from two nationally representative longitudinal studies. *Journal of Personality and Social Psychology*, 92: 717–30.

Lucas, R. E., Clark, A. E., Georgellis, Y. and Diener, E. (2003) Re-examining adaptation and the set point model of happiness: reactions to changes in marital status. *Journal of Personality and Social Psychology*, 84: 527–39.

Lucas, R. E., Diener, E. and Suh, E. (1996) Discriminant validity of wellbeing measures. *Journal of Personality and Social Psychology*, 71(3): 616–28.

Lupien, S. J. and Wan, N. (2004) Successful ageing: from cell to self. *Phil. Trans. R. Soc. Lond. B*, 359: 1413–26.

Lykken, D. and Tellegen, A. (1996) Happiness is a stochastic phenomenon. *Psychological Science*, 7(3): 186–9.

Lyubomirsky, S. (2006) Happiness: lessons from a new science. *British Journal of Sociology*, 57(3): 535–6.

Lyubomirsky, S. (2008) *The How of Happiness: A Practical Guide to Getting the Life you Want*. London: Sphere.

Lyubomirsky, S. (in press) Hedonic adaptation to positive and negative experiences. In S. Folkman (ed.) *Oxford Handbook of Stress, Health and Coping*. New York: Oxford University Press.

Lyubomirsky, S., Dickerhoof, R., Boehm, J. K. and Sheldon, K. M. (2009) Becoming happier takes both a will and a proper way: Two experimental longitudinal interventions to boost wellbeing. Manuscript submitted for publication.

Lyubomirsky, S., King, L. A. and Diener, E. (2005) The benefits of frequent positive affect: does happiness lead to success? *Psychological Bulletin*, 131: 803–55.

Lyubomirsky, S. and Lepper, H. (1999) A measure of subjective happiness: preliminary reliability and construct validation. *Social Indicators Research*, 46: 137–55.

Lyubomirsky, S., Sheldon, K. M. and Schkade, D. (2005) Pursuing happiness: the architecture of sustainable change. *Review of General Psychology*, 9: 111–31.

Lyubomirsky, S., Sousa, L. and Dickerhoof, R. (2006) The costs and benefits of writing, talking, and thinking about life's triumphs and defeats. *Journal of Personality and Social Psychology,* 90(4): 692–708.

Maddux, J. (2002) Self-efficacy: The power of believing you can. In C. R. Snyder and S. J. Lopez (eds) *Handbook of Positive Psychology* (pp. 277–87). New York: Oxford University Press.

Maddux, J. (2009a) Self-efficacy. In S. Lopez (ed.) *The Encyclopedia of Positive Psychology* (pp. 874–80). Chichester: Blackwell Publishing Ltd.

Maddux, J. (2009b) Self-regulation. In S. Lopez (ed.) *The Encyclopedia of Positive Psychology* (pp. 874–80). Chichester: Blackwell Publishing Ltd.

Magnus, K., Diener, E., Fujita, F. and Pavot, W. (1993) Extroversion and neuroticism as predictors of objective life events: a longitudinal analysis. *Journal of Personality and Social Psychology,* 65(5): 1046–53.

Marks, N. F. and Flemming, N. (1999) Influences and consequences of wellbeing among Australian young people: 1980–1995. *Social Indicators Research,* 46: 301–23.

Martin, P. (2009) *Sex, Drugs and Chocolate: The Science of Pleasure.* London: HarperCollins.

Maslow, A. H. (1954) *Motivation and Personality.* New York: Harper.

Mason, M. and Tiberius, V. (2009) Aristotle. In S. Lopez (ed.) *The Encyclopedia of Positive Psychology* (pp. 63–4). Chichester: Blackwell Publishing Ltd.

Matsunaga, M., Sato, S., Isowa, T. et al. (2009) Profiling of serum proteins influenced by warm partner contact in healthy couples. *Neuroendocrinology Letters,* 30(2): 227–36.

Matsunaga, M., Yamauchi, T., Nogimori, T., Konagaya, T. and Ohira, H. (2008) Psychological and physiological responses accompanying positive emotions elicited on seeing favorite persons. *Journal of Positive Psychology,* 3(3): 192–201.

Mayer, J., Roberts R. and Barsade, S. G. (2008) Human abilities: emotional intelligence. *Annual Review of Psychology,* 59: 507–5.

Mayer, J. and Salovey, P. (1993) The intelligence of emotional intelligence. *Intelligence,* 17(4): 433–42.

Mayer, J., Salovey, P. and Caruso, D. R. (2004) Emotional intelligence: theory, findings, and implications. *Psychological Inquiry,* 15(3): 197–215.

Mayer, J., Salovey, P., Caruso, D. R. and Sitarenios, G. (2001) Emotional intelligence as a standard intelligence. *Emotion (Washington DC),* 1(3): 232–42.

Mayer, J., Salovey, P., Caruso, D. R. and Sitarenios, G. (2003) Measuring emotional intelligence with the MSCEIT V2.0. *Emotion (Washington DC),* 3(1): 97–105.

McCullough, M. E., Emmons, R. A. and Tsang, J. A. (2002) The grateful disposition: a conceptual and empirical topography. *Journal of Personality and Social Psychology,* 82(1): 112–27.

McCullough, M. E. and Witvliet, C.V.O. (2002) The psychology of forgiveness. In C.R. Snyder and S. J. Lopez (eds), *Handbook of Positive Psychology* (pp. 446–58). New York: Oxford University Press.

McDonald, D. G. and Hodgdon, J. A. (1991) *The Psychological Effects of Aerobic Fitness Training: Research and Theory.* New York: Springer-Verlag.

McGrath, H. and Noble, T. (2003) *Bounce Back! Teacher's Handbook.* Port Melbourne, VIC: Pearson Education.

McGregor, I. and Little, B. R. (1998) Personal projects, happiness, and meaning: on doing well and being yourself. *Journal of Personality and Social Psychology,* 74(2): 494–512.

McMakin, D. L., Santiago, C. D. and Shirk, S. R. (2009) The time course of positive and negative emotion in dysphoria. *Journal of Positive Psychology,* 4(2): 182–92.

Meehl, E. (1975) Hedonic capacity: some conjectures. *Bulletin of the Menninger Clinic,* 39(4): 295–307.

Mei-Chuan, W., Lightsey, O. R., Pietruszka, T., Uruk, A. C. and Wells, A. G. (2007) Purpose in life and reasons for living as mediators of the relationship between stress, coping, and suicidal behavior. *Journal of Positive Psychology,* 2(3): 195–204.

Messer, S. B. and Wamplod, B. E. (2002) Let's face the facts: common factors are more potent than specific therapy ingredients. *Clinical Psychology: Science and Practice,* 9(1): 21–5.

Meston, C. and Buss, D. (2007) Why humans have sex. *Archives of Sexual Behaviour,* 36: 477–507.

Meston, C. and Buss, D. (2009) *Why Women have Sex: Understanding Sexual Motivations – From Adventure to Revenge (and Everything In Between).* New York: Times Books.

Michalec, B., Keyes, C. and Nalkur, S. (2009) Flourishing. In S. Lopez (ed.) *The Encyclopedia of Positive Psychology* (pp. 391–4). Chichester: Blackwell Publishing Ltd.

Milam, J. (2004) Posttraumatic growth among HIV/AIDS patients. *Journal of Applied Social Psychology,* 34(11): 2353–76.

Mink, J., Scrafford, C. G., Barraj, L. M. et al. (2007) Flavonoid intake and cardiovascular disease mortality: a prospective study in postmenopausal women. *American Journal of Clinical Nutrition,* 85(3): 895–909.

Mischel, W. (1978) How children postpone pleasure. *Human Nature,* 1(12): 50–5.

Mischel, W. and Ebbesen, E. B. (1970) Attention in delay of gratification. *Journal of Personality and Social Psychology,* 16(2): 329–337.

Mischel, W., Shoda, Y. and Rodriguez, M. L. (1989) Delay of gratification in children. *Science,* 244(4907): 933–8.

Miserandino, M. (1996) Children who do well in school: individual differences in perceived competence and autonomy in above-average children. *Journal of Educational Psychology,* 88: 203–14.

Moses, J., Steptoe, A., Mathews, A. and Edwards, S. (1989) The effects of exercise training on mental wellbeing in the normal population: a controlled trial. *Journal of Psychosomatic Research,* 33: 47–61.

Moskowitz, J. T. and Epel, E. S. (2006) Benefit finding and diurnal cortisol slope in maternal caregivers: a moderating role for positive emotion. *Journal of Positive Psychology,* 1(2): 83–91.

Moyer, C. A., Rounds, J. and Hannum, J. W. (2004) A meta-analysis of massage therapy research. *Psychological Bulletin,* 130(1): 3–18.

Mueller, C. M. and Dweck, C. S. (1998) Praise for intelligence can undermine children's motivation and performance. *Journal of Personality and Social Psychology,* 75(1): 33–52.

Murray, A., Knight, N., Cochlin, L. et al. (2009) Deterioration of physical performance and cognitive function in rats with short-term high-fat feeding. *Federation of American Societies for Experimental Biology Journal,* 23: 4353–60.

Mustafa, T., Sy, F. S., Macera, C. A. et al. (1999) Association between exercise and HIV disease progression in a cohort of homosexual men. *Annals of Epidemiology,* 9(2): 127–31.

Mutrie, N., Campbell, A. M., Whyte, F. et al. (2007) Benefits of supervised group exercise programme for women being treated for early stage breast cancer: pragmatic randomised controlled trial. *British Medical Journal,* 334(7592): 517–20B.

Mutrie, N. and Faulkner, G. (2004) Physical activity: positive psychology in motion. In A. Linley and S. Joseph (eds) *Positive Psychology in Practice.* London: Wiley.

Myers, D. G. (2000) The funds, friends, and faith of happy people. *American Psychologist*, 55(1): 56–67.

Nakamura, J. and Csikszentmihalyi, M. (2005) Engagement in a profession: the case of undergraduate teaching. *Daedalus: Journal of the American Academy of Arts and Sciences*, 134: 60–7.

Nelson, D. W. (2009) Feeling good and open-minded: the impact of positive affect on cross cultural empathic responding. *Journal of Positive Psychology*, 4(1): 53–63.

Nes, R. B., Czajkowski, N., Røysamb, E. et al. (2008) Wellbeing and ill-being: shared environments, shared genes? *Journal of Positive Psychology*, 3(4): 253–65.

NHS Sexual health (2010) www.nhs.uk/Livewell/Sexualhealthtopics/Pages/Sexual-health-hub.aspx.

Noble, T. and McGrath, H. (2005) Helping children and families 'bounce back'. *Australian Family Physician*, 9: 34.

Norem, J. K. and Cantor, N. (1986b) Defensive pessimism: harnessing anxiety as motivation. *Journal of Personality and Social Psychology*, 51: 1208–17.

Norem, J. K. and Chang, E. C. (2002) The positive psychology of negative thinking. *Journal of Clinical Psychology*, 58(9): 993–1001.

Nozick, R. (1974) *Anarchy, State, and Utopia*. New York: Basic Books.

Oishi, S. and Diener, E. (2001) Goals, culture, and subjective wellbeing. *Personality and Social Psychology Bulletin*, 27(12): 1674–82.

Oishi, S., Diener, E., Suh, E. and Lucas, R. E. (1999) Value as a moderator in subjective wellbeing. *Journal of Personality*, 67(1): 157–84.

Olds, J. and Milner, P. (1954) Positive reinforcement produced by electrical stimulation of the septal area and other regions of rat brain. *Journal of Comparative and Physiological Psychology*, 47: 419–27.

Oleson, T. and Flocco, W. (1993) Randomised controlled study of premenstrual symptoms treated with ear, hand and foot reflexology. *Obstetrics and Gynecology*, 82(6): 906–11.

Orlinsky, D. E., Grawe, K. and Parks, B. K. (1994) Process and outcome in psychotherapy. In A. E. Bergin and S. L. Garfield (eds) *Handbook of Psychotherapy and Behavior Change* (pp. 270–376). New York: John Wiley & Sons, Inc.

Otake, K., Shimai, S., Tanaka-Matsumi, J., Otsui, K. and Fredrickson, B. L. (2006) Happy people become happier through kindness: a counting kindnesses intervention. *Journal of Happiness Studies*, 7: 361–75.

Paffenbarger, R., Hyde, R., Wing, A. and Hsieh, C. (1986) Physical activity, all-cause mortality, and longevity of college alumni. *New England Journal of Medicine*, 314: 605–13.

Papageorgiou, C. and Wells, A. (2003) Nature, functions, and beliefs about depressive rumination. In C. Papageorgiou and A. Wells (eds) *Depressive Rumination: Nature,Theory, and Treatment* (pp. 3–20). Chichester: John Wiley & Sons, Ltd.

Park, C., Cohen, L. and Murch, R. (1996) Assessment and prediction of stress-related growth. *Journal of Personality*, 64: 71–105.

Park, N., Peterson, C. and Seligman, M. (2004) Strengths of character and wellbeing: a closer look at hope and modesty. *Journal of Social and Clinical Psychology*, 23(5): 628–34.

Parsloe, E. (1999) *The Manager as Coach and Mentor*. London: Chartered Institute of Personnel and Development.

Passer, M. and Smith, R. (2006) *Psychology: The Science of Mind and Behaviour*. Maidenhead: McGraw-Hill.

Pavot, W. and Diener, E. (2008) The Satisfaction With Life Scale and the emerging construct of life satisfaction. *Journal of Positive Psychology,* 3(2): 137–52.

Pawelski, J. (2009) William James. In S. Lopez (ed.) *The Encyclopedia of Positive Psychology* (pp. 537–8). Chichester: Blackwell Publishing Ltd.

Pawelski, J. and Gupta, M. (2009) Utilitarianism. In S. Lopez (ed.) *The Encyclopedia of Positive Psychology* (pp. 998–1001). Chichester: Blackwell Publishing Ltd.

Pennebaker, J. W. (1997) Writing about emotional experiences as a therapeutic process. *Psychological Science,* 8(3): 162–6.

Pennebaker, J. W. (2004) *Writing to Heal: A Guided Journal for Recovering from Trauma and Emotional Upheaval.* Oakland, CA: New Harbinger Press.

Pentland, W. E., Harvey, A. S., Lawton, M. P. and McColl, M. A. (eds) (1999) *Time Use Research in the Social Sciences.* New York: Kluwer Academic/Plenum Publishers.

Peterson, C. (2000) The future of optimism. *American Psychologist,* 55: 45–55.

Peterson, C. (2006) *A Primer in Positive Psychology.* New York: Oxford University Press.

Peterson, C. and Deavila, M. E. (1995) Optimistic explanatory style and the perception of health problems. *Journal of Clinical Psychology,* 51(1): 128–32.

Peterson, C., Park, N. and Seligman, M. E. P. (2006) Greater strengths of character and recovery from illness. *Journal of Positive Psychology,* 1(1): 17–26.

Peterson, C. and Seligman, M. (2003) Character strengths before and after September 11. *Psychological Science,* 14(4): 381–4.

Peterson, C. and Seligman, M. (2004) *Character Strengths and Virtues: A Handbook and Classification.* New York: Oxford University Press.

Peterson, C., Seligman, M., Yurko, K. H., Martin, L. R. and Friedman, H. S. (1998) Catastrophizing and untimely death. *Psychological Science,* 9(2): 127–30.

Peterson, C. and Vaidya, R. S. (2001) Explanatory style, expectations, and depressive symptoms. *Personality and Individual Differences,* 31(7): 1217–23.

Pöhlmann, K., Gruss, B. and Joraschky, P. (2006) Structural properties of personal meaning systems: a new approach to measuring meaning of life. *Journal of Positive Psychology,* 1(3): 109–17.

Porter, E. (1913) *Pollyanna,* 2nd edn. Rockville, MD: Tark Classic Fiction.

Positive Psychology Center (1998) Positive psychology network concept paper. Retrieved from http://www.ppc.sas.upenn.edu.

Pressman, S. D. and Cohen, S. (2007) The use of social words in autobiographies and longevity. *Psychosomatic Medicine,* 69: 262–9.

Prochaska, J. and DiClemente, C. C. (1984) Self-change processes, self-efficacy and decisional balance across five stages of smoking cessation. *Progress in Clinical Biological Research,* 156: 131–40.

Prochaska, J., Norcross, J. C., Fowler, J. L., Follick, M. J. and Abrams, D. B. (1992) Attendance and outcome in a work site weight control program: processes and stages of change as process and predictor variables. *Addictive Behaviors,* 17(1): 35–45.

Prochaska, J. and Prochaska, J. (2009) Stages of change. In S. Lopez (ed.) *The Encyclopedia of Positive Psychology* (pp. 125–8). Chichester: Blackwell Publishing Ltd.

Prochaska, J. and Velicer, W. F. (1996) Addiction versus stages of change models in predicting smoking cessation – on models, methods and premature conclusions – comment. *Addiction,* 91(9): 1281–3.

Prochaska, J., Velicer, W. F., Rossi, J. S. et al. (1994) Stages of change and decisional balance for 12 problem behaviours. *Health Psychology,* 13(1): 39–46.

Pury, C. (2009) Perseverance. In S. Lopez (ed.) *Encyclopedia of Positive Psychology* (pp. 678–82). Chichester: Blackwell Publishing Ltd.

Pyszczynski, T., Greenberg, J. and Goldenberg, J. (2002) Freedom versus fear: on the defence, growth, and expansion of the self. In M. Leary and J. Tangney (eds) *Handbook of Self and Identity* (pp. 314–43). New York: Guilford Press.

Ramarajan, L., Barsade, S. and Burack, O. (2008) The influence of organizational respect on emotional exhaustion in the human services. *Journal of Positive Psychology,* 3(1): 4–18.

Rashid, T. (2009a) Authentic happiness. In S. Lopez (ed.) *Encyclopedia of Positive Psychology* (pp. 71–5). Chichester: Blackwell Publishing Ltd.

Rashid, T. (2009b) Positive psychotherapy. In S. Lopez (ed.) *Encyclopedia of Positive Psychology* (pp. 749–52) Chichester: Blackwell Publishing Ltd.

Rasmussen, H. and Pressman, S. (2009) Physical health. In S. Lopez (ed.) *Encyclopedia of Positive Psychology* (pp. 695–701). Chichester: Blackwell Publishing Ltd.

Ratey, J. (2001) *A User's Guide to the Brain.* New York: Abacus.

Ratey, J. (2008) *SPARK: The Revolutionary New Science of Exercise and the Brain.* New York: Little, Brown Company.

Rath, T. and Harter, J. (2010) *Wellbeing – The Five Essential Elements.* New York: Gallup Press.

Rathunde, K. and Csikszentmihalyi, M. (2005) Middle school students' motivation and quality of experience: a comparison of Montessori and traditional school environments. *American Journal of Education,* 111: 341–71.

Redelmeier, D. A., Katz, J. and Kahneman, D. (2003) Memories of colonoscopy: a randomized trial. *Pain,* 104(1–2): 187–94.

Reed, G.M., Kennedy, M.E., Taylor, S.E., Wang, H.Y.J. and Visscher, B.R. (1994) Realistic acceptance: as a predictor of decreased survival time in gay men with Aids. *Health Psychology,* 13: 299–307.

Reivich, K., Gillham, K., Shatté, A. and Seligman, M. (2007) *Penn Resiliency Project: A Resilience Initiative and Depression Prevention Program for Youth and their Parents. Executive Summary.* Philadelphia, PA: University of Philadelphia.

Reivich, K. and Shatte, A. (2002) *The Resilience Factor: Seven Keys to Finding your Inner Strength and Overcoming Life's Hurdles.* New York: Broadway Books.

Rejeski, W. J. and Mihalko, S. L. (2001) Physical activity and quality of life in older adults. *Journals of Gerontology Series A – Biological Sciences and Medical Sciences,* 56: 23–35.

Rejeski, W. J., Shelton, B., Miller, M. E. et al. (2001) Mediators of increased physical activity and change in subjective wellbeing: results from the Activity Counseling Trial (ACT). *Journal of Health Psychology,* 6(2): 159–68.

Resnick, S., Warmoth, A. and Serlin, I. (2001) The humanistic psychology and positive psychology connection: implications for psychotherapy. *Journal of Humanistic Psychology,* 41(1): 73–101.

Reynolds, F. and Kee Hean, L. (2007) Turning to art as a positive way of living with cancer: a qualitative study of personal motives and contextual influences. *Journal of Positive Psychology,* 2(1): 66–75.

Reznitskaya, A. and Sternberg, R. J. (2004) Teaching students to make wise judgments: The 'Teaching for Wisdom' program. In P. A. Linley and S. Joseph (eds) *Positive Psychology in Practice* (pp. 181–96). New York: John Wiley & Sons, Inc.

Roberts, R. D., Zeidner, M. and Matthews, G. (2001) Does emotional intelligence meet traditional standards for an intelligence? Some new data and conclusions. *Emotion,* 1: 196–231.

Robson, C. (2004) *Small-scale Evaluation*. London: Sage Publications.

Rolls, E. T., O'Doherty, J., Kringelbach, M. L. et al. (2003) Representations of pleasant and painful touch in the human orbitofrontal and cingulate cortices. *Cerebral Cortex*, 13(3): 308–17.

Rosenberg, M. (1965) *Society and the Adolescent Self-image*. Princeton, NJ: Princeton University Press.

Rosenberg, M., Schooler, C., Schoenberg, C. and Rosenberg, F. (1995) Global self-esteem and specific self-esteem: Different concepts, different outcomes. *American Sociological Review*, 60: 141–56.

Ross, C. E. and Huber, J. (1985) Hardship and depression. *Journal of Health and Social Behavior*, 26(4): 312–27.

Rothschild, B. (2000) *The Body Remembers*. New York: W. W Norton & Company.

Rotter, J. (1966) Generalized expectancies for internal versus external control of reinforcements. *Psychological Monographs*, 80 (609).

Ruini, C. and Fava, G. A. (2004) Clinical applications of wellbeing therapy. In P. A. Linley and S. Joseph (eds) *Positive Psychology in Practice* (pp. 371–87). Hoboken, NJ: John Wiley & Sons, Inc.

Russell, J. A. (1980) The circumplex model of affect. *Journal of Personality and Social Psychology*, 39: 1161–78.

Ryan, R. and Deci, E. (2000) Self-determination theory and the facilitation of intrinsic motivation, social development and wellbeing. *American Psychologist*, 55: 68–78.

Ryan, R., Deci, E. and Grolnick, W. S. (1995) Autonomy, relatedness, and the self: their relation to development and psychopathology. In D. Cicchetti and D. J. Cohen (eds) *Developmental Psychopathology: Theory and Methods* (pp. 618–55). New York: John Wiley & Sons, Inc.

Ryan, R. and Grolnick, W. S. (1986) Origins and pawns in the classroom: a self-report and projective assessment of children's perceptions. *Journal of Personality and Social Psychology*, 50: 550–8.

Ryan, R. M., Huta, V. and Deci, E. L. (2008) Living well: a self-determination theory perspective on eudaimonia. *Journal of Happiness Studies*, 9: 139–70.

Ryff, C. D. (1989) Happiness is everything, or is it? Explorations on the meaning of psychological wellbeing. *Journal of Personality and Social Psychology*, 57(6): 1069–81.

Ryff, C. D. and Keyes, C. L. M. (1995) The structure of psychological wellbeing revisted. *Journal of Personality and Social Psychology*, 69(4): 719–27.

Ryff, C. D. and Singer, B. H. (2006) Best news yet on the six-factor model of wellbeing. *Social Science Research*, 35(4): 1103–119.

Sabiston, C. M., McDonough, M. H. and Crocker, R. E. (2007) Psychosocial experiences of breast cancer survivors involved in a dragon boat program: exploring links to positive psychological growth. *Journal of Sport and Exercise Psychology*, 29(4): 419–38.

Sackeim, H. A., Greenberg, M. S., Weiman, A. L. et al. (1982) Hemispheric-asymmetry in the experssion of positive and negative emotions: neurologic evidence. *Archives of Neurology*, 39(4): 210–18.

Salmela-Aro, K., Nurmi, J.-E., Saisto, T. and Halmesmäki, E. (2001) Goal construction and depressive symptoms during transition to motherhood: Evidence from two longitudinal studies. *Journal of Personality and Social Psychology*, 81: 1144–59.

Salonen, J., Puska, P. and Tuomilehto, J. (1982) Physical activity and risk of myocardial infarction, cerebral stroke and death: a longitudinal study in Finland. *American Journal of Epidemiology*, 115(4): 526–37.

Salovey, P., Caruso, D. and Mayer, J. D. (2004) Emotional intelligence in practice. In P. A. Linley and S. Joseph (eds) *Positive Psychology in Practice* (pp. 447–63). Hoboken, NJ: John Wiley & Sons.

Salovey, P., Mayer, J. and Caruso, D. (2002) The positive psychology of emotional intelligence. In C. R. Snyder and S. J. Lopez (eds) *Handbook of Positive Psychology* (pp. 159–71). New York: Oxford University Press.

Salovey, P. and Mayer, J. (1990) Emotional intelligence. *Imagination, Cognition and Personality,* 9: 185–211.

Sangsue, J. and Vorpe, G. (2004) Professional and personal influences on school climate in teachers and pupils. *Psychologie du Travail et des Organisations,* 10(4): 341–54.

Sarafino, E. P. (2002) *Health Psychology: Biopsychosocial Interactions.* New York: John Wiley & Sons, Inc.

Saroglou, V., Buxant, C. and Tilquin, J. (2008) Positive emotions as leading to religion and spirituality. *Journal of Positive Psychology,* 3(3): 165–73.

Scheier, M. and Carver, C. (1987) Dispositional optimism and physical wellbeing: the influence of generalised outcome expectancies on health. *Journal of Personality and Social Psychology,* 55: 169–210.

Scheier, M. F. and Carver, C. S. (1992) Effects of optimism on psychological and physical wellbeing: theoretical overview and empirical update. *Cognitive Therapy and Research,* 16: 201–28.

Scheier, M. and Carver, C. (2009) Optimism. In S. Lopez (ed.) *Encyclopedia of Positive Psychology* (pp. 656–63). Chichester: Blackwell Publishing Ltd.

Scheier, M. F., Carver, C. S. and Bridges, M. W. (1994) Distinguishing optimism from neuroticism (and trait anxiety, self-mastery, and self-esteem): a re-evaluation of the Life Orientation Test. *Journal of Personality and Social Psychology,* 67: 1063–78.

Scheier, M., Mathews, K., Owens, J. et al. (1989) Dispositional optimism and recovery from coronary artery bypass surgery: the beneficial effects on physical and psychological wellbeing. *Journal of Personality and Social Psychology,* 57: 1024–40.

Schmuck, P. (2001) Intrinsic and extrinsic life goal preferences as measured via inventories and via priming methodologies: Mean differences and relations with wellbeing. In P. Schmuck and K. M. Sheldon (eds) *Life Goals and Wellbeing: Towards a Positive Psychology of Human Striving* (pp. 132–47). Goettingen: Hogrefe & Huber Publishers.

Schmuck, P., Kasser, T. and Ryan, R. M. (2000) Intrinsic and extrinsic goals: their structure and relationship to wellbeing in German and US college students. *Social Indicators Research,* 50(2): 225–41.

Schulz, U. and Mohamed, N. E. (2004) Turning the tide: benefit finding after cancer surgery. *Social Science and Medicine,* 59(3): 653–62.

Schutte, N. S., Malouff, J. M., Simunek, M., Hollander, S. and McKenley, J. (2002) Characteristic emotional intelligence and emotional wellbeing. *Cognition and Emotion,* 16: 769–86.

Schwartz, B. (2000) Self-determination: the tyranny of freedom. *American Psychologist,* 55: 79–88.

Schwartz, B. and Ward, A. (2004) Doing better but feeling worse: The paradox of choice. In P. A. Linley and S. Joseph (eds) *Positive Psychology in Practice* (pp. 86–104). Hoboken, NJ: John Wiley & Sons.

Schwartz, B., Ward, A., Monterosso, J. et al. (2002) Maximizing versus satisficing: Happiness is a matter of choice. *Journal of Personality and Social Psychology,* 83(5): 1178–97.

Schwartz, S. H. (1994) Are there universal aspects in the structure and contents of human values? *Journal of Social Issues,* 50: 19–45.

Schwartz, S. H. and Sagiv, L. (1995) Identifying culture-specifics in the content and structure of values. *Journal of Cross-Cultural Psychology,* 26: 92–116.

Schwarzer, R. and Jerusalem, M. (1995) Generalized self-efficacy scale. In J. Weinman, S. Wright and M. Johnston (eds) *Measures in Health Psychology: A User's Portfolio. Causal and Control Beliefs* (pp. 35–7). Windsor: NFER-Nelson.

Schyns, P. (1998) Crossnational differences in happiness: economic and cultural factors explored. *Social Indicators Research,* 43: 3–26.

Seligman, M. (1998) *Learned Optimism: How to Change your Mind and your Life.* New York: Free Press.

Seligman, M. (2002a) *Authentic Happiness: Using the New Positive Psychology to Realize your Potential for Lasting Fulfilment.* New York: Free Press.

Seligman, M. (2002b) Positive psychology, positive prevention, and positive therapy. In C. R. Snyder and S. J. Lopez (eds) *Handbook of Positive Psychology* (pp. 3–9). New York: Oxford University Press.

Seligman, M. (2007) *The Optimistic Child.* New York: Houghton Mifflin.

Seligman, M. (2008) Positive health. *Applied Psychology,* 57: 3–18.

Seligman, M. and Csikszentmihalyi, M. (2000) Positive psychology – an introduction. *American Psychologist,* 55(1): 5–14.

Seligman, M. and Peterson, C. (2003) Positive clinical psychology. In L. G. Aspinwall and U. M. Staudinger (eds) *A Psychology of Human Strengths* (pp. 305–17). Washington, DC: American Psychological Association.

Seligman, M. and Schulman, P. (1986) Explanatory style as a predictor of productivity and quitting among life insurance agents. *Journal of Personality and Social Psychology,* 50: 832–8.

Seligman, M., Steen, T. A., Park, N. and Peterson, C. (2005) Positive psychology progress – empirical validation of interventions. *American Psychologist,* 60(5): 410–21.

Serafini, M., Bugianesi, R., Maiani, G. et al. (2003) Plasma antioxidants from chocolate – dark chocolate may offer its consumers health benefits the milk variety cannot match. *Nature,* 424(6952): 1013.

Sharp, D. M., Walker, M. B., Chaturvedi, A. et al. (2010) A randomised, controlled trial of the psychological effects of reflexology in early breast cancer. *European Journal of Cancer,* 46(2): 312–22.

Sheldon, K. (2009) Authenticity. In S. Lopez (ed.) *Encyclopedia of Positive Psychology* (pp. 75–8). Chichester: Blackwell Publishing Ltd.

Sheldon, K., Abad, N., Ferguson, Y. et al. (2010) Persistent pursuit of need-satisfying goals leads to increased happiness: A 6-month experimental longitudinal study. *Motivation and Emotion,* 34(1): 39–48.

Sheldon, K. and Deci, E. L. (1995) The Self-Determination Scale. Unpublished manuscript, University of Rochester.

Sheldon, K., Elliot, A. J., Kim, Y. and Kasser, T. (2001) What's satisfying about satisfying events? Comparing ten candidate psychological needs. *Journal of Personality and Social Psychology,* 80: 325–39.

Sheldon, K., Fredrickson, B., Rathunde, K., Csikszentmihalyi, M. and Haidt, J (2000) Positive Psychology Manifesto, revised at the Akumal 2 meeting, Mexico, January, www.ppc.sas.upenn.edu/akumalmanifesto.htm.

Sheldon, K. and Kasser, T. (1995) Coherence and congruence: two aspects of personality integration. *Journal of Personality and Social Psychology,* 68: 531–43.

Sheldon, K. and Lyubomirsky, S. (2004) Achieving sustainable new happiness: prospects, practices, and prescriptions. In A. Linley and S. Joseph (eds) *Positive Psychology in Practice* (pp. 127–45). Hoboken, NJ: John Wiley & Sons.

Sheldon, K. and Lyubomirsky, S. (2006a) Achieving sustainable gains in happiness: change your actions, not your circumstances. *Journal of Happiness Studies,* 7: 55–86.

Sheldon, K. and Lyubomirsky, S. (2006b) How to increase and sustain positive emotion: the effects of expressing gratitude and visualizing best possible selves. *Journal of Positive Psychology,* 1(2): 73–82.

Sheldon, K. and Lyubomirsky, S. (2007) Is it possible to become happier? (And if so, how?) *Social and Personality Psychology Compass,* 1: 129–45.

Sheldon, K. and Lyubomirsky, S. (2009) Change your actions, not your circumstances: An experimental test of the Sustainable Happiness Model. In A. K. Dutt and B. Radcliff (eds) *Happiness, Economics, and Politics: Toward a Multi-disciplinary Approach* (pp. 324–42). Cheltenham: Edward Elgar.

Shiota, M. N., Keltner, D. and John, O. P. (2006) Positive emotion dispositions differentially associated with Big Five personality and attachment style. *Journal of Positive Psychology,* 1(2): 61–71.

Shoda, Y., Mischel, W. and Peake, K. (1990) Predicting adolescent cognitive and self-regulatory competence from preschool delay of gratification: identifying diagnostic conditions. *Developmental Psychology,* 26(6): 978–86.

Shogren, K. A., Lopez, S. J., Wehmeyer, M. L., Little, T. D. and Pressgrove, C. L. (2006) The role of positive psychology constructs in predicting life satisfaction in adolescents with and without cognitive disabilities: An exploratory study. *Journal of Positive Psychology,* 1(1): 37–52.

Siev-Ner, I., Gamus, D., Lerner-Geva, L. and Achiron, A. (2003) Reflexology treatment relieves symptoms of multiple sclerosis: a randomized controlled study. *Multiple Sclerosis,* 9(4): 356–61.

Sin, N. L. and Lyubomirsky, S. (2009) Enhancing wellbeing and alleviating depressive symptoms with positive psychology interventions: a practice-friendly meta-analysis. *Journal of Clinical Psychology,* 65(5): 467–87.

Smith, J. and Eatough, V. (2006) Interpretative phenomenological analysis. In G. Breakwell, C. Fife-Schaw, S. Hammond and J. Smith (eds) *Research Methods in Psychology.* London: Sage Publications.

Smith, J., Flowers, P. and Larkin, M. (2009) *Interpretative Phenomenological Analysis: Theory, Method and Research.* London: Sage Publications.

Snyder, C. (2002) Hope theory: rainbows of the mind. *Psychological Inquiry,* 13: 249–75.

Snyder, C. and Lopez, S. (2007) *Positive Psychology: The Scientific and Practical Explorations of Human Strengths.* Thousand Oaks, CA: Sage Publications.

Solnick, S. and Hemenway, D. (1998) Is more always better? A survey on positional concerns. *Journal of Economic Behaviour and Organisation,* 37: 373–83.

Spence, G. B. and Grant, A. M. (2007) Professional and peer life coaching and the enhancement of goal striving and wellbeing: An exploratory study. *Journal of Positive Psychology,* 2(3): 185–94.

Spreitzer, G., Stephens, J. P. and Sweetman, D. (2009) The Reflected Best Self field experiment with adolescent leaders: exploring the psychological resources associated with feedback source and valence. *Journal of Positive Psychology,* 4(5): 331–48.

Steger, M. (2009) Meaning. In S. Lopez (ed.) *Encyclopedia of Positive Psychology* (pp. 605–10). Chichester: Blackwell Publishing Ltd.

Steger, M., Frazier, P., Oishi, S. and Kaler, M. (2006) The Meaning in Life Questionnaire: assessing the presence of and search for meaning in life. *Journal of Counseling Psychology,* 53: 80–93.

Stephenson, N., Dalton, J. A. and Carlson, J. (2003) The effect of foot reflexology on pain in patients with metastatic cancer. *Applied Nursing Research,* 16(4): 284–6.

Steptoe, A., Wardle, J., Pollard, T. M., Canaan, L. and Davies, G. J. (1996) Stress, social support and health-related behavior: A study of smoking, alcohol consumption and physical exercise. *Journal of Psychosomatic Research,* 41(2): 171–80.

Sternberg, R. (2009) Wisdom. In S. Lopez (ed.) *The Encyclopedia of Positive Psychology* (pp. 1037–44). Chichester: Blackwell Publishing Ltd.

Stiglitz, J. E., Sen, A. and Fitoussi, J. (2009) Report by the commission on the measurement of economic performance and social progress. Retrieved from http://www.stiglitz-sen-fitoussi.fr/documents/rapport_anglais.pdf.

Strauss, G. P. and Allen, D. N. (2006) The experience of positive emotion is associated with the automatic processing of positive emotional words. *Journal of Positive Psychology,* 1(3): 150–9.

Suh, E., Diener, E. and Fujita, F. (1996) Events and subjective wellbeing: Only recent events matter. *Journal of Personality and Social Psychology,* 70: 1091–102.

Sweetman, P. (1999) Anchoring the (postmodern) self? Body modification, fashion and identity. *Body and Society,* 5: 51–76.

Taylor, S. (1989) *Positive Illusions: Creative Self-deception and the Healthy Mind.* New York: Basic Books.

Taylor, S. (2001) Positive psychology and humanistic psychology: a reply to Seligman. *Journal of Humanistic Psychology,* 41: 13–29.

Taylor, S. (2009) Positive illusions. In S. Lopez (ed.) *Encyclopedia of Positive Psychology* (pp. 727–30) Chichester: Blackwell Publishing Ltd.

Taylor, S. and Brown, J. (1988) Illusion and wellbeing: a social psychological perspective on mental health. *Psychological Bulletin,* 103(2): 193–210.

Taylor, S. and Brown, J. (1994) Positive illusions and wellbeing revisited: separating fact from fiction. *Psychological Bulletin,* 116: 21–7.

Taylor, S., Kemeny, M. E., Reed, G. M., Bower, J. E. and Gruenewald, T. L. (2000) Psychological resources, positive illusions, and health. *American Psychologist,* 55: 99–109.

Tedeschi, R. G. and Calhoun, L. G. (1995) *Trauma and Transformation: Growing in the Aftermath of Suffering.* Thousand Oaks, CA: Sage Publications.

Tedeschi, R. G. and Calhoun, L. G. (1996) The posttraumatic growth inventory: measuring the positive legacy of trauma. *Journal of Traumatic Stress,* 9: 455–71.

Tedeschi, R. G. and Calhoun, L. G. (2003) Routes to posttraumatic growth through cognitive processing. In D. Paton, J. M. Violanti and L. M. Smith (eds) *Promoting Capabilities to Manage Posttraumatic Stress: Perspectives on Resilience* (pp. 12–26). Springfield, IL: Charles C. Thomas.

Tedeschi, R. G. and Calhoun, L. G. (2006) Foundations of posttraumatic growth. In R. G. Tedeschi and L. G. Calhoun (eds) *Handbook of Posttraumatic Growth* (pp. 3–23). Mahwah, NJ: Lawrence Erlbaum Associates.

Tedeschi, R. G. and Calhoun, L. G. (2008) Beyond the concept of recovery: growth and the experience of loss. *Death Studies,* 32: 27–39.

Tedeschi, R. G., Park, C. and Calhoun, L. G. (1998) Posttraumatic growth: Conceptual issues. In R. G. Tedeschi, C. Park and L. G. Calhoun (eds) *Posttraumatic Growth* (pp. 1–22). Mahwah, NJ: Lawrence Erlbaum Associates.

Tellegen, A., Lykken, D. T., Bouchard, T. J. et al. (1988) Personality similarity in twins reared apart and together. *Journal of Personality and Social Psychology,* 54: 1031–9.

Tennen, H. and Affleck, G. (2002) Benefit-finding and benefit-reminding. In C. R. Snyder and S. Lopez (eds) *Handbook of Positive Psychology* (pp. 584–96). Oxford: Oxford University Press.

Thompson, S. C. (2002) The role of personal control in adaptive functioning. In C. R. Snyder and S. J. Lopez (eds) *Handbook of Positive Psychology* (pp. 202–13). Oxford: Oxford University Press.

Thornton, A. A. (2002) Perceiving benefits in the cancer experience. *Journal of Clinical Psychology in Medical Settings,* 9: 153–65.

Thornton, A. A. and Perez, M. A. (2006) Posttraumatic growth in prostate cancer survivors and their partners. *Psycho-Oncology,* 15(4): 285–96.

Tiberius, V. and Mason, M. (2009) Eudaimonia. In S. Lopez (ed.) *Encyclopedia of Positive Psychology* (pp. 351–5). Chichester: Blackwell Publishing Ltd.

Tkach, C. and Lyubomirsky, S. (2006) How do people pursue happiness? Relating personality, happiness-increasing strategies, and wellbeing. *Journal of Happiness Studies,* 7: 183–225.

Tomarken, A. J., Davidson, R. J., Wheeler, R. E. and Kinney, L. (1992) Psychometric properties of resting anterior EEG asymmetry: temporal stability and internal consistency. *Psychophysiology,* 29(5): 576–92.

Tomes, N. (1986) Income distribution, happiness and satisfaction. A direct test of the interdependent model. *Journal of Economic Psychology,* 7: 425–46.

Tudor-Locke, C. and Bassett, D. R., Jr. (2004) How many steps/day are enough? Preliminary pedometer indices for public health. *Sports Medicine,* 34: 1–8.

Tugade, M. M., Fredrickson, B. and Barrett, L. F. (2004) Psychological resilience and positive emotional granularity: examining the benefits of positive emotions on coping and health. *Journal of Personality,* 72(6): 1161–90.

Updegraff, J. A. and Suh, E. M. (2007) Happiness is a warm abstract thought: self-construal abstractness and subjective wellbeing. *Journal of Positive Psychology,* 2(1): 18–28.

Urcuyo, K. R., Boyers, A. E., Carver, C. S. and Antoni, M. H. (2005) Finding benefit in breast cancer: relations with personality, coping, and concurrent wellbeing. *Psychology and Health,* 20(2): 175–92.

Vaillant, G. (2004) Positive aging. In P. A. Linley and S. Joseph (eds) *Positive Psychology in Practice* (pp. 561–78). Hoboken, NJ: John Wiley & Sons.

Van Deurzen, E. (2009) *Psychotherapy and the Quest for Happiness.* London: Sage Publications.

Veenhoven, R. (1991) Is happiness relative? *Social Indicators Research,* 24(1): 1–34.

Veenhoven, R. (2010) World Database of Happiness, Erasmus University Rotterdam. Available at http://worlddatabaseofhappiness.eur.nl Accessed at: (November, 2010).

Vittersø, J. (2004) Subjective wellbeing versus self-actualization: using the flow-simplex to promote a conceptual clarification of subjective quality of life. *Social Indicators Research,* 65(3): 299–331.

Vittersø, J., Overwien, P. and Martinsen, E. (2009) Pleasure and interest are differentially affected by replaying versus analyzing a happy life moment. *Journal of Positive Psychology,* 4(1): 14–20.

Vohs, K. D., Schmeichel, B. J., Nelson, N. M. et al. (2008) Making choices impairs subsequent self-control: A limited-resource account of decision making, self-regulation, and active initiative. *Journal of Personality and Social Psychology,* 94(5): 883–98.

Wampold, B. E. (2001) *The Great Psychotherapy Debate: Models, Methods, and Findings.* Mahwah, NJ: Lawrence Erlbaum Associates.

Wampold, B. E. (2005) Do therapies designated as ESTs for specific disorders produce outcomes superior to non-EST therapies? Not a scintilla of evidence to support ESTs as more effective than other treatments. In J. C. Norcross, L. E. Beutler and R. F. Levant (eds) *Evidence-based Practices in Mental Health: Debate and Dialogue on the Fundamental Questions* (pp. 299–308, 317–19). Washington, DC: American Psychological Association.

Wasko, L. and Pury, C. (2009) Affective forecasting. In S. Lopez (ed.) *Encyclopedia of Positive Psychology* (pp. 24–6). Chichester: Blackwell Publishing Ltd.

Waterman, A. S. (1993) Two conceptions of happiness: contrasts of personal expressiveness (eudaimonia) and hedonic enjoyment. *Journal of Personality and Social Psychology,* 64: 678–91.

Waterman, A. S., Schwartz, S. and Conti, R. (2008) The implications of two conceptions of happiness (hedonic enjoyment and eudaimonia) for the understanding of intrinsic motivation. *Journal of Happiness Studies,* 9: 41–79.

Watkins, C., Cruz, L., Holben, H. and Kolts, R. L. (2008) Taking care of business? Grateful processing of unpleasant memories. *Journal of Positive Psychology,* 3(2): 87–99.

Watson, D., Clark, L. A. and Tellegen, A. (1988) Development and validation of brief measures of positive and negative affect: the PANAS scales. *Journal of Personality and Social Psychology,* 54(6): 1063–70.

Waugh, C. E. and Fredrickson, B. L. (2006) Nice to know you: positive emotions, self–other overlap, and complex understanding in the formation of a new relationship. *Journal of Positive Psychology,* 1(2): 93–106.

Waugh, C. E., Wager, T. D., Fredrickson, B. L., Noll, D. C. and Taylor, S. F. (2008) The neural correlates of trait resilience when anticipating and recovering from threat. *Social Cognitive and Affective Neuroscience,* 3(4): 322–32.

Weert, E., Hoekstra, J., Grol, B. et al. (2005) A multidimensional cancer rehabilitation program for cancer survivors. Effectiveness on health related quality of life. *Journal of Psychosomatic Research,* 58: 485–96.

Wehmeyer, M. and Little, T. (2009) Self-determination. In S. Lopez (ed.) *Encyclopedia of Positive Psychology* (pp. 868–74). Chichester: Blackwell Publishing Ltd.

Weinberger, J. (1995) Common factors aren't so common: the common factors dilemma. *Clinical Psychology: Science and Practice,* 2: 45–69.

Weiss, T. (2004) Correlates of posttraumatic growth in husbands of breast cancer survivors. *Psycho-Oncology,* 13(4): 260–8.

Wells, J., Barlow, J. and Stewart-Brown, S. (2003) A systematic review of universal approaches to mental health promotion in schools. *Health Education,* 103: 197–220.

Werner, E. E. (1993) Risk, resilience and recovery: perspectives from the Kauai longitudinal study. *Development and Psychopathology,* 5(4): 503–15.

Werner, E. E. (1996) Vulnerable but invincible: high risk children from birth to adulthood. *European Child and Adolescent Psychiatry,* 5: 47–51.

Wessman, A. E. and Ricks, D. F. (1966) *Moods and Personality.* New York: Holt, Rinehart & Winston.

Whalen, S. P. (1999) Finding flow at school and at home: a conversation with Mihaly Csikszentmihalyi. *Journal of Secondary Gifted Education,* 10: 161–6.

Wheeler, R. E., Davidson, R. J. and Tomarken, A. J. (1993) Frontal brain asymmetry and emotional reactivity: a biological substrate of affective style. *Psychophysiology,* 30(1): 82–9.

Wilkinson, S. (1998) Focus groups in feminist research: power, interaction and the co-construction of meaning. *Women's Studies International Forum,* 21: 111–25.

Williams, G. C., Grow, V. M., Freedman, Z., Ryan, R. M. and Deci, E. L. (1996) Motivational predictors of weight loss and weight-loss maintenance. *Journal of Personality and Social Psychology,* 70: 115–26.

Williamson, J., White, A., Hart, A. and Ernst, E. (2002) Randomised controlled trial of reflexology for menopausal symptoms. *International Journal of Obstetrics and Gynaecology,* 109(9): 1050–5.

Willig, C. (2008) *Introducing Qualitative Research Methods in Psychology,* 2nd edn. Maidenhead: McGraw-Hill/Open University Press.

Wills, T. A., Sandy, J. M. and Yaeger, A. M. (2001) Time perspective and early-onset substance use: a model based on stress-coping theory. *Psychology of Addictive Behaviours,* 15: 118–25.

Wincour, G. and Greenwood, C. (2005) Studies of the effects of high fat diets on cognitive function in a rat model. *Neurobiology of Aging,* 6: 46–9.

Winkelmann, L. and Winkelmann, R. (2008) Personality, work, and satisfaction: evidence from the German Socio-Economic Panel. *Journal of Positive Psychology,* 3(4): 266–75.

Wolk, A., Larsson, S., Johansson, J. and Ekman, P. (2006) Long term fatty fish consumption and renal cell carcinoma incidence in women. *Journal of the American Medical Association,* 296: 1371–6.

Wong, P. (2009) Existential psychology. In S. Lopez (ed.) *Encyclopedia of Positive Psychology* (pp. 361–8). Chichester: Blackwell Publishing Ltd.

World Health Organization (1948) Preamble to the constitution of the World Health Organization as adopted by the International Health Conference 1946. Retrieved from www.who.int/about/definition/en/print.html.

Yeager, J. (2007) The Culver model – positive psychology and wellbeing in the independent high school. *Positive Psychology News Daily,* 10 October 2007, http://pos-psych.com/news/john-yeager/20071010436.

Zaleski, Z., Cycon, A. and Kurc, A. (2001) Future time perspective and subjective wellbeing in adolescent samples. In P. Schmuck and K. M. Sheldon (eds) *Life Goals and Wellbeing: Towards a Positive Psychology of Human Striving* (pp. 58–67). Goettingen: Hogrefe & Huber.

Zimbardo, G. (2002) Just think about it: time to take our time. *Psychology Today,* 35: 62.

Zimbardo, G. and Boyd, J. N. (1999) Putting time in perspective: a valid, reliable individual-differences metric. *Journal of Personality and Social Psychology,* 77: 1271–88.

Zimbardo, G., Keough, K. A. and Boyd, J. N. (1997) Present time perspective as a predictor of risky driving. *Personality and Individual Differences,* 23: 1007–23.

Zullow, H. M., Oettingen, G., Peterson, C. and Seligman, M. E. P. (1988) Pessimistic explanatory style in the historical record: CAVing LBJ, presidential candidates and east verus west berlin. *American Psychologist,* 43(9): 673–82.

Index

Locators shown in *italics* refer to boxes, figures.

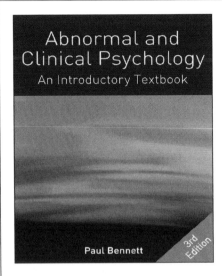

ABNORMAL AND CLINICAL PSYCHOLOGY
An Introductory Textbook
Third Edition

Paul Bennett

9780335237463 (Paperback)
March 2011

eBook also available

Extensively updated, this popular textbook includes the latest research and therapeutic approaches, including CBT, as well as developments in clinical practice. The book introduces and evaluates the conceptual models of mental health problems and their treatment, and provides valuable analyses of various disorders, such as schizophrenia and paedophilia.

Key features:

- Provides new case formulations to illustrate discussion of clinical work
- Includes new chapter on cognitive theory and therapies
- Lists further reading extended with web links

www.openup.co.uk

OPEN UNIVERSITY PRESS
McGraw - Hill Education

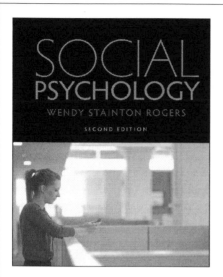

SOCIAL PSYCHOLOGY
Second Edition

Wendy Stainton-Rogers

9780335240999 (Paperback)
June 2011

eBook also available

Social Psychology is an introductory text, uniquely acknowledging that there are two different approaches to social psychology – experimental and critical. The new edition explores the increasing dominance of the critical approach, while still providing the reader with a holistic view and understanding of social psychology.

Key features:

- Introduces a new Online Learning Centre
- Provides up-to-date coverage of developments in the field
- Includes a new chapter exploring values, culture and 'otherness'

www.openup.co.uk

OPEN UNIVERSITY PRESS
McGraw - Hill Education

CONSUMER PSYCHOLOGY

Cathrine V. Jansson-Boyd

9780335229284 (Paperback)
2010

eBook also available

Informed by psychological theory and supported by research, this book provides an overall understanding of consumer behaviour and underlying thought processes. Psychology is central to an effective understanding of consumer behaviour and this book shows how it can be used to explain why people choose certain products and services, and how this affects their behaviour and psychological well-being.

Key features:

- Incorporates chapters with an introduction, key terms and a summary
- Includes study questions or class exercises
- Comprises topics illustrated with real-life examples, including adverts and case studies

OPEN UNIVERSITY PRESS
McGraw - Hill Education

www.openup.co.uk

QUALITATIVE RESEARCH METHODS IN PSYCHOLOGY

Combining Core Approaches

Nollaig Frost

9780335241514 (Paperback)
June 2011

eBook also available

Qualitative Research Methods in Psychology: From Core to Combined Approaches provides research students with practical guidance and thoughtful debate on carrying out qualitative research in psychology. The book is written in a clear and accessible manner designed to support students from the beginning of their research experience at undergraduate level through to postgraduate research and beyond.

Key features:

- Includes case studies and group projects
- Provides problem-based questions
- Incorporates reference lists

www.openup.co.uk

 **OPEN UNIVERSITY PRESS**
McGraw - Hill Education

24880071R00155

Made in the USA
Lexington, KY
04 August 2013